Anthropologists in the Securityscape

Anthropologists in the Securityscape

Ethics, Practice, and Professional Identity

Editors

Robert Albro
George E. Marcus
Laura A. McNamara
Monica Schoch-Spana

Walnut Creek, CA

Left Coast Press, Inc.
1630 North Main Street, #400
Walnut Creek, CA 94596
www.LCoastPress.com

ISBN 978-1-61132-012-1 hardcover
ISBN 978-1-61132-013-8 paperback
ISBN 978-1-61132-014-5 electronic

Library of Congress Cataloging-in-Publication Data:

Anthropologists in the securityscape : ethics, practice, and professional identity / Robert Albro... [et al.].
p. cm.—Includes bibliographical references and index.
ISBN 978-1-61132-012-1 (hardcover :alk. paper)
ISBN 978-1-61132-013-8 (pbk. : alk. paper)
ISBN 978-1-61132-014-5 (ebook)
1. Anthropological ethics. 2. Anthropology—Research. 3. Government agencies. 4. Intelligence service. I. Albro, Robert.
GN33.6.A49 2012
301.072—dc23
2011030569

Printed in the United States of America

∞™ The paper used in this publication meets the minimum requirements of American National Standard for Information Sciences—Permanence of Paper for Printed Library Materials, ANSI/NISO Z39.48—1992.

Cover design by Allison Smith

CONTENTS

INTRODUCTION

This volume began as an ethics casebook, inspired by casebooks in such applied fields as law, medicine, psychology, or the forensic sciences. If it had remained an ethics casebook, it might have resembled the "Cases and Comments" chapter in Joan Cassell and Sue-Ellen Jacobs' *Handbook on Ethical Issues in Anthropology* (1987), but with an orientation toward anthropological practice in the military, intelligence, and broader national security communities. Along the way, however, the project evolved into something quite different. Why this happened is germane to understanding what this book is about and how we hope people will read it.

In 2006, the Central Intelligence Agency (CIA) submitted a job advertisement for publication in the American Anthropological Association's (AAA) newsletter, *Anthropology News.* Given anthropology's long-standing distrust of military and intelligence activities, the job ad generated lively discussion among members of the AAA Executive Board. The ad was ultimately posted on the AAA's website, but the Executive Board recognized that this was probably not the last time that the AAA would be asked to broker or to facilitate connections between anthropologists and the national security state. Its members agreed that a better understanding of the "complex terrain linking anthropology to national security policy in the U.S." would be invaluable in helping the AAA and its membership to respond appropriately to further overtures (Goodman 2006); hence, the idea for a Commission on the Engagement of Anthropology with the U.S. Security and Intelligence Communities (CEAUSSIC), which was formed in late 2006, was born. CEAUSSIC's work continued for four years, through two incarnations and multiple research products, presentations, and reports. All four of this volume's editors were also CEAUSSIC members.[1]

CEAUSSIC started out as a fact-finding body, but it became what fellow CEAUSSIC member Kerry Fosher referred to tongue-in-cheek as a "journey of discovery." CEAUSSIC was created when criticism about the post-9/11 intersection of anthropology and national security was beginning to crescendo. If a small minority of anthropologists argued publicly for engaging military, intelligence, and other functions in the United

States' multifront war on terror, others, such as the Network of Concerned Anthropologists, argued that Vietnam had amply demonstrated why anthropologists should entirely avoid any such entanglements. The same tensions were present in CEAUSSIC itself. Its membership included people working in various capacities with or in the security sector, critics of such arrangements, and academic as well as applied practitioners. The group brought diverse perspectives and strong opinions to bear on the risks and benefits of anthropological engagement with military and intelligence activities.

Even though some of CEAUSSIC's early exchanges were quite intense, these conversations created an atmosphere of trust in which we gradually came to understand and appreciate each other's positions, despite deep differences of opinion. And, although we all agreed that it was important to account for the fraught history of anthropology vis-à-vis military and intelligence functions in the United States, we also recognized that these domains had also evolved significantly since the Vietnam era. As a group, we began to appreciate the extent to which "security" was an arrangement of moving frontiers that included much more than might first catch the eye.

However, CEAUSSIC members were also concerned that discourse within the AAA was so polarized as to preclude any civil, grounded, or judicious discussion about whether and how anthropologists might have a role in the work of the national security state (or not, as the case may be). At the same time, we often felt that the center of gravity of this unfolding debate was largely stuck on implications of the problematic U.S. Army Human Terrain System program to the detriment of wider-ranging discussion of the varieties of disciplinary practice associated with the many moving parts of the security universe. For this reason, we understood our charge to include effectively communicating the "multi-voicedness" of CEAUSSIC's work, a point we foregrounded in our 2007 report (CEAUSSIC 2007).

These commitments thus laid the groundwork for both iterations of CEAUSSIC's inquiries. Moreover, they also provide the grounding orientation for this volume. In preparation for our 2007 Report to the AAA, we pursued an empirical, even ethnographic, approach to describing the varieties of intersections of security with anthropology, while at the same time pursuing research into the history of anthropology and the formulation of our ethical codes. This included data gathering about the institutions comprising the "national security state," and the kinds of activities that might engage anthropologists in these settings, alongside a snowball sampling of the kinds of work of anthropologists found in various institutional settings affiliated with national security, from private contractors to academic departments to the CIA.

What these initial efforts revealed was a heterogeneity and diversity that belied often sweeping generalizations about what "anthropology" would bring to "security" and what "security" would do to "anthropology." We observed some striking parallels between anthropologists working inside and outside the security domain. In particular, the security-oriented anthropologists we met and interviewed described fieldwork and career challenges that would sound quite familiar to most anthropologists. They described developing projects, winning funding, negotiating access to research participants, getting Institutional Review Board (IRB) approvals, balancing confidentiality and publication, how to pursue advocacy, carrying out research in different settings, and introducing students to anthropology. They were facing these challenges in proximity to institutions of state power that are often the focus of vociferous anthropological critique, but in ways not altogether well described by such critique. We felt that the strategies they had developed for negotiating these challenges, and the associated arrangements of anthropological practice in these domains, were worth documenting, because such accounts could add nuance and balance to these matters and constructively ground the wider ongoing discussion and debate.

Along the way, the idea that an ethics casebook might be the most effective vehicle for communicating the broad range of circumstances of professional experience and practice in the security domain began to percolate in our discussions. Anthropology had not had an ethics casebook for a very long time; why not revive the genre with an ethics casebook illustrating the kinds of challenges facing anthropologists in the domain of military and/or intelligence work? We imagined a collection of short, anonymized narratives, each structured around a particular ethical dilemma elicited from anthropologists working in or around the national security domain; each case would be accompanied by a brief editorial commentary and a set of discussion questions. Ultimately, we aimed for a book that could be used in classrooms to provoke discussion and debate. We put out a "call for cases" that we disseminated as broadly as we could, using the AAA's publication mechanisms. It was also picked up by blogs dedicated to anthropology and elsewhere.

This initial emphasis on ethical dilemmas stemmed from CEAUSSIC's charge to examine the ethical dimensions of the anthropology-security nexus. However, as we continued to discuss the project, we began to feel constrained by the requirements of keeping "ethics" at the center of the casebook. As we waited for responses to our initial call for cases, some potential participants seemed taken aback by our interest in ethical dilemmas. Several told us that they simply could not identify a specific dilemma. Most described an ongoing effort to negotiate the boundaries and goals of anthropological practice among coworkers and managers, who had little familiarity with anthropology in any of its forms. This feedback told us that we were mistaken in the assumption that any anthropologist working in any domain of security must have some distinctively paradigmatic ethical set of dilemmas they could easily share, simply because of their institutional affiliations and associated work.

Despite our extensive dissemination efforts, eliciting cases proved difficult, and we received surprisingly few responses. This suggested to us that initiating a dialogue based on describing what anthropologists actually do in these contexts and at this more intimate level was at an odd angle to the prevailing terms of our disciplinary discussion. For us, on the contrary, this lack of response pointed to the limits of the discussion we had been having and underscored the need for a project of just this sort. Moreover, as we discussed these challenges and learned more about these anthropologists' careers and the kinds of work they were performing, we realized that these exchanges themselves should really form the basis of our casebook project, which now was a quite different project than that which we had originally conceived. Pursuing this, we found it necessary to be more proactive in the elicitation of representative cases. Abandoning our formal call, we used personal networks and snowball techniques to arrive at our present roster of cases—representative if by no means exhaustive.

The resulting casebook is an experiment in representing and extending our dialogical experience beyond the confines of CEAUSSIC so that we can engage other stakeholders—anthropologists, nonanthropologists, AAA members, and stakeholders in the security sector—in a productive conversation about what it means to practice anthropology in the domain of security. Our project's shift away from an anonymized ethics casebook to a more autoethnographic one reflects the volume's emphasis upon disciplinary self-reflexivity, where ethnographic sensibilities are brought to bear in a critical engagement with, and performance of, the self (see Reed-Danahay 1997)—in this case, the "professional self"—as a way for contributors to explore the contours, limits, and constitutive possibilities of professional practice in the securityscape, along with anthropology's changing situatedness in the overlapping contexts of security.

These essays, however, are not simply a compilation of subjective experiences, personal narratives, or autobiographical sketches. Instead, these collected narratives, as self-reflections about professional contexts, are also the basis for a print dialogue (with the editors and, we hope, readers), in turn, set within current disciplinary and extradisciplinary dialogue and debate. The purpose of this arrangement is to foreground multiple voices and points of view within, across, and about the encompassing circumstances of security, in which we collectively attempt to locate, describe, critique, reflect upon, and assess what it means to "practice anthropology" in the multiple overlapping locations of what we have taken to calling the securityscape.

As we developed the book, we decided that the term "national security" was too narrow to describe the various complicated local, national, and global intersections, networks, nodes, institutions, and agencies that our interlocutors had described to us. We decided to use the term "securityscape" to situate our contributors' essays in this broader and more diffuse territory, with its moving frontiers. We did not coin this term; instead, we borrowed and amended Hugh Gusterson's original description of a securityscape as comprising "asymmetrical distributions of weaponry, military force, and military-scientific resources among nation-states and the local and global imaginaries of identity, power, and vulnerability that accompany these distributions" (Gusterson 2004:166).[2]

Gusterson's definition has a sharp critical edge that prioritizes the role of the state in the construction of relations of power and production of violence. We expand the term "securityscape" to invoke a broader geographic and institutional expanse of heterogeneous, hybrid, interconnected state and nonstate, public and private, agencies and resources, which variously organize professional expectations, notions of expertise, activities, and goals, through which technology and training are distributed, and knowledge circulates, often but not simply in relationship to the interdiction of threats to the nation-state.

For us, an important difference is a scalar one. We have chosen to give characteristically disciplinary attention to the particular contexts of professional practice within the many corners of the securityscape rather than to apprehend the "security state" as a monolithic actor. We feel it is critical to remind the reader of the many and varied corners of this expansive heterogeneity, since the essays in this volume demonstrate that anthropologists can encounter and engage the securityscape in a multitude of settings, and that its edges or frontiers are often not stationary or easily defined. The problems associated with what it means to operate professionally in these complex arrangements of security often look different from this vantage point.

The 16 chapters of this volume are thus dialogically engaged autoethnographic essays in which anthropologists describe the intersection of anthropology and security in their work and lives. Some are affiliated professionally with the national security community; others are not. But all have something to tell us about the shifting relationships among scholarship and practice in the domain of security. Because we are all citizens of the United States who have practiced anthropology in the United States, and because our contributors are similarly situated, this volume is heavily skewed toward the concerns of anthropology in the United States. We expect, however, that similar volumes could be assembled for other countries, illustrating different kinds of state-specific professional situations and entanglements while also demonstrating the overlapping facts of what is increasingly a global securityscape.

Throughout this volume, our collegial dialogue with its contributors makes a point of exploring the different questions raised by the essays, even as it also points to family resemblances as well as differences between anthropological practice as conventionally perceived and work by anthropologists in the security context. The order of essays is also designed to take the reader through a linked set of discussions, with successive essays sharing one or another key issue in common, if often in contrasting ways. Throughout, the editorial commentary aims to help facilitate the dialogue among these essays and to exhibit their intertextuality.

We hasten to emphasize, however, that the assembled essays can in no way be considered a representative sample of the kinds of professional expectations, challenges, entanglements, and possibilities of security spaces as work environments. There are significant omissions here of other ways in which anthropologists have been involved with the security sector, including the work of forensic anthropologists; work on post-traumatic stress disorder and with veterans; research on military families; the use of remote or high-risk ethnography; work for a large military contractor such as MITRE, Booz-Allen, or SAIC; or work on development, reconstruction, and stabilization, to name some of the more evident omissions.

There are multiple ways these essays could have been organized, and interesting comparisons and contrasts to make between them all. If not always organized side-by-side, a significant group of contributors work in the Professional Military Education system (see the essays by Fujimura, Holmes-Eber, Simons, and Turnley) and raise sometimes unexpected issues for the familiar work of teaching and the less-familiar work of training military personnel. Still others are concerned with ethnography and the research mode, offering a glimpse of the circumstances of "studying up" and of "organizational ethnography" in/on the securityscape (in particular, see the essays of Miller, Abramson, McNamara, and Rubinstein). Another group of essays are found in close proximity—if in very different ways—to the work of the intelligence analyst (see essays by Dawson, again Abramson and McNamara, and in a different way, Miller). Along a different tack, we also have a cluster of essays exploring the role of the nongovernmental organization (NGO) community, civil-military relationships (or their absence), and the humanitarian contexts in which militaries are often present. These include the essays by Van Arsdale, Omidian, and Rubinstein. Several essays are situated in what we might call the growth industry of para-academic centers and institutes (Schoch-Spana and, again, Van Arsdale). Others pursue implications of the teaching and resourcing of "culture" in the securityscape (see Albro, Fujimura, Rush, Milliken, and Turnley). Still others focus on the challenges of program building and funding in often large security bureaucracies (e.g., Goolsby, and again, Turnley and McNamara).

These are certainly not the only ways in which these essays can be read, or intertextually speak to one another. Also cropping up are some less obvious themes, such as what composes common sense or "practical reason" in different security contexts (see Milliken on "tools," Van Arsdale and Dawson on "skills," and Albro and Turnley on "clients" and "customers"), what is legible and/or can be communicated in this environment (see Albro on "dialogue," Schoch-Spana on "notional publics," and Simons on "critical thinking"), and the challenges of interdisciplinarity for anthropology (in particular, see McNamara, Simons, Milliken, Albro, Turnley, and Goolsby). But we invite the reader to make these and other connections.

Notes

1. The original Commission was chaired by Jim Peacock and included Kerry Fosher, Laura McNamara, Rob Albro, Carolyn Fluehr-Lobban, George Marcus, David Price, and Monica Heller. The second iteration was chaired by Rob Albro, included all the previous members with the exception of Monica Heller (whose tenure on the AAA's Executive Board had ended), and added Laurie Rush, Jean Jackson, Monica Schoch-Spana, and Laura Graham (as the new Executive Board representative). Further details about the extent and products of CEAUSSIC's work can be found at http://www.aaanet.org/cmtes/commissions/CEAUSSIC/index.cfm, including its two reports to the AAA (CEAUSSIC 2007, 2009).
2. Gusterson, in turn, extended Appadurai's (1996) well-known recitation of anthropology's expansion into a series of "-scapes"—hybridized cultural flows and local-global connections and disjunctions—as settings for multiple global imaginaries.

References

Appadurai, Arjun

1996 Modernity at Large: Critical Dimensions of Globalization. Minneapolis, MN: University of Minnesota Press.

Commission on the Engagement of Anthropology with the U.S. Security and Intelligence Communities (CEAUSSIC)

2007 Report of the Commission on Anthropology and the Military and Intelligence Communities. Arlington, VA: American Anthropological Association.

Commission on the Engagement of Anthropology with the U.S. Security and Intelligence Communities (CEAUSSIC)

2009 Final Report on The Army's Human Terrain System Proof of Concept Program. Arlington, VA: American Anthropological Association.

Goodman, Alan

2006 Engaging with National Security. Arlington, VA: American Anthropological Association.

Gusterson, Hugh

2004 People of the Bomb: Portraits of America's Nuclear Complex. Minneapolis, MN: University of Minnesota Press.

Cassell, Joan

1987 Cases and Comments. *In* Handbook on Ethical Issues in Anthropology, Joan Cassell and Sue-Ellen Jacobs, eds. Washington, D.C.: American Anthropological Association. Available at http://www.aaanet.org/committees/ethics/ch4.htm. Accessed August 15, 2011.

Reed-Danahay, Deborah

1997 Auto/Ethnography: Rewriting the Self and the Social. Oxford: Berg Publishers.

1

The Winds of Politics, Change, and Social Science Transformation in a Military Research Institution

Rebecca Goolsby

One of the most important goals of the American Anthropological Associations (AAA) Commission on the Engagement of Anthropology with the U.S. Security and Intelligence Communities (CEAUSSIC) activity was to provide the AAA Executive Board and membership with a richer and more detailed understanding of what it means to "practice" anthropology in the context of military-funded research and development. This was how we came into contact with Rebecca Goolsby, a cultural anthropologist who manages a major social science research program for the Office of Naval Research (ONR). While searching for literature related to the intersection of national security, social science, and research ethics, we came across an article in which Goolsby quite frankly assessed the major ethical challenges of defense funding for social science research (Goolsby 2005). Given her position at ONR, we found this quite intriguing, and asked Goolsby if she would be willing to be interviewed about her work at ONR for the CEAUSSIC report. That interview led to a subsequent phone call, in which Albro and McNamara asked Goolsby to submit an autoethnographic essay for this volume.

Goolsby's essay appears first in the volume because she provides such a detailed overview of the Department of Defense (DoD) research-and-development landscape. Moreover, her story illuminates the complex positions and relationships that exist among researchers and their funding sponsors. Goolsby is a program officer, a position of some significance in the military science and technology community (and analogous to the role of program officer at the National Science Foundation). In this role, Goolsby advocates that ONR invests resources into social science research, negotiates programmatic goals, then issues calls for proposals, awards project funds, and oversees the research projects that her program supports.

Of particular interest is her program's emphasis on computational social modeling and simulation as a research approach for social science in military domains. This is important because, as several contributions to this volume indicate, so many social science projects in the securityscape involve some element of computational modeling and simulation. This is an interdisciplinary methodology that is probably unfamiliar to many anthropologists, even those with more quantitative backgrounds. In contrast, Goolsby has a background in computer science, and her methodological toolkit includes social network analysis, a quantitative methodology more familiar to sociologists than cultural anthropologists. Coupled with her training in ethnological theory and method, and ONR's orientation to mathematical and physical sciences, it is perhaps not surprising that Goolsby has successfully developed and maintained a 10-year counterterrorism social science research program that includes a strong emphasis on computational methodologies. These days, Goolsby is known for advocating the value of social network analysis and social media to facilitate interagency coordination and situational awareness during natural disasters, a problem of significant concern to the Navy given its role in responding to earthquakes and tsunamis.

Prior to joining ONR in 2000, Goolsby taught at universities on the west coast. She received her doctorate in cultural anthropology at the University of Washington in Seattle (1992). Her dissertation research was conducted under a Fulbright award and concentrated on gender, class, and ethnicity and the differential impact of social change and modernization in Northeastern Thailand.

I came to the Office of Naval Research (ONR) in August of 2000 with the original intention of helping to manage programs in organizational culture and social change, including computational modeling projects. By October, the U.S.S. Cole disaster—a particularly naval event—had struck, a situation in which I immediately saw that social science could have an important impact. But where do military research projects come from?

An aircraft carrier takes a great deal of forethought to slow down, let alone turn. So, too, do the huge bureaucratic levers of change at the Department of Defense. When I came to my boss, the great Willard S. Vaughan, with the proposal that we start a research program addressing counterterror, he patiently explained the budgetary planning process—how it takes years to get new programs into the budget, the steadying hand of Congressional oversight committees, and how the problem of counterterror was not "in ONR's lane." Counterterrorism, he explained, was the responsibility of the State Department. There would not be any possibility of funding such a program without years of patient effort, even with the tragedy of the U.S.S. Cole. However, because Dr. Vaughan thought there might be some potential as a training exercise—and he could see the need, despite the enormous obstacles—he gave me permission and even encouragement to develop a rationale for such a program. This would include developing an argument for "naval need," "naval impact," and objectives and technologies to be developed, with the caveat that, although it would be good practice for me to learn about program development, funding issues and policy challenges would be insurmountable. For him, it was a modest bet on a long shot that the Navy would be interested in such a program within the calendar year, something like a three-dollar bet on a hundred-to-one shot. I needed to learn the ropes and this was as good an exercise as any, and the bet itself was modest—a few hours of my time a week doing something I found interesting.

Military research funding agencies have different histories, mandates, and "customers" for their science and technology products. ONR is the oldest agency and has a wide variety of research projects from basic to highly advanced; "highly advanced" means research ready to move from the lab into the Fleet, for use by military operators. Funding is coded by Congress as Budgeting Activity (BA) 1, 2, 3 (formerly "6.1, 6.2, 6.3," etc.), with BA 1 representing the most basic research and BA 2 representing applied research. These codes are derived from their funding lines in the military's research budget. The Office of the Secretary of Defense is in charge of military research funds, through The Office of the Assistant Secretary for Defense (Research & Engineering), also known as ASD (R&E). Congress provides funds to research funding offices like ONR and to the DoD laboratories, such as the Naval Research Lab, and to a variety of other research projects and programs. ONR is given BA 1, BA 2, and BA 3 funds, whereas the Air Force Office of Scientific Research (AFOSR), a "sister" organization, has only BA 1 funds. Research funding agencies have different cultures (reflecting the services they serve) and different perspectives on what makes for a "good" research project.

Essentially, I learned that in this project I would be chasing a rabbit down a hole, much like Alice in Wonderland—a learning exercise, but this did not deter me. Computational social science was on the new side to me, though I did, coincidentally, have a computer science as well as an anthropology background. The terrorism project was something I could research "on the side" during my down time in program management (which I was also learning).

I began to build a case. I reviewed the history of Al Qaeda and similar groups in Southeast Asia, my old stomping grounds. The embassy bombings in Africa, the problems in South and Central Asia, and the opinions of scholars of terrorism pointed to a disturbing trend with explosive potential. The world was changing. Discontent and frustration, not unlike what I'd found in my research in Thailand, were beginning to find voice in violent discourses and acts against the United States as well as against other nation-state authorities. On September 11, 2001, a little less than a year later, Dr. Vaughan's longshot bet was, unfortunately, less of a longshot than he, or most anyone, had figured, even me.

What made this program possible were several things: first, a culture that valued inquiry and basic research and that encouraged exploration of issues just over the horizon; second, my difference was highly valued (ONR as an institution has a history of tackling new and even heretical thinking and of coming at a problem from a new direction; letting someone have ownership of that direction was part of the culture); third, my education, background, training, and experience enabled me rapidly to prepare and develop a strong foundational understanding of the technological, historical, and sociological bits and pieces of Islamism and its direction; and fourth, the devastating power of the situation itself revealed the enormous gap of knowledge about the world, about non-Western cultures, and the social changes afoot in the world affecting America's position, status, and security. The ability to see the problem coming was not so much visionary as it was a natural outcome of being placed where I was, looking at the problems of the military in international situations at a time when a number of high-placed and brilliant people were beginning to put their finger on the issues. Dr. Vaughan hired me to address his growing intuition about problems that would require social science training. I walked into the living room and easily located the elephant. The U.S.S. Cole incident was the bellwether for 9/11, but no one appreciated this at the time.

Of course, after 9/11, no one cared much about the background of the problem (unless it was to find the "root causes" and dig them out); the scramble was on to do something. My job was to put together a practical, relevant, ethical, and affordable program of research that would yield information analysis tools as quickly as possible, founded on the best scientific foundation available. All over the Department of Defense, meetings were convened, workshops were held, and every kind of idea in the world was explored. Social science had a weak but secure place in the form of terrorism experts, from academics to working intelligence analysts in any of the "three-letter" (Federal Bureau of Investigation [FBI], Central Intelligence Agency [CIA], Defense Intelligence Agency [DIA], etc.) agencies, who were in high demand. However, psychology was better represented in the funding agencies, since virtually all social science except psychology had been shut down in military research when the National Science Foundation took on these responsibilities. The computer models being pursued by the military were mostly based on psychological or social-psychological foundations. The exception was the team organization-modeling program that had been nurtured in my department at ONR in the 1990s, which had a multidisciplinary approach that included mathematical sociology and social network analysis as part of its disciplinary base.

By February of 2002, I had a plan. Based on ONR's prior work in social network modeling, I proposed to "cleave" off a new specialized program in social network analysis, with a special focus on the computational modeling of terrorist organizations. I put together the plan in a language that the military could understand—PowerPoint—with a list of objectives and a plan to fund research that would lead to social network tools for better intelligence analysis. My refined plan was presented together with a number of proposed counterterrorist programs of research in June of 2002. It was given the go-ahead several weeks later.

It is difficult to recall the changes that I underwent as a scholar and as an anthropologist in those first five years. I learned the term "warfighter" and began to use it in everyday language. I shunned the word "occupation" because it made the military uncomfortable (at best), I grew tall and I grew small to try to understand the viewpoints of people caught in a variety of roles and contradictions in the frantic rush to "solve" the situations in Iraq and Afghanistan. I was surprised (given my West Coast, "Birkenstock" roots) to find myself inspired by many military officers with a deep concern for the Iraqi and Afghan peoples. Finding brilliant minds was easy, and finding deeply committed and ethical officers was a matter of just looking for them; the preconceptions I had of military culture being one shade of green fell away rapidly.

The diversity of military culture(s) is astonishing. The Department of the Navy alone has many clans: blue-water (surface), air, and submariners, Marines, and SEALs, each with their rituals and traditions, distinct world-views, and dispositions. The different training academies have differing perspectives and understanding of their role of the military. And each class is shaped by the political world in distinctive ways, so that people ask about what class so-and-so was in, so as to understand that person better. Pentagon culture is bewilderingly diverse, one huge building housing a wide variety of differing opinions, perspectives, and experiences that somehow must be hammered together in committees to create a solid, unassailable foundation for going forward. From my vantage point, I would not say there are doves and hawks; nothing is that simple anymore. Military officers in my experience tended to lack education in the social sciences prior to 9/11. The conflicts in Iraq and Afghanistan made a significant impact on that. Further, General Petraeus's doctorate in political science certainly has given him a deep appreciation of social factors, and this has no doubt also spurred more interest in social science by young military officers as the ranks of young people who think of themselves as "soldier-scholars" has swelled.

Talking to social scientists and military officers and intelligence analysts involved multiple frames of reference and mutually unintelligible vocabularies. In the early days (2002–2005), getting people together was always fraught with the potential for misunderstanding and missed engagements. Some of the social scientists feared I was there to help the military with targeting, whereas the military—who knew all about targeting, thank you very much—wanted to know what else was important to know for "winning" and getting home as soon as possible. Thoughtful people (both military and scientist) struggled to understand the "native's point of view" in both the science as presented and the discussion that followed about how that science might be applied.

I funded the first workshop for social network analysis in 2002 at the National Academy of Sciences; a great deal of progress in developing shared frameworks of understanding was made through this and subsequent workshops. The first five years were particularly important in beginning to teach the military about social science—and social scientists, in turn, about the wide variety of needs and interests of the military in the products of their work—which was less and less about targeting as time went on. As the military began to have a deeper understanding of social science, their demands changed, and their questions changed. Military research programs, developed and run by psychologists and engineers, grew in size and sophistication. The AFOSR is particularly to be commended for its commitment to basic research in computational modeling in social science.

It has not all been easy or pleasant. I have had to stand up, on occasion, in workshops, meetings, and committees to explain research ethics and point out why this or that program would not or could not be done according to federal laws. Oh, nothing evil or vile, just misguided or lacking in education that the people involved could not be expected to have. Simple issues such as having to divulge that one's funding source is a military funding institution, even if you are collecting data on the Internet, had to be reviewed carefully. The problematic nature of deception research—and the question of whether it is a good idea at all—and other controversial issues had to be brought to the surface, and the full panoply of "why this or that is a bad idea" had to be laid out. My experience went something like this: I would get up, tell the bad news, then listen to the 45 seconds of silence as people mulled this over. Finally, someone, typically a psychologist, would clear his throat and point out that I was correct. Everyone would sigh dramatically, and then incorporate that new fact point into the emerging program. Program officers and research managers now are subjected to rigorous ethics training. If one is very fortunate, one gets a good mentor like Dr. Vaughan for a boss. No one means to give you bad advice or to provide you with a limited view.

But a limited view of the Department of Defense behemoth is the only view that anyone ever has. I learned to keep asking questions and reevaluating the situation. The Department of Defense is not only immense, it is always moving. Working at ONR under Dr. Vaughan, I was kept fairly busy with my own small "patch" of funding and did not look far afield for new programs, aside from sitting on boards, reading proposals, and consulting with other agencies who were leaping on the bandwagon of social network analysis and computational modeling. I consulted everywhere and frequently recruited other social scientists to serve on boards, research studies, and committees. In 2006, I was asked to help with a program at the Army's Foreign Military Scholarship Office (FMSO) by being its anthropology lead, aiding to develop it as a small military test project. It was called the "Human Terrain System," and it involved training military officers and soldiers in civil affairs to improve their collection of social and cultural data for a new information tool called Map-Human Terrain. It was a short-lived relationship, full of confusion. In the three months while it existed, I worked feverishly to develop workshops and get together people to provide training and information tools. Then, without any warning, the Army collapsed the activity, and a new activity with the same name leaped forward that was related to intelligence activities (not civil affairs) funded by the Joint Capability Technical Demonstration line of funding. Further, it would hire anthropologists to go out and collect field material, rather than train soldiers. The Human Terrain System project I worked on was not the Human Terrain System project that would go on to fame and funding.

At the time, I refused the offer to become part of their new collective. In its prior incarnation, FMSO, the agency in charge, had a very supportive leadership that understood the ethical and practical issues very well. The program management of the new Human Terrain Teams did not share that understanding as well and changed many aspects to secure funding. The new program was promoted as a means to provide better advice to combatant commanders, rather than assistance to civil affairs. Putting professional social scientists in the field was not seen as problematic. This disturbed me because in the past the military had experienced ethical flaps in social science–related research, as long ago as Project Camelot and as recently as Total Information Assurance. Today, the ONR has in place a Human Research Protections Unit, and other research units of the military have similar boards and policies. But Human Terrain was an Army activity outside of those units; there were no external ethical review boards and no academic advisory panels to provide guidance and boundaries, only the general oversight of the Joint Capability Technical Demonstration. FMSO had originally planned such boards and panels. I am convinced that if the original Human Terrain Team vision had gone forward, it would have been a stronger scientific effort. Though there would still have been significant ethical struggles, they would have been different struggles.

After 10 years, I still feel as if I have only just arrived. I am beginning to see how funding agencies can transform science. I still publish. I still do a modest amount of (mainly library) research. But most of all, I am privileged to propose programs for meaningful social science research to benefit scientists and universities—and science itself. My research and engagement in social science allow me to transpose the military's needs and problems into the problem space of the sciences. Because I am a subject matter expert in anthropology and computational social science, I know the edges of the disciplines, the gaps: we need better ethnographic inputs into models, social science models of disaster with better biophysical connections to the realistic world of non-Western cultures, to understand how cell phones affect people's patterns of mutual assistance in times of hardship, and a dozen other topics, from illicit networks to humanitarian assistance collaboration.

The Vision Thing: What's Ahead for Social Science and the Military?

There is still no real career path for social science within the Department of Defense, and that is a significant issue. I believe that more trained social scientists working in research at many different levels would improve national security, humanitarian assistance, and civil affairs greatly. And it is up to the Department of Defense to create those career paths, especially for young people. I would like to see agencies create postdoctoral positions for social scientists, especially combatant commands like SOUTHCOM and AFRICOM, where improvements in understanding people in fragile and failing nation-states is critical to developing the right kinds of plans and interventions (when needed). If the jobs exist, then the universities will need to step up. I look forward to the day when I have 10 postdocs and a big workshop on "Ethics and Practice in Human Security" will end in a job fair. I want to see people with a postdoc at AFRICOM, followed by five years working for a nongovernment organization (NGO) in drought or agriculture, followed by 10 years at a research institution, and side consultancies with SOUTHCOM, with research funded by the NSF, Wenner-Gren, and AFOSR or ONR. I want to see researchers step back and forth across the aisle, within reason and within ethical boundaries that make sense.

Social science must change and shift as well as the Department of Defense. Hot prejudices on all sides must be tempered with common sense and proportion. In my experience, the new, young military is astonishingly open to change and genuinely interested in being part of the solution to humanitarian problems. This is a teaching moment. I hope that the social science community can appreciate this.

For my part, I have a wish list that is a mile long: postdoctoral appointments for social scientists in military research labs, funding units, combatant commands. If our social scientists can step into many roles and many situations over the course of a career, then their understanding will be more comprehensive. Consortiums, workshops, and advisory groups to help the military do their job better and smarter are another possibility, because the military's problems are, today, totally within the problem space of social science: civil affairs, governance, how to build the capacity of poor countries in health and economic welfare, how to promote peace, work collaboratively, and understand non-Western norms, values, and life situations. The Department of State problem space and the Department of Defense problem space have not so much collided as overlaid each other, a kind of arranged marriage rather than a collision of adversaries, with challenges and significant issues ahead—but with good intentions on every side. Of course, this is only my personal view of the elephant. Your mileage may vary.

Editorial Commentary

In her narrative, Goolsby positions "anthropology" in a strong way in the specific institutional context of the ONR, for which the role and purpose of the social sciences—anthropology included—remains significantly ambiguous. Goolsby emphasizes the advantages of her ability as a program officer to bring anthropology to bear on the Navy's mission space, a kind of advocacy that represents "new and even heretical thinking" within ONR. As a self-described "subject matter expert in anthropology," Goolsby uses the authoritative language of "science" to create room for maneuvering in ONR politics so that she can propose and build up new ONR programs; in particular, a post-9/11 program combining computational modeling and social network analysis designed to produce "information analysis tools" to better understand terrorist groups.

Goolsby's essay illustrates a theme that characterizes many of the experiences detailed in this volume: a realization by the authors of how heterogeneous "the military" or "military culture" is. Like Clementine Fujimura, Robert Rubinstein, Paula Holmes-Eber, and Jessica Glicken-Turnley, Goolsby's interactions with military personnel overturn preconceptions about the armed forces as a monocultural, monolithic institution singularly bent on killing people. In Goolsby's case, she tells us, "Finding brilliant minds was easy, finding deeply committed and ethical officers was a matter of just looking for them; the preconceptions I had of military culture being one shade of green fell away rapidly." Like several of our contributors, Goolsby's essay alerts us to the role of military personnel in providing humanitarian aid, conducting civil affairs, and supporting health and economic development. Goolsby's experience suggests the military must be ethnographically understood before the hot-button ethical issues of participation engagement can be coherently and responsibly discussed.

Equally interesting, Goolsby's description of the military evokes an entire parallel universe, replete with funding agencies, universities, scholars, standards, and ethics of its own. Her funding sources are ones with which we do not normally interact, but they are extremely important sources of funding for a great deal of academic and private research. This is a bafflingly complicated world. And even as Goolsby is in a position to effect change and support research, she is also subject to a set of constraints—"rules, clearance, and by protocols and manners"—that practitioners in other environments are unlikely to encounter. Goolsby's ethnographic sensibility perhaps enables her to mediate among "multiple frames of reference and mutually unintelligible vocabularies" (e.g., between those of the military and of the social sciences) and among "the military's needs and problems and the problem space of sciences," as she puts it.

This seems to require that she interpret the concerns of anthropology (or of professional social science, generally) for the benefit of military decision makers in her domain. She describes this process as telling "the bad news." In this case, the "bad news" appears to include frank discussion of the ethical guidelines of research for professional social scientists, which of course makes one wonder about the extent to which social scientists are free to practice their vocation as such in ONR, as well the kinds of ethical frameworks that operate in institutions like ONR. In anthropology's disciplinary conversations about such matters, the topic of military and/or intelligence ethics is discursively intertwined with language like "kill chains" and "deception." We expect that there is more to these ethical frameworks than such blatantly problematic constructs, but it is difficult to discern from Goolsby's narrative.

Last, we read Goolsby's essay just after the AAA's controversy over the excision of the word "science" from one paragraph in its mission statement. Perhaps this controversy heightened our sensitivity to the ways in which Goolsby deploys the language of science, and the importance of science as a discursive currency to justify programmatic agendas and funding support. Moreover, Goolsby's identity seems to be that of "subject matter expert" and "scientist" rather than anthropologist, suggesting that these are professional categories that make particular institutional sense for ONR. This led to a discussion of the extent to which Goolsby's programmatic agenda at ONR is conversant with ethnographic research that is more narrative, qualitative, and descriptive in form, as well as other kinds of anthropology and the broader universe of social scientific research in academia, other federal settings, and the private sector.

This, in turn, raised the question: To what extent do the requirements upon Goolsby to act in the role of mediator between worlds transform her own disciplinary investment in ways beyond the recognition of her disciplinary peers? As she herself notes: "There is still no real career path for social science within the Department of Defense." As such, to be a social scientist is, in some significant sense, to be something else within the Department of Defense at this time, even when such a background is explicitly valued. What this entails may bear further exploration.

Goolsby Response

My sense is not only of a "parallel universe" (which anyone who engages with significant bureaucracy has experienced) but also a universe in juxtaposition to the universes of science and practice. Military operators and military scholars with less experience and education in social sciences often stumble on ideas (such as structural functionalism) that appear to have great utility and insight; the limitations of these notions are not implicitly apparent. The "bad news" I refer to in this essay refers to ideas that seem wonderful, groundbreaking, new, and, further, an idea or approach that will make a difference in the military understanding of their problem space; sometimes it included ideas about how to "get around" the fact that the military were involved as funding sources or as partners. Whether it was a naive approach or a naive conception about some aspect of social science, bringing the bad news that that such-and-such cannot work always means bursting someone's bubble. But in my experience, people got over this rapidly. A friend redirects you if you're headed the wrong way. Were there instances in which good advice was ignored? Yes. But at ONR, at least, there are checks and balances in place that do an excellent job in protecting research subjects, and Freedom of Information Act (FOIA) requests help to make sure non-social scientists pursuing programs of social science research (in targeting, for example) must always be concerned about the high level of transparency in military-funded research in this institution. I have never felt constrained in my vocation, and the ethical frameworks in play are as high, if not higher, than any university in the United States.

As to whether I am more a "subject matter expert" than an anthropologist, I have conducted research—mostly in social media, humanitarian operations, and sociotechnical behavior—and it is from that research that I derive the knowledge and understanding of the scientific issues that need further study. I attend conferences and workshops in many disciplines; I present papers, and I publish; my specialties are simply more in line with what has become the field of computational social science, a new disciplinary specialty that has relatively few anthropologists. Anthropologists who study highly urban cultures are remarkably different than those who study rural or small-scale cultures; linguists are different from archaeologists. My disciplinary specialty is merely novel, and I bring to it the ethnographic and ethnological education, the problems and advantages of qualitative research, and the theoretical depth of a full and rigorous training in culture and society. I do agree that the military committees on which I have sat have used me primarily as they do other social scientists, as subject matter expert. But in exploring the world of social behavior, as limited as I am by my armchair, my age, and my life situation, I feel I remain fully engaged as a researcher whose foundations are fully rooted in the masters (Boas, Mead, Bourdieu, Mauss, Malinowski, et al.) and with contemporary anthropologists. And, like many, I would point to others, from Herb Simons to Marshall McLuhan, as having influenced my perspective. Is anthropology a "job"? Or a vocation?

Personally, I often find that it is my disciplinary peers who have in some cases transformed beyond recognition. As many move away from the paradigm of science, I am concerned that anthropology will be considered more like poetry; very pretty, nice things to think, but on the whole, not useful in the real problems such as social cohesion and community stability. But then, perhaps I am outdated, following the path of Margaret Mead, Ruth Benedict, and others now long gone. And yet, when I spend time with graduate students, talking about community and social media, I get the distinct feeling that we still have a great deal to learn about human behavior, and that science does provide the best toolset, metaphors, and ways of seeing that we need to engage the world constructively.

Reference

Goolsby, Rebecca

2005 Ethics and Defense Agency Funding: Some Considerations. *Social Networks* 27:95–106.

2

Identity Management in the Federal Government: How an Andean Archaeologist Became a Social Scientist

Charlene Milliken

Charlene Milliken was introduced to us through a colleague of Laura McNamara's at Sandia National Laboratories, who had encountered Milliken while interacting with research project partners in the federal agency where Milliken works (which is not named in this essay, at Milliken's request). Recognizing that Milliken and McNamara had similar disciplinary backgrounds, he put them in touch with each other. Subsequently, McNamara asked Milliken if she would be interested in contributing an essay to the volume.

Milliken is the only postdoctoral candidate represented in this book, and is one of the few anthropologists that we know to hold a postdoctoral position in a U.S. government agency. Her experience intrigued us for two reasons: first, we had not considered the vehicle of the "postdoc" as a point of entry into the world of national security work; and second, Milliken's training was in archaeology. Milliken has a B.A. in international relations from the University of Southern California, but pursued a Ph.D. in archaeology. Her doctoral fieldwork involved multiple excavations in Peru, Bolivia, Ecuador, and Colombia; and her academic research interests include mortuary rituals, ancestor veneration, corporate group dynamics, household status and wealth, gender, and the legitimization of local power through the co-option and transformation of state ideology and religious practices. As she describes in her essay, her orientation and interests have changed dramatically in the past few years, and she currently works on issues of science and technology policy in a large government bureaucracy responsible for a broad range of security functions.

Shortly after completing her Ph.D. in Anthropology at the University of Pittsburgh, Milliken won an American Association for the Advancement of Science (AAAS) fellowship and was soon working in the Science &

Technology Directorate of a federal government agency. The annual AAAS competition is one of the few regularly available sources of flow-through of academic capital into government institutions, and one way in which Ph.D.s in the social sciences come to work in security settings. During her AAAS fellowship, Milliken participated and worked on projects related to terrorism, risk communication, community resilience, and technology transfer. When the fellowship ended, Milliken continued working in the same agency. Her work is mainly focused on identifying barriers and developing solutions to technology transfer of university-based research to end-users. She plans to continue developing a career in science and technology issues related to national security, either in a government or a think-tank setting.

I always thought I'd go the traditional academic route of teaching and research upon completing my Ph.D. in anthropology. However, by the end of graduate school, I had decided against pursuing a career in academia for many reasons. My specialization was narrow enough that the available teaching jobs were few, not to mention the fact that I lacked the experience and publication record to successfully compete against my colleagues for most of these jobs. Like many, I had become disillusioned about how disconnected academia was from the problems and concerns of the real world. Finally, though I love conducting research and the excitement of discovery, I felt that it would be self-serving to spend my life doing research that would interest only a handful of people.

During my last semester in graduate school, I had a memorable conversation with a trainer at my gym. He had recently returned from Iraq. Being sent out of state for military training in his late teens before being deployed to Iraq was probably the farthest he had ever traveled in his life. When I spoke to him, there was nothing but venom in his voice when he talked about the Iraqi people. It was unfortunate that his first experience in another country was in the context of war. And it was clear that he had not received much, if any, cultural training to prepare him for Iraq and the Iraqi civilians he would no doubt encounter. After my brief conversation with this veteran, I felt that anthropologists were morally obligated to help teach these young, inexperienced warfighters about the dangers of ethnocentrism, the inevitability of culture shock, and the beauty of cultural diversity. This conversation made me realize that as an anthropologist, I had the background and skills that would allow me to do something that could have a positive impact, both at home in the United States and internationally. Wars happen. But I remain convinced that better cultural understanding will reduce conflict during wartime and make wars less common.

During my last year in graduate school, I started looking for job opportunities in the private and public sectors. I reached out to an anthropologist who had made the transition from academia to the "real world" to ask for advice about how to make this transition and suggestions of career pathways to pursue. She had received a fellowship through the American Association for the Advancement of Science (AAAS) Science & Technology Policy Fellowship Program and suggested I apply for it. I applied and was selected for the National Defense/Global Security Fellowship. This fellowship program gave me an opportunity to work in the federal government as a postdoctoral fellow, and I ended up in the science and technology division of one of the large federal agencies.

After 9/11, U.S. troops overseas were contending with the challenges of improvised explosive devices (IEDs) and the federal government became focused on preventing another act of terrorism within U.S. borders. For my AAAS fellowship experience, I was offered an opportunity to learn about and get involved in IED research and policy. In addition to learning new research areas, I hoped that the experiences I gained through the AAAS fellowship program would make me more marketable outside of the academic world. I was certainly enthusiastic about working in the public sector and making a difference where it would really count. I knew I was taking a risk with my academic reputation working on a national security topic, but I have always believed that sometimes the best way to make a positive impact and bring about change is to become part of the system you want to change or do not agree with. Though I learned a lot about IEDs and terrorism through my AAAS fellowship, I was also able to expand my opportunities and participate in a variety of programs and projects related to risk communication, community resilience, and technology transfer.

About six months after I started my fellowship, the spouse of a fellowship cohort was looking for an anthropologist to consult on a project his organization wanted to pursue. I was asked to work as an independent consultant to help put together a grant proposal to develop an assessment tool that could be used by the U.S. military to better understand a local cultural context while carrying out Security, Stabilization, Transition and Reconstruction (SSTR) missions. I struggled with whether or not I should use my anthropological expertise to help develop a cultural assessment tool for the military. How could I be sure the tool would not be used in some way to root out enemies, subjugate a local population, or overthrow a government? But what if this tool actually helped the U.S. military better understand a local culture, enabling it to minimize conflict, establish greater security, build culturally and environmentally appropriate infrastructure, and provide more successful humanitarian assistance? As I thought about the potential impacts such a tool could have, I realized that the use of any tool could result in negative or positive outcomes. I decided to help put together the grant proposal because I believe that people who have a better and more intimate understanding of a culture become more protective, respectful, and empathetic toward that culture. And I know that people in the military are no different than the rest of us: they want to do good rather than harm, have peace rather than war, and protect rather than kill.

In all honesty, I was surprised to find out that we won the grant. Now that we had the funds to move forward on the project, I was faced with the dilemma again. Should I use my anthropological expertise to develop a cultural assessment tool for the military? Putting forth an idea for a tool in a proposal is different than actually developing a prototype of the tool. By participating on this project, how could I be certain that the tool I was helping to develop would not be used to compromise the safety of, eliminate, or destroy individuals or groups deemed dangerous by the U.S. military?

I decided to work on the project. I felt an important outcome that could result from using the tool was a more culturally aware, prepared, and empathetic warfighter—characteristics we strive to instill in our undergraduate students through teaching them about other cultures. In addition, a good proportion of warfighters probably spend more time "in the field" interacting with local populations than many anthropologists, and this tool would simply provide them with a framework within which to better make sense of and organize their own observations and impressions. Ultimately, I hoped using this tool would enable warfighters to make better decisions when carrying out SSTR missions. All the resources I used to develop the tool were open and available to anyone with access to libraries, bookstores, or the Internet. I did not provide information. Nor did I have any privileged or confidential information, about any culture or society that could result in betrayal of or specifically harm a certain individual or group. In fact, the tool could be used to assess a U.S. college fraternity, hunter-gatherer group in southern Africa, or kibbutz in Israel. Finally, in the spirit of Scheper-Hughes' "militant anthropology" (Scheper-Hughes 1995), I felt that developing a tool that would make warfighters more culturally sensitive would be one small contribution toward protecting a society that found itself in the midst of a conflict or war.

Many will argue that the United States is often the instigator or cause of that conflict or war. But the individuals sent to fight in that war should not be denied the tools or knowledge to better understand the cultural contexts or the people of the conflict area, especially if these tools or knowledge will ultimately benefit the local population. We anthropologists seem to believe that it is against our principles and morals to help the powerful, and that we are obligated to help the powerless, the underdogs, or the exotic "other." Yet sometimes the biggest impact can be made by changing the "culture" of the powerful, and by becoming part of the system to transform it so that the less powerful benefit. I believe that working in the federal government and working on developing this tool for the U.S. military is how I can make a positive impact by nudging the system to take one tiny step that would benefit "the other" in a context that was literally one of life and death.

Not long after I started my AAAS fellowship, I had another memorable conversation. My contact information was provided to prospective AAAS fellows looking for placement in the federal government. A professor of anthropology was trying to decide which federal agency he wanted to be placed in and he called me to ask about my experience. Specifically, he asked if I had ever been asked to do intelligence work or to help find "bad guys." I told him that I had never been asked, nor had I ever been confronted with those types of scenarios. Further, I told him that if I had been or am asked to find bad guys or do anything that I didn't feel comfortable doing, that I would refuse to do it. His response was, "Wow. So you haven't lost your morals since you've been working in the federal government." His comment represents a viewpoint held by some in the anthropology community about people who work on national defense/global security issues. When I started learning about IEDs at the beginning of my fellowship, I began following the debate within the anthropology community about the role of anthropology and anthropologists in national security and the military. But I had never been personally affected by it until talking to this prospective AAAS fellow. Though this anthropology professor knew nothing about me, he had made an assumption about my character solely based on my place of employment.

However, this was not the only comment I received about my moral integrity since I started my fellowship. Not long after my discussion with the anthropology professor, I was talking to one of my anthropology graduate school advisors who asked me how I was enjoying working in the federal government and then playfully scolded me, "I hope you're not doing anything illegal!"

Conversations like these make me feel liminal. After my AAAS fellowship, I have continued working in the federal government as a postdoc. I am no longer part of the academic community, but as a postdoctoral fellow neither am I a federal employee. I am an anthropologist who works in the federal government. I am not working in the federal government as an anthropologist. During my AAAS fellowship, I was often referred to and introduced as "the anthropologist." Like many people with little knowledge about anthropology or the social sciences in general, many of the people I interact with in the federal government—whether in meetings or at conferences or workshops—assume all anthropologists are cultural anthropologists (my subfield is archaeology). Anthropologists are often seen as experts on almost everything related to human behavior, culture, or interaction. We are presumed to understand how the human mind works, know every detail of the most obscure tribal group in Africa, have expertise in social network analysis, and carry around an extensive toolbox of methods to tackle terrorism, white-collar crime, community relations, public health problems, poverty, or any other topic that involves working with or understanding humans.

Like most jobs, my day-to-day activities mainly consist of the mundane: writing and answering emails, attending endless meetings, and going down the checklist of getting a project completed. Once in a while, my day or week is punctuated by attending a conference, traveling to meet with partners on collaborative efforts, participating in a brainstorming session to develop a new project, taking a brief detour to explore an interesting research question, or dropping everything to complete an urgent task due at the end of the day. I share an office, socialize with coworkers, have a Blackberry, wear a business suit, and occasionally go out for lunch to sample the lunch fare offered up by the myriad specialty food trucks that congregate around Washington, D.C.'s city parks.

For the past couple of years, I have been struggling with how to separate being an anthropologist from doing anthropology. Because I was trained as an anthropologist, can all the work I do be characterized as anthropological? Or, are my perceptions and ways of looking at the world a result of my life experiences and personal history, which gave me an affinity for and ultimately led me to study anthropology? I often use my social science research skills (e.g., literature reviews, writing, developing hypotheses, etc.), but I do not use any specific anthropological skills, methodologies, or knowledge to carry out my day-to-day work. The only time I specifically used my anthropological skills and knowledge was in the development of the aforementioned cultural assessment tool for the military. Yet both my federal and academic colleagues assume that I must be regularly using my anthropological knowledge and skills on the job. Lately I have found it more authentic to identify myself as a "social scientist with a degree in anthropology" for two reasons. First, "social scientist" is a broader label under which an anthropologist can be categorized, and calling myself a social scientist helps deter people from automatically making assumptions about me as an anthropologist. And second, the skill set I sometimes use to carry out my work is more accurately associated with that of a general social scientist than with that of a specific social science discipline such as anthropology.

The anthropology community is distrustful of the federal government, especially the national security agencies and the military services.

Many people in the national security agencies and the military recognize the importance of culture and have been reaching out to anthropologists for the past several years. I believe that anthropology can make a valuable contribution within the U.S. military context and in other homeland and national security efforts. But I also firmly identify with the ideals and values of my collective anthropology community. Anthropologists, like many other social scientists, are bound by a professional ethical code to do no harm and to consider the potential negative consequences of our research efforts. Indeed, I find myself wondering where to draw the line between the enormous amount of good that anthropologists hope and expect to come out of our research, against the endless possibilities of potential harm or unintended consequences our research efforts might bring about.

Like many anthropologists, I want to use my skills and knowledge to make this world a better place. Leaving academia for the federal government does not mean that I have given up my morals, my integrity, or my ethical training as an anthropologist. However, I do feel as though I have had to give up membership in my kin group—anthropology—because I have chosen to work in the federal government and, specifically, in the area of security.

Editorial Commentary

Like many of the contributors to this volume, Charlene Milliken describes pursuing work that is meaningful, consequential, and transformative. In multiple passages, she relates searching for a professional opportunity to "have a positive impact." She sees herself as sharing in an anthropological ethos that values knowledge production that "make[s] this world a better place."

Although Milliken emphasizes moral considerations and a desire for personal agency as salient forces shaping her career decisions, we sensed that her choices have been as pragmatic as idealistic. Coming out of graduate school, she believed that her narrow specialization and lack of research experience and publications precluded seeking an academic career. Milliken is not unique in this regard; many graduate students decide at some point that academia is not a good fit and, upon completion of their degrees, decide to pursue careers in other institutional settings. Indeed, the fact that anthropologists are pursuing so many kinds of work in such a wide range of institutional settings is a grounding theme of this book.

In any case, what is interesting is that Milliken, trained as an archaeologist, takes a position as an AAAS postdoctoral science policy fellow for a large federal agency in Washington, D.C. Postdoctoral positions are common in the physical, mathematical, and biological sciences as mechanisms to help new Ph.D.s transition from graduate school into professional careers. They are less the norm in anthropology (quite rare in cultural anthropology, less unusual in archaeology and physical anthropology). But in government agencies, postdocs are commonly used to provide relatively inexpensive but knowledgeable labor to support existing research and development projects. We wonder if Milliken's experience signals that anthropologists are joining the flow of professionals who transition into government work via the postdoctoral position.

For Milliken, the postdoctoral position may be a mechanism through which she permanently transitions out of academic anthropology, cultivating a career in what many anthropologists would consider "nontraditional" institutions. At the same time, we find it potentially significant that the AAAS and the federal agency sponsoring the postdoctoral program selected someone trained in anthropology for a federal science policy position. For this agency and AAAS, Milliken's postdoctoral position may serve an array of institutional purposes, including a relatively low-risk way of exploring how anthropology might be made to usefully intersect with the concerns of national security. Milliken hints at this when she describes a range of "programs and projects related to terrorism, risk communication, community resilience, and technology transition" to which her postdoctoral position exposes her.

Along these lines, it is worth pointing out that the position also exposes these projects to Milliken as an anthropologist. This raises the question of what kinds of expertise her colleagues held, and what understandings and expectations they had of Milliken. We know she learned to present herself as a "social scientist," and she draws a distinction between "being an anthropologist" and "doing anthropology." However, we wondered what this distinction looked like in practice. For one thing, Milliken isn't interacting with the agency as an institution. She is interacting with groups of people in an organization, and they are the ones who hold these expectations and communicate them to her. We wondered who these people are, and what their backgrounds were, and if she is the only social/behavioral scientist in her group. In other words, how does she think their expectations of her as an anthropologist were formed? Moreover, we can easily imagine her struggling to find ways of making her training and expertise in archaeology—she is an Andeanist by training—relevant to the projects in which she participated; we wondered if she sees herself as successful in doing so, or if she ultimately sought other ways of bridging between the worlds of the agency where she worked and her recent academic training.

Since roughly the 9/11 attacks, anthropologists have been engaged in an often-charged disciplinary discourse about whether or not anthropologists can and should contribute to the projects of the "national security state." These debates are rendered visible in editorials, resolutions, and conference presentations, but also occur in the internal dialogues that anthropologists have with themselves about how their work meets the ethical, methodological, and political norms of the discipline as well as the one-on-one interactions we have with each other.

Milliken's essay is fraught with these tensions. She imagines herself to be crossing a boundary that many anthropologists would not be willing to breach, by stepping into the national security arena. She is deeply self-conscious about how her career decisions have affected her reputation among academic colleagues. She finds herself countering stereotypes from at least two colleagues, as demonstrated in the conversation with an anthropologist who seemingly assumed that her position in a national security environment would entail doing "intelligence work or [helping] find 'bad guys.'" When she explains this is not the case, he jokes—perhaps only semihumorously—that she has not lost her moral compass. Perhaps conversations like this are why Milliken spends so much of her essay emphasizing her internal ethical debates and justifications, and less time detailing what she does on a daily basis.

In any case, Milliken emphasizes that the costs she feels are worth the effort, because she has an opportunity to affect "a difference where it would really count." Implicit in this statement is a differentiation between "what academics do" and "what really counts." One might read this as a suggestion that academic work does not "count" in the way that government service does; or, perhaps, that academics do not think about justifying their work in the way that Milliken's career decisions seem to be forcing her to do; or that the space of justification is more consciously fraught in the public sector. Indeed, Milliken's narrative raises some provocative questions about anthropology as a kind of public practice, beyond the routine academic-versus-applied distinction. Reading her essay, we identified three interrelated ways in which Milliken's work is public: first, she is translating anthropological knowledge from a form that might otherwise be inaccessible for the consumption of nonanthropologists; second, she is doing so to have a public impact; and third, she is doing so as a federal or "public" employee.

Regarding the issue of translation, one of the major issues that anthropologists are examining is not just the ethics of making cultural knowledge accessible and useful to individuals and institutions representing the state, but the practicalities of doing so. This is a massively complicated problem. Not only do most government institutions fail to recognize that anthropology is as much an ethical and political project as it is a scientific one, but that anthropology has developed its own narrative, linguistic, and semantic conventions. And these are unlikely to translate cleanly into the politicized pragmatics of governance in places like the large, bureaucratized, federal workplace where Milliken is located. This is important, because from what we can tell, Milliken's work seems very much about translation. Of particular importance in this regard is her vignette of the "tool," which raises a number of important themes and questions.

First, Milliken tells us that she was asked to work as a "private consultant" to develop this "tool." We take this to mean that her consultancy was either outside her main employment in the federal government or that her position as an AAAS postdoctoral fellow entailed consulting work for other government programs external to the agency sponsoring her postdoctoral position. In any case, Milliken's self-described role as "consultant" speaks to the diverse array of relationships through which information is transmitted in policy and decision-making circles inside Washington, D.C., and the multiple roles that a single individual may assume either sequentially or simultaneously in a policy career: postdoctoral fellow, consultant, contractor, federal employee.

Second, the use of the word "tool" hints at a rather jarring difference between the way that anthropologists perceive their knowledge products and the way that Milliken's interlocutors in the national security community make things "useful." Milliken frames this "tool" project more as a problem of ethical/moral/personal choice than as an opportunity to describe how anthropological/social science knowledge is treated as something that can be instrumentalized. The fact that she's asked to develop "a tool" may say a great deal about the organizational culture that Milliken has entered into. What is this "tool?" What is its format; where will it circulate; how is it constructed; who is negotiating what is considered appropriate for inclusion in a "tool" and what is not; who is contributing to it? Milliken seems more focused on presenting the "tool" as something that can have a positive moral valence and outcomes; we wish she had instead used this as a chance to enter into a discussion about how the knowledge regimes of the federal government differ from (1) archaeology (arguably and somewhat ironically, archaeologists are anthropology's tool experts) and (2) the idea of "cultural assessment tools," more generally vis-à-vis the kind of tropes and structures that we use in anthropology. The "tool" story could mark a potentially significant difference in the disciplinary/organizational culture.

Related to the "tool" is the largely unexplored assertion that working for the federal government is actually a form of militant anthropology. We can easily hear Nancy Scheper-Hughes taking umbrage to this assertion, as "militant anthropology" is a construct that entails very explicit political and ideological commitments. Milliken seems to be provocatively reframing it to legitimize work with the very "systems" that Schepher-Hughes has spent most of her career criticizing.

In her response, Charlene Milliken told us that she tried to address the main questions that we had asked her: what she does (which, as she put it, is "pretty much what people do in an office setting"); what anthropological things people expect from her ("Nothing," she told us); and how being trained as an archaeologist has relevance ("We actually have a few good transferable skills!"). She told us that the people she works with are more interested in her background as an archaeologist, perhaps because it evokes images of Indiana Jones. Her response to our commentary is below.

Milliken Response

After 9/11, the importance within the federal government of understanding the "other," which in many cases implied the "enemy," once again pushed the subject matter experts of the "other"—anthropologists—to the forefront. I think this has unfortunately resulted in a common belief that anthropologists who work in the federal government on security-related issues or in homeland or national security agencies or departments spend their days developing effective methods to help the military, intelligence analysts, national security officials, or investigative agents identify and find bad guys. However, as in my case, I believe many anthropologists who work in the federal government spend most of their time doing generalized day-to-day tasks typical in any office setting: email, attending meetings, managing projects, returning phone calls, putting together presentations, writing reports, etc. Some, like me, are lucky enough to occasionally participate in a research project. Many people—anthropologists included—assume that anthropologists working in the federal government are applying their specialized skills, capabilities, and knowledge to perform their jobs. However, the typical day-to-day activities that need to be accomplished to make an office run smoothly and accomplish its goals almost always trump the need for specialized anthropological insight, knowledge, or contribution. As a postdoctoral fellow working in the federal government, the number of times I have been asked to develop or conduct an anthropological study or to do any kind of anthropological research or analysis on an individual, country, or ethnic community, group, or organization has been zero.

Since I've been working in the federal government, if specifically asked what my Ph.D. is in, I inform people that I am an anthropologist. Most of the time, I get the polite response of how important culture is. Only when people assume I am a cultural anthropologist do I correct them and tell them I actually studied archaeology. Of course, this almost always provokes evokes visions of Indiana Jones, and most people are fascinated to learn about my experiences as an archaeologist. I have never had anyone question what an archaeologist was doing working in this agency or on that project. As an archaeologist, I do possess a transferable skill set: data collection methods, developing and managing large databases, statistical analyses to identify relationships within datasets, and interpretation of data analysis results. These are skills that most social scientists have and ones that are relevant to many types of jobs and organizations. Though I am not a cultural anthropologist, I have spent several years living (or doing archaeological research) in the Andean region of South America. Like cultural anthropologists, I had to study contemporary societies and anthropological methods and theories. The skills and training I gained as an archaeologist are easily transferred to many employment contexts. These transferrable skills are what I emphasized to transition out of academia, though I did capitalize on the value placed on being an anthropologist to get a foot in the door.

One last note about the "tool" project. It was a project I worked on outside of my fellowship as an independent consultant for a private firm. As with any tool, technology, methodology, vaccine, etc. developed by a private company, specific information about that product is proprietary.

Reference

Scheper-Hughes, Nancy
1995 The Primacy of the Ethical: Propositions for a Militant Anthropology. *Current Anthropology* 36(3):409–40.

3

Public Anthropology and Multitrack Dialoguing in the Securityscape

Robert Albro

Trained in political, legal, and linguistic anthropology, Robert Albro received his Ph.D. in sociocultural anthropology from the University of Chicago. He maintains a 20-year research focus on popular and indigenous politics in Bolivia, with particular attention to the changing terms of citizenship, political participation, and the role of indigenous movements. Albro is the author of Roosters at Midnight: Indigenous Signs and Stigma in Local Bolivian Politics *(Albro 2010).*

In 2004 and 2005, Albro received consecutive fellowships at the Carnegie Council for Ethics in International Affairs and at the Smithsonian Institution, respectively. If in different ways, each included sustained attention to the practice of multilateral cultural policy, with a focus on cultural rights and intangible cultural heritage, respectively. Overlapping with this was Albro's tenure on the American Anthropological Association's (AAA) Committee for Human Rights, including as its Chair (2005–2007). These experiences moved Albro into overlapping worlds of public policy, with particular attention to culture as a subject of policy, ethics, and human rights advocacy. These activities coincided with a move to Washington, D.C. where many of the U.S. cultural institutions also active in cultural policy are located. Albro's regular involvement with the AAA, background in human rights, cultural policy, and his location in Washington, D.C. all contributed to the invitation to participate in CEAUSSIC in 2006. This experience has extended Albro's work at the borders of anthropology, public policy, and cultural policy, adding attention to the security sector.

Albro's current research has been driven by this work with national and multilateral cultural policy-making. His efforts pay attention to the advancement of cultural claims by grassroots social justice efforts but also by state actors, as culture is now regularly made the subject of new legal and regulatory efforts to define and to protect it and as culture is viewed as a critical problem-solving instrument. Albro's work is informed by an effort to understand how and why the culture concept—formulated in terms of soft power, property, terrain, heritage, and as a right—is increasingly conceived less as an intransigent obstacle to progress and more as a resource, an intangible asset, information capital, and as a source of expert knowledge by new social movements and for work in public diplomacy, international development, human rights, emerging cultural industries, and military planning, as well as the relationships among these projects. Albro regularly engages with counterparts in these arenas about the roles of culture and of anthropological practice as a part of such efforts, an experience he reflects on in this essay.

Over the years, Albro's work has been supported by the National Science Foundation, Mellon Foundation, Rockefeller Foundation, and the American Council for Learned Societies, among others. Albro has also been a Fulbright scholar and an International Fellow at the Kluge Center of the Library of Congress. From 2008 to 2009, Albro was Chair of the Commission on the Engagement of Anthropology with the U.S. Security and Intelligence Communities (CEAUSSIC). He was recently a member of the National Research Council's Committee on Unifying Social Frameworks, and serves on the American Association for the Advancement of Science (AAAS) Science and Human Rights Coalition Steering Committee. In 2009, Albro received the AAA President's Award for outstanding contributions to the Association. He has taught at a number of colleges and universities, and he is currently in residence at the School of International Service at American University in Washington, D.C.

I don't work in any capacity for the security sector. Nor have I ever consulted for, or been funded by, any organization (public or private) associated with this sector, unless we count the National Science Foundation, but that was for ethnographic research on local Bolivian politics. My relationship to anything having to do with the intersection between anthropology and the U.S. national security state, therefore, is not something I actively set out to pursue. It is fairly serendipitous and indirect. And it has been professionally relatively late to emerge.

It might not be obvious, then, why I was asked in early 2010 to serve on a National Research Council committee with the inauspicious name of "Unifying Social Frameworks," sponsored by the Office of Naval Research. Since the mid-2000s, in fact, I have been regularly solicited to participate in a wide variety of conversations—public, formal, and informal—about the relationship of anthropology to different parts of the security state. This includes academic meetings, departments, academic centers and institutes, Pentagon briefings, talks at RAND, at the National Defense University, and the Military Operations Research Society, among others. These are not consulting gigs. They are different locations that, collectively with others, compose a challenging conversation across historically fraught fault lines between anthropology (and the social sciences, with some exceptions) and the military.

Often I am invited to participate with the expectation that I will "represent" anthropology for constituencies across this landscape largely unfamiliar with the discipline. I am asked in most cases as a direct result of my participation in CEAUSSIC. Here, I want to consider some of the practical, conceptual, and ethical implications of this role as, let's say, a public policy interlocutor in the securityscape, and how this is different from more typical academic debate, which is usually conducted in print, at conferences, and sometimes through the media.

CEAUSSIC and Dialogue

The CEAUSSIC work included a modest intervention in the anthropological public sphere in the form of two reports to the AAA on matters anthropological-military, participation in a variety of public forums and press conferences (including at annual meetings of the AAA, two public forums at Brown University's Watson Institute, and the United States Institute of Peace), and interviews with media following the story. CEAUSSIC as a group mixed professionals from various academic and nonacademic vantage points, including people working within the security context and without, for the military and on the military, critics as well as agnostics. Our conversation, too, departed from a variety of not always compatible perspectives, and it was a steep learning curve for all. In our work together, in the main we did not seek to resolve these tensions into a unitary account so much as we tried to convey this "multivoicedness"—if with varying success—to colleagues inside and outside of anthropology, as part of an effort to promote a more grounded and far-ranging back-and-forth.

Notable was the fact that anthropological colleagues from academic walks of life and journalists were very much interested in the controversy attending the U.S. Army's Human Terrain System (HTS) program, but little else. From our location, promoting regular conversation about the context, diversity, and wider implications of anthropology's engagement with security, broadly conceived, was challenging. And as we discussed periodically, the public debate over these issues was in particular ways overdetermined and overshadowed by the litmus test of HTS. This, in turn, obscured pertinent and wider-ranging discussions about, among other things, the shifting fault lines of academic versus nonacademic disciplinary practice with respect to the security domain and the various relationships of anthropology, as a social science, to these unfolding exigencies. As such, in our first report to the AAA (2007:6), we encouraged "openness and civil discourse on the issue of engagement." In addition to the written reports, public forums, and media engagement, we regularly submitted short articles to *Anthropology News* and blogged. Our success was, at best, partial. The present volume, in part, continues these efforts.

The "multivoicedness" often characterizing the discussions that were part of the CEAUSSIC experience contrasted with the at times alarmingly agonistic character of our wider disciplinary discourse, among ourselves and with others. At least with regard to the U.S. military, as an association we did not always seem inclined to listen to counterparts from the security sector then actively engaging with our discipline, its methods, and key concepts—or at least we did not appear to want to listen very closely. This reminded me of Norwegian anthropologist Thomas Eriksen's critique of anthropology's withdrawal from public discourse—self-imposed "cocooning," he had called it (Eriksen 2006).

As I have discussed elsewhere (Albro 2008), in effect, the ways the discipline conducted these debates actively contributed to a dramatic lack of public dialogue between the social sciences and the military, leaving the military to make of anthropology what it would. It increased the likelihood that military decision makers would cherry-pick the kinds of social science that best mirror image what it already thinks it knows, and that military planners would continue to hear what they wanted to hear rather than what they might need to hear. It also increased the likelihood of the entrenchment of a parochial and mediocre "military social science" largely conditioned by the goals of the military establishment itself. And, through a lack of engagement, it sanctioned a traditional role for academic social scientists as "useful idiots" who only occasionally contribute—in compartmentalized fashion and only at a distanced remove—to potentially ill-conceived military anthropological adventures.

That it was important to have a constructive discussion with counterparts working in security contexts was, for me, distinct from the question of whether, and how, anthropologists might work in these contexts. Critique certainly has a place in these discussions. Yet, although I had no designs on work in the security sector, the fact that anthropology's debate about these matters was at times largely driven by its own just-so stories about the history of this problematic relationship—with special attention reserved for the Vietnam era—was disquieting. Often this did not seem to be a good-faith dialogue, but instead too narrow in scope, often politicized, on occasion even inquisitional, and self-serving.

As a result of this relatively long association, I've both developed new research interests at the intersection of cultural policy with the U.S.

security state—largely stumbled into on the job as part of the CEAUSSIC work—and become a regular participant, typically recruited, in ongoing dialogues with different interlocutors, including with other anthropologists, the AAA, journalists, or people working in different capacities across the military, as well as different organizations in these sectors. I cautiously describe these as "policy"-type dialogues. That is, they are about what happens when anthropological ideas, concepts, and methods are put into play among decision makers and users in different security arenas. That I have been drafted into this role, and taken it up it in certain ways, is a testament to the paucity of dialogue frequenting this anthropology-security frontier. Evidently, there aren't many people doing this.

Public Policy Anthropology?

And so my question: Why might anthropologists talk with different communities transecting the national security state, and what are the potential implications of these conversations? I am talking about dialogues with interlocutors, particularly where the discipline of anthropology, its methods and subjects, have been actively identified as a desirable capacity, expertise, asset, competency, knowledge base, or data source, and in ways that are often at odd angles to disciplinary sensibilities. Often this is a matter of the potential application of a disciplinary conceptual apparatus, method, or technique to potentially controversial state activities and interventions like intelligence work and wars. From the outset, then, a basic feature of these conversations is that multiple ideas about "anthropology" are in play at the same time, often subject to translation, typically among stakeholders with significantly different versions of what the social sciences, in essence, are. One risk, of course, is that "all translation is mistranslation."

This, then, got me thinking seriously about what we might credibly call a "public anthropology." I labeled my participation in these dialogues as serendipitous. But this isn't entirely true. My disciplinary genealogy, as a student at the University of Chicago and afterward, has included a preoccupation with "dialogue" and periodic thinking about anthropology's methodological and functional relationships to dialogue. This comprises both what different disciplinary developments have had to say about dialogue as an ethnographic and theoretical project of sorts and how to connect these developments to ways of imagining and of pursuing worthwhile kinds of public engagements.

There have been several recent disciplinary articulations making the case for dialogue as at the center of disciplinary practice. I don't want to rehearse these here in any detail. I do, however, want to note how this set of preoccupations is part of an immediate context of ideas for my identification with the discipline and suggests avenues for public engagement. Formative was the influence of coadvisors Jim Fernandez—his abiding concern with the "arguments" at the heart of culture—and Paul Friedrich, who worked out the concept of "dialogic breakthrough." Important as well were dialogically inclined anthropologists and linguists, including Peirce, Geertz, Bakhtin, and others. I was trained, too, during the so-called "writing culture" moment, sophisticated as it was about the intimate engagement between ethnography and dialogue. Jakobson's memorable reference to monologue as a social pathology has always stayed with me. And these ideas inform how I interpret Geertz's well-known observation about ethnography, "We are seeking, in the widest sense of the term in which it encompasses very much more than talk, to converse with them" (Geertz 1973:13). What this has added up to, for me, is a basic conviction that anthropological knowledge and practice in all its forms is fundamentally dialogically engaged and produced (see Tedlock and Mannheim 1995).

Another genealogical connection here is to Cold War conceptualizations of what we would today refer to as public anthropology, in the context of the formulation of area studies, post–World War II public diplomacy efforts like Voice of America, and the proliferating hyperrational security discourse of so-called defense intellectuals, ably critiqued by Carol Cohn (1987). Again, a Chicago connection: Robert Redfield's 1950s-era antidote to area studies in the form of his intercultural studies project, as he spelled this out in "Does America Need a Hearing Aid?" (Redfield 1953). Redfield translated his concern for the one-sidedness of U.S. diplomacy efforts of the time into a comparative project dedicated to promoting a "dialogue of civilizations," where, as he put it, "Mutual security depends on mutual understanding, and for understanding you have to have a conversation" (Redfield 1953:11). Redfield emphasized the crossing of disciplinary boundaries, cross-cultural engagement, and cross-fertilization of ideas. I lived with these ideas for several months in 1992 when, as a graduate student, I coordinated a conference organized by Milton Singer—a close associate of Redfield's—and Jim Fernandez, exploring "the conditions of reciprocal understanding" (Fernandez and Singer 1995). These precedents have continued to percolate in my thinking.

If conversation is a precondition for mutual security, then this includes a role for listening. We might find Redfield's formulation uncritical, even naive. But we might bring this together with the recent dialogic turn in anthropology, with its close attention to the pragmatics of dialogue and to the contributions of context to meaning. In this way, the essentially dialogical sensibilities of ethnography amount to more than a research method. They compose a principle of public disciplinary conduct: or at least for me, a location in discussions with counterparts across the securityscape. If the dialogic turn locates our interpretations in reciprocal engagements, often as discrepant and where our own voice provisionally contends with those of others, than we cannot only talk in terms of our own choosing, on our own turf, determined to maintain our own purity-at-distance.

To call these engagements public because they address looming extra-disciplinary social issues is insufficient. Nor, as has been argued, is it enough to suggest that a more effective public anthropology needs to tell better or more accurate stories than, say, the punditocracy. The error this makes is that it still assumes a unilateral projection of a recognizable disciplinary "voice" and makes no accommodation for the plural voices of consociates in a conversation. In disciplinary ethical terms, it is notable that there is little legible room for public engagements except in this way. If the AAA's Code of Ethics notes the importance of ongoing "dialogue and negotiation" with research subjects and on the matter of informed consent, with publics it restricts comment to an unproblematic concept of dissemination. As important are the terms of reference of our interlocutors, their discursive habits and language ideologies. Stripping away all the meta-talk, this amounts to an injunction to meet people where they are rather than just on our own terms.

The NRC Experience: Interdisciplinarity in the Securityscape

The National Research Council (NRC) is part of the National Academies, which are nonprofit and independent from the U.S. government, in contrast, say, to the Congressional Research Service. NRC's URL, for example, uses ".edu." Nevertheless, the government does fund a large percentage of the NRC's work. As part of the National Academies, the NRC's mission is to "advise the nation" regarding "questions of science, technology, and health policy." In practice, this means particular federal agencies, including military, security, and intelligence agencies. The NRC is responsible for most of the "study projects" within the National Academies, on the basis of committees filled out by highly vetted if uncompensated non-NRC volunteers from across the academic universe. Typically, a particular agency will bring a problem to the NRC about which it would like further clarification, and ask that a committee be organized to address it. If the NRC decides to accept the task, this agency becomes the "sponsor." In the case of the committee in which I participated, on "Unifying Social Frameworks," the statement of task was the following:

> The Office of Naval Research (ONR) requested the Committee on Human-Systems Integration to appoint an ad hoc committee to plan and conduct a public workshop focused on the methods and tools relevant to

> the subject of Unifying Social Data Frameworks. The workshop will feature invited presentations and discussions that will include: 1) an analysis of what sorts of data are needed to provide a comprehensive picture of a given region or country (e.g. Iraq, Afghanistan) in order to provide cultural and diplomatic knowledge for DoD [Department of Defense] personnel, 2) an examination of current frameworks and data bases used by ONR, while considering alternatives and additions which may prove to be more useful, and 3) an analysis of methods and tools that may effectively combine disparate data sources into a meaningful whole (e.g. through data management and data mining) (National Academies 2010).

As it happened, I was the only anthropologist on the committee. My name had come to the attention of the NRC study director managing the committee's work on the basis of my role in CEAUSSIC. The rest of the committee was composed of four psychologists, a political scientist, a criminologist, and a professor in a business school with a focus on organizational behavior and conflict management and a background in psychology. The committee's work from the beginning was—sometimes interestingly and sometimes problematically—an interdisciplinary undertaking. This ensured a range of departure points and attitudes about the virtues of our task. It is important to note that we were not tasked with producing a consensus report, and so did not have to agree.

As our work commenced, it was quickly clear that our interaction with the sponsors at ONR was highly mediated through the NRC. In part, this was about ensuring the independence of the committee's work. If the sponsoring agency might dictate the statement of task, as it was put to me, it has "little/no involvement in the way the specifics come together." To ensure this as well, committee members were asked to fill out confidential conflict of interest forms, and the committee discussed potential conflicts or biases each might have. We had a day-long meeting early in the committee's tenure, part of which was a presentation by the relevant ONR program. Between then and the workshop itself, communication with ONR was a lot like a sequestered jury to a judge: formally transacted by NRC via written statements. As a group, we had little face time with the sponsor, and it was the NRC staff's job to "manage the sponsor's expectations," not ours.

Nevertheless, the sponsor's expectations for our work were clear enough. Whatever the general statement of task specifically, we were to provide ONR with a sharper appreciation for the sources and best methods of acquiring desirable "sociocultural data." Since, as was noted by an ONR employee, "We drink our own Kool Aid too often," our committee was supposed to provide "outside-the-box" thinking on the question of "data." This was, in other words, an ONR fishing expedition. ONR hoped to benefit from our "cache of scientific expertise," as it in turn sought to grow the "applied science" space in DoD, and to come away at the very minimum with a "vague outline of the elephant." In other words, tell us what to make of "all this culture stuff," please. Interestingly, from the ONR point of view, useful scientific expertise was explicitly contrasted to the "literariness"—read: uselessness—of anthropology. What was useful, in other words, was data that could be relatively straightforwardly applied; contemporary ethnography apparently did not exhibit this characteristic.

Within our committee itself, this exhortation was variously interpreted. Several members were skeptical, both of the "unifying" frame and about the idea that we might provide ONR a "comprehensive theory of culture," as others had interpreted our task. Along these lines, one suggestion was to show ONR "what's being ground up in the sausage factory": that is, the fact of distinct and sometimes incompatible disciplinary investments in the sociocultural. Another committee member voiced the need to debunk "snake oil salesmen," that is, to suggest to ONR that it might be investing in junk science. As things developed, I had at least one clear ally in this group. From a distinct disciplinary perspective, in our discussions, his departure points were often complementary to my own: to engage with ONR about what the social sciences—ethically, methodologically, theoretically—could do, but more important, could not be expected to deliver in this regard. This seemed particularly important, given that ONR was actively seeking more DoD support for its applied science programs.

These committee conversations were often difficult. Here, I note just two ways that this was the case, pointing to institutional and interdisciplinary constraints, respectively. Throughout the experience, it was hard to miss what I'll call the entrepreneurial—others might say neoliberal—discourse that often framed our work. The NRC's staff referred to the sponsor as the "client," and we spent time considering our "deliverables." We were encouraged to see our mandate as the "supply side," not the "demand side." Among committee members, there was enthusiasm for drawing upon lessons from such fields as business negotiations, contract negotiations, and marketing. And we were urged to privilege parsimony over complexity, or as was said, to deliver "good, fast, cheap."

More challenging still was sorting through the different disciplinary sensibilities that committee members brought to this work. On the one hand, we collectively quickly agreed that suggesting any "unifying framework" was a bad idea. We also agreed that, generally, our ONR sponsor "wants humans to operate in a more deterministic fashion" than they do. On the other hand, at least some members were happy to pursue how to support the military's "armed social work"—using David Kilcullen's problematic term in discussions—and related social engineering projects.

I could engage constructively with some of these interventions, but not with all. And I often had misgivings about much of our conversation.

Perhaps my main misgiving, and the most difficult to address, was that my conception of culture was definitely in the minority. A major critical mass on our committee was generated by the fact that it was dominated by academic psychologists, most of whom had received DoD funding. Two of these had appointments in business schools. These represented, if you will, the contemporary version of what we might call the defense intellectual, if without the rational choice myopia of decades past. But, they did make different assumptions than I did about the culture concept. They discussed "cultural competence" as a "critical skill." They moved easily between "cognition" and "culture," taking for granted that people act on collectively shared "traditional cultural norms," which could be broken out into a taxonomy. They assumed that "psycho-social needs" à la Maslow were drivers for cultural meanings. If one identified the drivers, therefore, one could manipulate cultural beliefs. And so forth. All of this struck me in much the same way as it has struck anthropological colleagues who have criticized the military culture concept as derived from mid-twentieth century "culture and personality."

In our committee work, I went to some lengths to push back against this conception of culture. This included penning a lengthy eight-page single-spaced internal memo sketching out my concerns. In the end, our day-long workshop did represent these ideas, alongside others. But, I had also managed to ensure that at least one of the day's five panels was given over to a more skeptical appraisal of whatever we might mean by "sociocultural data" and its availability for the applied science tools ONR had in mind. The workshop ended up not being organized in terms of identified "competencies." I successfully argued that categories of cultural competence (e.g., trust, negotiation, or persuasion) were arbitrary, promoted "skills" in misleading ways, slighted tremendous variations in the ways these categories might be used and understood, and narrowly prioritized a cognitivist approach to culture in ways already conversant with how DoD tended to treat the question. The panel I organized certainly complicated any notion that the "data" were simply available to be collected in straightforward fashion, and did not support such an account. In fact, to the evident dismay of the sponsor, one position coming out of our panel was that "all data are inherently debatable."

Moving Centers of Gravity?

So what happened? The workshop took place. A variety of different perspectives from across the social sciences were represented. From my own standpoint, I found much of this work problematic in different ways. There was serious talk of methods of clandestine research, the Protestant ethic, more taxonomies, questions like "What makes people tick?," confident statements offered about prediction, social engineering, "honor cultures," and the like. And all of this was incorporated into the published workshop summary (NRC 2011). Government—including military—agencies like to have such published reports by the NRC because they can be used for legitimating purposes, giving agencies something to point to in the budget wars. Our publication's title also optimistically suggests—with Talcott Parsons' ghost—that we are indeed moving toward some sort of "unified" social science, and that the "data" merely await its collection by the DoD.

However, the summary's narrative reads differently. That same project of the summary's title is described several times between its pages as a "fool's errand." Among other critical interventions, I was able to organize a panel—which included two participants in this volume, Laura McNamara and Jessica Glicken Turnley—that took a fairly skeptical line, if while also talking with our ONR interlocutors. This included repeatedly drawing attention to the problems with a predictive social science and limits of technological black boxes, underscoring likely irresolvable tensions between the assumptions informing empirical data collection and those of the interpretive social sciences, and pointing to misconceptions in the extent to which ethnography can address the DoD data deficit in the "sociocultural." In large part as a result of our panel's intervention, the final chapter on the workshop's "Implications" concluded: "Attempts to create broad, integrated, approaches to social science issues or to base practical applications on such integrated theoretical foundations are not likely to succeed" (NRC 2011:90).

In debates about the identity of anthropology, part of what a public anthropology can include is attention to the particular conditions of dialogue: the terms of internal disciplinary discussion and debate as well as the possibilities of, and configurations for, sustained dialogue along emerging and often ill-defined disciplinary frontiers. In our own vernacular, this translates as a concern for the shape of dialogue in contact zones, or as folded into the structure of the conjuncture, in this case, as often interdisciplinary in character and conducted with agencies of the security state. This includes meeting people where they are and listening and responding to "their" terms of reference, prevailing lexicons, operative knowledge frames, conceptions of "subject matter" expertise, and "lessons learned" while also critically engaging them. This can, and should, include conversations about relationships drawn between anthropology and claims about culture advanced in the interests of security, with associated instrumentalities. But, this is hard to do through routine academic channels, and it is often necessary to participate in forums like this one in the hope of moving discussion to a different place.

Editorial Commentary

Unlike many of this volume's contributors, Albro does not identify himself as "national security" anthropologist, military or otherwise. However, in the wake of his involvement with CEAUSSIC—which was a very public exercise—Albro gained a reputation for being an informed discussant about national security anthropology. Given Albro's involvement in CEAUSSIC, his residence near Washington, D.C., and his employment at the School of International Studies at American University, the role is something of a natural one for Albro, who is institutionally and geographically proximate to the institutional settings in which national security theory and policy are formulated, promulgated, examined, and taught. Indeed, in the past five years, Albro has become a kind of "go-to" figure for the military professionals and policy makers who see themselves as advocates for the incorporation of social science theory, knowledge, methods, and experts into a range of national security activities. As a result, Albro finds himself in forums where he witnesses military, intelligence, academic, and other experts discussing and debating the deployment of the social sciences in general, and anthropology in particular, as a "desirable capacity, expertise, asset, competency, knowledge base, or data source," as he puts it.

In this regard, Albro's experience is unique, as he has created a role for himself that enables him to maintain a certain independence from the institutional commitments—academic, government, private contracting—that others have described. Albro describes himself as committed to the idea and practice of dialogue among anthropologists and the many individuals who comprise the national security state. His disciplinary training primed him for this role, he tells us. He was trained in cultural anthropology at the University of Chicago, and describes his advisers' emphasis on knowledge production as conversation, dialogue, display, interactions, and arguments. Moreover, Albro came of age when anthropology in general, and cultural anthropology in particular, was engaged in a difficult assessment of its identity, relationships to research subjects, and representational practices. For Albro, dialogue and conversation are anthropological practice, and anthropological knowledge is fundamentally dialogical.

At the same time, Albro's dialogic projects are more than extensions of theoretical commitments that were hammered into him during graduate school. Instead, Albro takes the discipline of anthropology at its word when thought leaders and professional associations assert the importance of a publicly engaged anthropology. He believes we need to interact with the institutions from which anthropology seeks the greatest distance, including the military, intelligence, and other forms of national security. After all, members of these institutions are claiming a stake in the translation of anthropological research and knowledge to military, intelligence, and other domains. For Albro, a public anthropology demands engagement with the self-identified stakeholders that are in the public sector, including meeting with them on their "turf," if only to understand what these institutions expect of anthropology. After all, if dialogue and negotiation are foundational principles for our work with research subjects, they probably have a grounding role in other interactions that we have with our many publics, even those that challenge anthropology's core sensibilities.

So how does this work? Albro's vignette is his experience on an NRC committee, in which he was the lone anthropologist-expert on a committee of social scientists charged with organizing a workshop oriented around "unifying" social frameworks, so that the ONR can develop comprehensive and integrated examinations of regions and countries of interest. As a participant-observer in the intersection of academic knowledge and military policy, Albro learns several things. First, the NRC sees ONR as a client, which means that it is unlikely to challenge the ONR's conceptualization of social science, despite the fact that many of the committee members object to the premise of "unifying" social theory. Second, he finds that some of the committee members are willing to support what he refers to as the DoD's "social engineering" projects, for which Albro has little enthusiasm, making it difficult to connect productively with these committee members. Finally, he is dismayed to discover that most of the committee members are unsympathetic to his anthropologically rooted understanding of "culture." Most of these are psychologists whose orientation to Maslow's needs dovetails with the operational orientation that the DoD brings to culture: as something to be documented, or a skill to be attained, or a form of cognitive activity to be manipulated.

Despite this trying context, Albro successfully leverages his committee role to organize a workshop panel in which social scientists (including McNamara, one of the coeditors of this volume, and Turnley, one of our contributors) presented skeptical critiques of the ONR sociocultural research mission. In the end, Albro says, the report seems to have been heavily influenced by the skeptical voices his panel brought to the discussion. One comes away from the NRC/ONR case with an appreciation of Albro's determinism to see his vision of public anthropology through—and how hard it is to execute. Just how many people have the diplomatic disposition and the discipline (both social and intellectual) to match these efforts is an open question. We wonder about the extent to which anthropology rewards this type of behavior and whether we have enough people in the field who model this kind of practice. We were curious whether Albro has tried to foster these attitudes and behaviors in his anthropology students, and if so, how.

As illustrative as Albro's NRC story is, we wished that there were more examples of the forums and relationships in which Albro is engaging in the exchanges the importance of which he stresses repeatedly throughout the essay. Moreover, we wondered how security experts find out about his work and interests; if so, are they sharing information among themselves about which anthropologists will "talk" to the security sector, in the way that we anthropologists talk about the military intellectuals who are promoting culture for operational and strategic imperatives? Also, what kind of messages does Albro bring back to anthropology, and how does he communicate these? And last, is he seen as "representing" anthropology in any corporate sense? If so, how does he deal with being seen as a representative or spokesperson for the discipline?

Albro Response

What I refer to as "multitrack dialoguing" is a purposeful allusion to "multitrack diplomacy," and to the fact that regular engagement with counterparts across the securityscape is certainly not just talk. The phrase is also meant to suggest that traditional academic stock-in-trade (e.g., published articles in the usual journals or conference presentations at the regular meetings) does not usually rise to the level of meaningful dialogue in this instance. At best, that amounts to an indirect dialogue-at-a-distance vis-à-vis often highly preoccupied counterparts across security institutions. Sometimes it is necessary to circumvent these turf wars by accepting the terms and conditions of where exchanges of ideas most often happen among counterparts. It has most often been the case that I have been brought into such interactions referred by established colleagues within security institutions. At this point, then, at least my own participation has been largely determined by the vagaries of informal networks.

These dialogues have been had mostly in person and mostly as part of invited meetings. One set of these has been sponsored by agencies that form a part of the U.S. government or are partly funded by it, including the NRC, but also the U.S. Institute of Peace (USIP), the National Defense University, the Military Operations Research Society, Sandia National Laboratory, and the Wilson Center. Others have been convened by nonmilitary academic institutions, including the University of California–Irvine, Columbia University, George Washington University, and American University. Several of these, including CEAUSSIC, were convened by professional scientific associations and advocacy organizations, including the AAA and the Social Science Research Council. This has included regular interaction with journalists, most fishing for sound bites for short articles, with the vast majority entirely about the HTS controversy. In fact, one quickly encounters a journalistic iron cage of sorts if wanting to raise other issues.

Perhaps the most frequent location for these conversations has been that of "centers and institutes" attached to universities. CEAUSSIC was invited to Brown University's Watson Institute on two occasions. Otherwise, I have been invited to small meetings at the Triangle Institute (a consortium of Duke University, the University of North Carolina, and North Carolina State), the Krasnow Institute (George Mason University), the John Hope Franklin Institute (Duke University), and the Eagleton Institute (Rutgers University), among others. It appears to me that these centers and institutes are one primary type of location for such dialogues, on the margin both of the university proper and of security institutions, though often with a foot in both. These dialogues can also fail, as was the case with an ill-conceived USIP-sponsored effort framed as a dialogue about the need for dialogue. No one had any idea how to proceed, so it went nowhere. These discussions tend to work better when sharply delimited by a particular topic or issue.

These dialogues are also inextricable from acts of representation: of kinds and availability of knowledge; of disciplinary specificity; of different perspectives at play within anthropology; of where the intersections of the social sciences and of security might be, what they look like, and what this might mean for the goals of colleagues in the securityscape; and of the ethical, methodological, conceptual, epistemological, and practical limits of anthropological engagement with these domains. Interlocutors, obviously, often want specific things from you and from anthropology. They are not in the room or at the table simply to listen to your (my) critiques, however constructive. They are often people without extensive training in the social sciences (though, often they do possess such training), and they are actively engaged in advancing their projects and their programs. This fact, of course, explains a basic tension built into any such dialogue. Individual academic anthropologists are rarely responsible for directly advancing projects in the same ways when speaking publicly about their research.

This raises the specter of "naive dialogue," which goes something like this: colleagues in these institutions and agencies pay attention when you say things they might want to hear, and/or minimally need to perform due diligence, for which such conversations—public or private—are merely a pro forma expression. Disciplinary critiques of "military anthropology" often appear to take the fact of naive dialogue for granted or conclude that the powerful institutions of the U.S. security state tend to interpellate—in the manner of Althusser—the people working in these institutions. Therefore, real dialogue—a frank exchange of perspectives—becomes almost impossible. With respect to the interpellation argument, I am an agnostic. The people with whom I have interacted in these institutions have expressed variable combinations of self-reflexivity, institutional critique, toeing the line, policy skepticism, or blinkered commitments, in ways not fundamentally different from, say, typical voices across the more traditional academic setting.

I will say, however, that a regular challenge is effectively conveying internal disciplinary diversity as a way to invite further consideration of the sources of knowledge claims about the social sciences, as these are part of ongoing work in the security sector. This has to do with directing dialogue to what, for colleagues in this arena, is the assumed value of the social sciences (and anthropology) in the first place. Here, I often encounter the expectation that I should represent a relatively unitary "discipline" boasting specific methods, key concepts, and subject matter expertise—all easily transalatable across multiple priorities and programs. "Anthropology," in this mode, takes on a familiarly generic and modular plug-in characteristic. This predicament is perhaps familiar to anyone who teaches introductory undergraduate courses about the discipline—an activity with which I've always been uncomfortable, since I've long felt anthropology in particular among the "liberal arts" translates poorly in this setting.

Although I have taught those courses, most recently I have been in an interdisciplinary school of international affairs. This means I am rarely teaching "anthropology students," and so whatever might be anthropological about my work in the classroom is rarely the course's subject matter. Instead, it is conveyed through choices about the introduction of concepts, framing of topics, and the uses of cases. In an introductory course I have often taught, "Cross-Cultural Communication" (yes, in the tradition of Hall, Hofstede, and Trompenaars), I routinely use a short 2008 video clip by the journalist John McHugh called "Afghanistan: Lost in Translation," which dramatically shows U.S. soldiers unable effectively to communicate with an Afghan elder, despite the presence of a translator, then becoming irate. I show the clip in the context of a discussion of "culture shock"—a standard topic for such a course but also a concept I find highly dubious for many reasons. And the video can be understood as an "example" of such but also as an implicit critique of the ways U.S. soldiers are primed to interact with Afghan civilians: give me the who, what, and where, now. While it makes sense for soldiers, this language ideology of dialogue as fact-driven and instrumentally purposive is an important source of the friction exposed in the video. It is, in fact, a fundamental way in which "culture" matters here.

Students find the video compelling, but typically either blame the interpreter as incompetent or treat the friction as an "example" of communication failure, given culture shock and the soldiers' lack of cultural competence. That is, whereas I might view aspirations of "cultural competence" as misguided, this is often not the lesson for students. Why show the video if not to demonstrate that more cultural competence adds up to better communication? "Culture" is treated as a vehicle of communication. There is, in short, very little room for the self-interrogation of one's own working assumptions about the utility of talk. This might be an anthropological lesson of sorts and an implicit critique of the assumptions underwriting the project of cross-cultural communication. But, although I might note this and some students perceive this, totally convinced as they are of the virtues of culturally competent dialogue, most do not. Hence, the video is available for interpretation in several ways. But since this particular classroom environment makes the culture shock-competence frame more available, students tend to seize on it.

This, then, poses the problem of naive dialogue or interpellation when discussing anthropology, ethnography, or the culture concept, with counterparts in DoD, the intelligence community, or other security agencies. As an anthropologist, it is not the case that I can simply authoritatively lay out what I understand to be the relevance and limits of anthropology in these contexts. Counterparts often already have definite commitments, say, about culture, conversant with their institutional setting and priorities. These need to be recognized and made a part of our dialogue. But what I have found most challenging is to broaden discussions with counterparts in security settings beyond ethics to include appreciation for multiple conceptions of culture and accompanying critiques, and to ask fruitful questions about why one such conception might have purchase there while another appears altogether absent.

References

Albro, Robert

2008 Minerva and Critical Public Engagement. *In* The Social Science Research Council's online forum "The Minerva Controversy." Available at: http://essays.ssrc.org/minerva/2008/11/14/albro/.

2010 Roosters at Midnight: Indigenous Signs and Stigma in Local Bolivian Politics. Santa Fe: School of Advanced Research on the Human Experience (SAR Press).

Cohn, Carol
1987 Sex and Death in the Rational World of Defense Intellectuals. *Signs* 12(4):687–718.
Eriksen, Thomas Hylland
2006 Engaging Anthropology: The Case for a Public Presence. Oxford, U.K.: Berg.
Fernandez, James W., and Milton Singer (eds.)
1995 The Conditions of Reciprocal Understanding. Chicago, IL: The Center for International Studies at the University of Chicago.
Geertz, Clifford
1973 The Interpretation of Cultures. New York: Basic Books.
McHugh, John
2008 Afghanistan: Lost in Translation [videorecording]. Available at: http://www.guardian.co.uk/world/video/2008/jun/11/afghanistan.johndmchugh. Accessed August 15, 2011.
National Academies
2010 Committee on Unifying Social Frameworks Project Objectives. Available at: http://www7.nationalacademies.org/dbasse/Committee%20on%20Unifying%20Social%20Frameworks.html. Accessed August 15, 2011.
National Research Council (NRC)
2011 Sociocultural Data to Accomplish Department of Defense Missions: Toward a Unified Social Framework Workshop Summary. Washington, D.C.: The National Academies Press.
Redfield, Robert
1953 Does America Need a Hearing Aid? *Saturday Review* 36 (September 26): 11–45.
Tedlock, Dennis, and Bruce Mannheim (eds.)
1995 The Dialogic Emergence of Culture. Urbana, IL: University of Illinois Press.

4

Blurring the Boundaries between Anthropology and Intelligence Analysis

David Abramson

David Abramson is an analyst at the U.S. Department of State in the Bureau of Intelligence and Research. In 2008–2009 he was a Woodrow Wilson International Center Public Policy Scholar working on transnational trends in Islamic education and their impact on the future of Islam in Central Asia. He published his findings with the Central Asia-Caucasus Institute in Washington (Abramson 2010).

Abramson received his doctorate in cultural anthropology from Indiana University, where he specialized in community and conflict in post-Soviet Uzbekistan. Before coming to Washington in 2001, Abramson spent four years at Brown University's Watson Institute for International Studies and directed the undergraduate Development Studies major. From 2001 to 2005, he worked in the State Department's Office of International Religious Freedom, monitoring the status of religious freedom in the Middle East, promoting religious freedom as an element of U.S. foreign policy, advising on outreach to the Muslim world, and engaging with Muslim-American communities. Abramson frequently lectures and has published on Islam in Uzbekistan, religious-secular tensions, the politics and culture of foreign aid to Central Asia, the role of religion in U.S. foreign policy, and anthropologists working in security and the military.

Like Clementine Fujimura, later in this volume, Abramson participated in a 2008 conference at George Washington University on the U.S. military's conception of culture, co-organized by Robert Albro. Albro and Abramson have maintained this conversation since. As someone working at State in what he describes as the most publicly engaged of the intelligence services, Abramson is in a good position to reflect upon what it means to move from an academic space to the State Department, and into the intelligence community. After spending considerable time as a student and faculty in academia, he moved to State, and actively brokers these spaces while maintaining an academic trajectory at State. Abramson, therefore, can be particularly thoughtful about the role of the "analyst" in the U.S. government. What does it mean to do analysis; what are the activities of the analyst; what kind of practice is this; how is it similar to but distinct from academic forms of interpretive practice? With Dawson in this volume, his case interestingly reflects upon some implications of the practice of analyst-type activities and their relationship to academic practice.

This case examines boundaries, blurred or otherwise, between field research for scientific and U.S. government consumption. I make three points. First, given that they are not so far apart, there's room—indeed, a need—in the intelligence community (IC) for the kind of creativity anthropologists bring to research and analysis. Second, government work, whether related to security, military, or diplomatic affairs, provides useful experience and insights for effectively harnessing some of that creativity. Finally, it is possible to conduct work that is relevant to and meets both anthropological and security goals.

Intelligence Has a Need for Anthropology

As a trained anthropologist working as an intelligence analyst at the U.S. Department of State's Bureau of Intelligence and Research (INR), I am not a "collector." The term "collector" in the IC refers very specifically to those who use sensitive methods to gather information (intelligence) for the purpose of protecting national security. Given the sensitivity and need to maintain the secrecy of such work, the IC usually draws stark distinctions and creates firewalls between the work of analysis and collection. Moreover, due to its particular position in the IC as an intelligence agency that is located in the State Department and serves policy makers, INR produces analysis and does not engage in collecting intelligence. I highlight this fact because, in some ways, the availability and quantity of publicly accessible (open source) information and the ways in which acquiring information is being reorganized in the contemporary world are blurring this distinction. Today, analysts can collect data more easily than in the past. Indeed, intelligence analysts are encouraged to use open source material as part of the all-source approach to analysis, drawing on foreign language skills and a deep familiarity with the Internet, including social media. Analysts are also urged to travel to the countries they monitor and to conduct interviews with officials, political activists, scholars, and others.

Analysts who use anthropological methods (e.g., social network analysis) to gather information blur these lines even more. My experience as an analyst conducting field research simultaneously for U.S. government and public consumption raises provocative questions both inside and outside the IC that I shall address. For whom does an analyst write? In what situations does it make sense, or not make sense, to distinguish between government and citizen audiences? What impact, if any, does or should such a distinction have on anthropological research? Whom does my research benefit? And how? And what are the ethical implications of such research for the field of anthropology?

I began my work at the Department of State as an American Association for the Advancement of Science (AAAS) Diplomacy Fellow in 2001 in the Office of International Religious Freedom (IRF), where my responsibilities included engaging foreign governments to promote religious freedom as part of the U.S. government's larger human rights platform. The AAAS program is designed to give academics, mostly in the natural and social sciences, exposure to policy-making. After a two-year fellowship period I transitioned to the more permanent "civil service" status, and in 2005 took a position in the Office of Analysis for Russia and Eurasia (INR/REA).

Prior to applying for the AAAS fellowship, I had never planned to work for the government, instead intending to use my credentials as a cultural anthropologist who had focused on Central Asia since 1991 to try to get an academic position. Nevertheless, once I arrived at the State Department, I realized it offered me a unique perspective on the world of international relations, diplomacy, and policy-making. I had no reservations about working in INR because of the bureau's relatively (for the intelligence community) open environment, the fact that many of its analysts shared an academic background, and my superiors' support for publishing—several of my colleagues have published academic books. Indeed, the work raises fewer ethical questions than many policy positions at the State Department. I view it as an analytical job that has allowed me to continue participating in academic and policy-oriented workshops and conferences, teach, and take time off to write and publish articles and chapters for edited volumes. Maintaining an academic identity, in particular staying on colleagues' radar screens, has taken extra work—I occasionally hear someone comment that I "disappeared," most likely because I rarely participate in anthropology conferences. The reasons for this is that I do not have the time to maintain my credentials as a "professional anthropologist" (i.e., keeping up with the broader literature, publishing in academic journals, and making the high-cost of membership in discipline-based organizations worthwhile). Furthermore, my publications are divided between very different audiences—academic and policy-oriented—whereas the writing I do exclusively for work is not for public consumption.

In 2008, three years after starting work in INR, I applied for and received an intelligence community fellowship to conduct research on a project of my own design—the role of foreign religious education in the Central Asian Islamic revival. My intention was to use this sabbatical-like yearlong opportunity to engage in the kind of doctoral and postdoctoral anthropological research I no longer have time for when engaged with my usual responsibilities as a foreign affairs analyst at the State Department. Although I occasionally make short research trips to the field and regularly write very short assessments on matters of Islam in Central Asia, having a year to examine this issue afforded me the time to conduct more densely descriptive research and write more extensive pieces for both IC and public consumption. My fellowship year was much the same as any academic research: it involved the generation of a research question to secure funding for "sabbatical" release from regular duties, short research in the field, extensive secondary research, and a writing-up period. Moreover, I was offered a position as a policy scholar at the Woodrow Wilson International Center for Scholars, a nonpartisan research center in Washington, D.C. Consistent with a long-standing tradition involving some of my colleagues from INR/REA, the Wilson Center generously offered me a desk and other assistance in exchange for contributing to and being a part of their community of scholars from academia, journalism, government, etc. In short, I would like to highlight the point that I was in fact engaging in "fieldwork"—the focal point for those who would distinguish professionals in the IC from anthropologists.

My dual affiliation with the U.S. government and an independent research center posed some ethical quandaries. Would my government affiliation negatively affect the reputation of the research center? How would I present myself to my informants? Would my government affiliation hinder my research efforts and, if so, should I emphasize my research center affiliation and disguise my government one? In the end, I found that these questions were not the challenges I had anticipated.

I first secured a letter from the research center in advance stating that they understood fully the sources of my funding and that had no qualms about hosting me for the year. In fact, they welcomed my presence there because it added to the diversity of their scholars. In return—and there was no presumption of obligation on my part to the center—I had no intention to hide my government affiliation behind my temporary affiliation with the center.

I resolved to explain to informants in advance, if possible, that I was on leave from my usual responsibilities as an analyst at the State Department and was based at a research center to pursue my project. I did not reveal the fact that part of my sabbatical money originated in the IC (specifically with the Office of the Directorate of National Intelligence), but outside the State Department—my regular salary comprised the majority. Presumably, anthropologists who receive money from the U.S. government for research do not necessarily identify the source of that money (e.g., Fulbright, National Science Foundation) in the process of conducting interviews, in part because the fruits of the research belong to the researcher and the researcher alone. Moreover, the details of research funding in the United States can elude anyone who has not participated. In my case, the fruits of the research were also my own since 100 percent of my research was based on unclassified material. Following two straightforward mandatory internal review processes (for the Directorate of National Intelligence [DNI] and the State Department) that required me to make no substantive changes, I was able to publish my findings entirely for public consumption. I chose to publish my research in an occasional paper series produced by the Nitze School for Advanced International Studies in part because I knew it would be Internet accessible and available to the many informants whose emails I had collected during my fieldwork. I also asked U.S. embassies in Central Asia to distribute my paper to counterparts in their host governments (Abramson 2010).

As for the impact of my affiliation as a State Department employee or member of the IC on my access to informants, this was a problem in just one of the six countries where I conducted research—Uzbekistan. For example, the people who did not want to meet with me because I was a U.S. official tended to be government officials. Some individuals outside the government warily met with me. In one case, the individual wondered whether it was legal to discuss the topic with Americans at all. The climate in Uzbekistan was such that my government affiliation mattered little. Due to a combination of leftover Soviet attitudes of suspicion toward religion, state politicization of Islam, and regime fears about terrorism and extremist threats, many people were afraid to talk about the topic with strangers, foreigners, and those outside of their immediate, trusted social circle. The one sector where people were slightly less afraid was academia, but those contacts usually had only tangential connection to people who studied Islam abroad, given that academia is a relatively secular sphere in the post-Soviet space. Some of these contacts, especially the younger ones, had a relative or knew someone who knew someone who had studied abroad. Accessing those contacts often required more time than I had for the research, so I had to make do with a relatively small sample in that country.

In the other countries, my affiliation and research topic occasionally scared people away. But in the vast majority of cases, it either had no effect or inspired curiosity. It is not clear to me whether my research center affiliation had any impact at all. Tajikistan, for example, has a recent history of Islamic-secular dialogue dating back at least to the Tajik civil war in the 1990s. Although this history is rife with tension, intellectuals and religious leaders nevertheless have preserved some space for exploring religion's role in Tajikistan's future. Kyrgyzstan has had a very different history: its relative openness and limited experience with terrorist threats has also created an environment in which most people are comfortable discussing Islam.

Applying Government Experience to Research

I have found that my conversations with Muslims abroad about religion, especially given the post-9/11 climate, have been very useful. My four years beginning immediately after 9/11 in IRF prepared me well for this. I had regional monitoring and reporting responsibilities that included the Middle East, Turkey, parts of South Asia, and Indonesia. I traveled to Turkey, Egypt, Saudi Arabia, and Bangladesh, where I met with government officials, nongovernmental organizations (NGOs), academics, religious preachers, and community leaders. Despite concern about the "sensitivities" of U.S. government officials discussing religion, the conversations were almost always amicable, intellectually stimulating, usually very productive, and insufficiently long. In Washington I spoke about U.S. religious freedom policy and fielded questions from approximately 30 State Department–sponsored International Visitor Program Muslim groups (ranging from 1 to 30 participants from nearly every country in the world) on topics pertaining to Islam or Muslims in America. In addition, conducting outreach to American Muslim leaders and organizations through roundtables and other events and serving as a liaison for their interactions with the State Department comprised another part of my portfolio (for an excellent overview, see Farr 2008; Johnston and Sampson 1994).

These experiences prepared me well for the kinds of meetings I would have on the topic of religion, especially Islam, after joining INR. I addressed interlocutors' curiosity about Muslim life in the United States, attitudes about the United States, and the U.S. government's relations with the "Muslim world," including from some of the United States' harshest critics (at least, those willing to engage).[1] In particular, I learned that:

- Listening first and answering their questions about why the U.S. Government, State Department, or I was interested in knowing about Muslims in Central Asia or Muslim students studying abroad helped build trust at the start of the conversation.
- Sharing information about Muslim-American life (statistics about immigration, demographics, diversity, interfaith relations, civil rights, and

conflict resolution) piqued interlocutors' curiosity and demonstrated that I was knowledgeable and cared about their coreligionists.
- Outlining the U.S. Government's religious freedom policy and its roots in American history helped put U.S. foreign policy in perspective and balanced some of its more controversial aspects.

It might seem like these three points should be part of any elementary understanding of diplomacy. Where religion in diplomacy is concerned, however, there often remains a degree of discomfort, even when one's personal religious beliefs are immaterial. These conversations, in which both my interlocutors and I functioned as virtual peers, achieved something like a genuine conversation. Anthropologists, often separated by a professional divide from those they engage, struggle with the lack of parity.

Anthropological and Security Goals are Not Mutually Exclusive

My research project had several goals that could benefit different constituencies. These were:

- Refining, deepening, and refocusing relevant intelligence analysis and policy concerning religious dynamics in Central Asia to make U.S. government efforts more efficient and steering government resources away from being deployed in pursuit of red herrings, such as conservative Islamic movements that do not employ or support violence;
- Building and expanding U.S. ties with current and future Central Asian Muslim community leaders and experts via my contacts with them and conveying that U.S. interests in "the Muslim world" and Islam do not fit well with U.S. war on Islam narratives, such as those propagated by Al Qa'eda;
- Persuading Central Asian governments that their own domestic "wars on Islam" need not be so repressive, and that their policies sometimes foster conditions that strengthen opponents.

Although I have no idea what impact my work will have, the project has deepened my grasp of these issues, a grasp I expect I will be able to deploy in multiple briefings and other interactions with a range of government and nongovernment actors over the coming months and years. The project's potential to meet some of these objectives and therefore benefit multiple consumers and participants links it and me to the purpose of both anthropology and national security. My goal of informing analysts and policy makers makes the project relevant to U.S. national security interests. My goal of improving conditions for Muslims in Central Asia makes the project relevant to anthropologists' concerns about benefitting the people with whom they work. And my goal of building bridges and expertise, hopefully, makes the project relevant to both. My point here is that research sponsored by the IC, conducted by IC personnel, and made publicly available does not exclusively benefit the IC. It is not a black and white issue. Moreover, anthropologists can work in the securityscape without abandoning or even seriously compromising their disciplinary or fieldwork-originated values.

Security Work Can Benefit Anthropology

Working for two decades on a region that was on "the other side" of the Iron Curtain throughout the Cold War taught me that anthropology's neglect of socialist bloc countries, which comprised the United States' enemy and which the United States' relations with shaped international politics for decades, was the ultimate example of a head in the sand approach. Of course, access to field sites was nearly nonexistent and, when possible, could easily have endangered informants. Nevertheless, the field's lack of interest in international politics generally produced generations of anthropologists with a disregard for larger political contexts of colonialism and war.

I wonder whether anthropologists are not making similar mistakes again with regard to the leading issue shaping U.S. domestic and foreign policy today—namely, the threat of extremist violence in the name of Islam against American interests. There are many ways to study actual and perceived threats, popular and state reactions, transnational terrorist narratives, narratives about terrorism, and narratives about combating terrorism. Anthropologists doubtless have something to contribute to, and to gain from, engaging U.S. policy-making, security, and military institutions as anthropologists, as practitioners, and as both.

Final Thoughts

The thoughts I have outlined here do not pertain to all parts of the IC. INR is one of the least clandestine of the intelligence agencies. This is largely because it is part of the State Department, whose climate is one of engagement—provided the policy message is controlled—and because our primary audience is policy makers whose own constant global engagement sets a standard that INR analysts must match in comparable ways to be of service. INR encourages its analysts to engage with experts and other informants outside the U.S. government, recognizing that such contacts comprise a critical component of acquiring the information we need to produce quality analysis. Analysts at other agencies also do this to varying degrees, but usually under greater constraints.

The future of the IC may well involve a reorganization of how intelligence is gathered, processed, and disseminated. Its emphasis on and adaptation to collaborative tools, open source materials, and new social media challenges old ways of conducting business and presents opportunities that might be more palatable to anthropologists and academics in general. The current emphasis on outsourcing certain forms of data collection and analysis to software is one answer, but it will likely prove inadequate, at least in terms of qualitative analysis. When it does, the IC may need to draw more extensively on the kind of research and expertise intelligence analysts and academics already have in common to make up for the shortfalls that characterize much of today's analysis.

Editorial Commentary

Abramson complicates and nuances our appreciation for the challenges of "dual affiliation." He explores what is at times a balancing act between his disciplinary training and background as an anthropologist and his work as an intelligence analyst at the U.S. Department of State. Abramson's case takes us right to the heart of regularly expressed concerns for the integrity of anthropological practice in extra-academic contexts working for state institutions. This is especially true of the IC, given the disciplinary injunction against "secret and clandestine" research.

As with Mark Dawson's narrative, which follows this one, Abramson seeks to demystify the practice of anthropologically trained government analysts as a category of work. But Abramson's description of his work differs dramatically from Mark Dawson's more "day-in-the-life" narrative. The larger context is, of course, very different: intelligence analysis to inform diplomatic policy-making versus front-line military activity. Abramson also writes primarily of a self-conceived and directed research project, whereas Dawson describes the contours of his military headquarters support staff position.

But, Abramson makes the case that anthropology's creative combination of both method with analysis is something that the IC needs at present. And he stresses that his government career at State also has prepared him well for his fellowship research, which we are invited to understand as at once a product of the things he has been doing inside and outside of the academy but also of government during his career. His ethnography, in short, is complexly situated across these environments, seeking to maintain a conversation among them. Abramson's research commitment also takes on anthropology's historical lack of interest in international politics, which, as others have pointed out, has helped to maintain a significant disciplinary knowledge gap in this area (Weldes et al. 1999).

In the 2007 Commission on the Engagement of Anthropology with the U.S. Security and Intelligence Communities (CEAUSSIC) report we argued that, if it might be possible, performing research for powerful institutions like the U.S. government with foreign populations is perhaps the most fraught intersection of anthropology with the security sector (CEAUSSIC 2007). But Abramson blurs easy distinctions. On the one hand, he points to the changing demands made of analysts in the IC. This includes a growing emphasis on collaborative tools, open source materials, and new social media as part of research that might also include data collection. As such, his research confounds the traditional firewall maintained between so-called "collectors" and "analysts" in the IC. It also makes the case that intelligence analysts can, at least in Abramson's case, take up activities that look a lot more like ethnography.

Abramson's case is one indicator that the IC is regularly reconsidering the ways it thinks about data collection and analysis, which has given him some professional room for maneuver. And he suggests research sponsored by the IC and conducted by IC personnel, which is made publicly available, does not just benefit the IC but can also participate in a wider public discussion, including with anthropology. Such a case invites us to appreciate the extent to which the IC, as a set of state institutions and research activities, is in fact best understood as a dynamically changing environment rather than monolithically as the state's intelligence arm. Abramson's work, too, reminds us of the ways that analysts and anthropologists share commitments both to research and to writing in social scientifically informed ways. If often for different publics, these efforts coexist in many environments, as with think tanks like the Wilson Center. As a discipline, we have given little thought to what we might call this para-academic universe of institutions and analysis.

At the same time, Abramson's is a case that invites us to continue our dialogue on the relationship of ethics to research. His is not traditional fieldwork, where the "field" is clearly defined, and where field notes are carried back to relatively autonomous universities to be written up in dialogue with an "intercommunicating cluster" of disciplinary peers. Rather, the fault lines of his engagement overlap multiple purposes, forms of data, arenas of encounter, professional interlocutors, and constituencies. This includes multiple ethical frames, of the state and of anthropology. Abramson undertakes ethnographic research in ways meant to meet the requirements of his several professional communities of interest, carrying out research of relevance both for the U.S. government but also for the academic public. Abramson's case invites us to do more thinking about the ethics of dual affiliation among anthropologists (see Albro 2009).

Key to this is the availability of a sabbatical-like fellowship, funded with monies from the IC, which allows Abramson to pursue a research project on the role of foreign religious education in the Central Asian Islamic revival, a project he is able to define not merely by the narrow end-user demands of his usual job description. On the one hand, this is the kind of fellowship that any academic anthropologist working in this area might crave. On the other, Abramson depicts this as a once-in-a-long-while opportunity and certainly not typically part of his normal routines of work. This, in turn, suggests that Abramson's is an exceptional case and not particularly representative of his regular junket.

One wonders to what extent is this fellowship opportunity an exception to other prevailing day-in-day-out expectations for Abramson's work as an analyst? As he notes, he has ownership of his research in this case in part because "100 percent of my research was based on unclassified material." But is this normally the case? And if not, what does his balancing act of dual affiliations routinely look like? Abramson is clear that his space of maneuver is facilitated by his particular vantage point within the Department of State and at INR—perhaps the least clandestine of U.S. intelligence agencies. What about the rest of the IC? The impression is that things might be different elsewhere.

Unlike another contributor, Paula Holmes-Eber, who also works in the Arab-Islamic world, Abramson did not find ethnography in Central Asia impossible. Even so, here it is notable that one of the particular challenges "in the field" for Abramson was negotiating his status as a State employee. As he tells us, interviews with peers in government were sometimes facilitated by his own government affiliation. And he reminds us that the internal dynamics of the countries he visited—both the history and the political climate of each country—fundamentally shaped his research interactions in ways often more important than his government affiliation.

Nevertheless, talking with counterparts, as he described it, took on a quality of diplomacy that it otherwise might not have had. Whereas anthropologists, along with many others, have long taken advantage of government-sponsored exchange programs with undercurrents of diplomacy to carry out their research (e.g., Fulbrights), here the issue of diplomacy vis-à-vis how the researcher is situated appears to be much more front-and-center, which raises a pertinent question about scholarly independence and the relative autonomy of state-sponsored research agendas.

Can the priorities of U.S. diplomacy be disambiguated from Abramson's project, given his funding source and topic, along with his national and government affiliations? Abramson's is a less-recognized variant of so-called public anthropology. It is less an activist intervention and more an ethnographic engagement with public policy, in this case, better understandings of terrorism. His work is a good litmus test of the extent to which such a policy-engaged, quasi-diplomatic public anthropology is in fact possible.

Abramson Response

The editors ask to what extent U.S. diplomatic priorities (1) inform and (2) bias my research questions and ethnography, given the fact that I work at the Department of State and in the intelligence community. First, on a day-to-day basis I work for two masters. My primary audience is the policy community, although I also write for IC analysts and managers. In either case, analysts ideally address a given issue or set of circumstances in their country or region of focus from the perspective of the actors involved, assessing the impact on and implications for U.S. interests. As analysts, we generally do not "do us," meaning we do not explicitly assess the success or wisdom of U.S. policy implementation or U.S. actions. Moreover, we also do not make policy recommendations. This varies across the IC, and there is a certain degree of flexibility, such as when an analyst discusses foreign government and popular reactions to U.S. actions or engages in what is referred to as "opportunity analysis." Opportunity analysis is tantamount to making policy recommendations, which policy makers sometimes request of the IC. Conversely, policy-makers are expected not to "interfere" with "policy-neutral" intelligence analysis by criticizing assessments or asking for alternative analyses until they get something that conforms to their own view of a given issue. Although such interference occasionally happens, it is generally considered within both communities to be unacceptable. In sum, analysts and policy makers consider the separation of policy formulation and intelligence analysis as described here to be the norm.

What does this look like in practice? At the time I conducted my research on Islamic education and Central Asia, I was no longer engaged in policy-making or the diplomacy of promoting religious freedom abroad. Consequently, although I was well versed in religious freedom policy: that is, its origins and justifications grounded in both American history and the language of international agreements (e.g., the Universal Declaration of Human Rights) as well as religious tolerance, sectarian conflict, and conflict resolution in American history, and religious dynamics in contemporary American society and foreign policy, I felt no obligation to push a religious freedom agenda or to justify my research in terms of religious freedom. Nevertheless, the somewhat oversimplified narrative of the United States being founded on the principles of religious freedom by immigrants who fled religious persecution in other parts of the world did occasionally creep into my own accounting of why I was pursuing the topic I had chosen. This religious freedom "bias" informed by diplomacy could be said to have influenced my research findings—that Central Asian regimes' approaches to the Islamic revival and threats to political stability exaggerate the threat of citizens who go abroad to study Islam and take unnecessarily repressive measures against observant Muslims—which depart from the assumption that individual rights trump collective security. In the end, however, my "biases" differ little from those of scholars "embedded" in the academy.

Finally, I wish to address the observation raised by this volume's editors that my "ethnographic engagement with public policy" is by definition a "less activist" intervention. I like to think of my work as forms of both scholarly and activist engagement with policy-making. I seek to write in a way that allows research findings to be more easily converted into recommendations. It is a challenge for the academically trained, myself included, to navigate between the regurgitation of stale and nonnuanced policy "recommendations" that abandon the truly innovative nature of scholarship on the one hand, and indigestible conclusions that speak solely to disciplinary literature on the other. As a result, I have begun to develop a series of presentations on how academics might package their research in ways that are more relevant to policy, more applicable to policy, and more user-friendly to those formulating policy. Thus, I hope this contribution helps to interrogate not only the dichotomy between public and scholarly anthropology, but also the presumption that activist interventions necessarily are burdened by ideological bias, or conversely that ethnographic engagement is free of such bias. I am grateful to the editors for giving me the opportunity to illuminate the complexities and issues created by the juxtaposition of public anthropology and "pure academic" research that is inherent in most of our disciplinary discourse about anthropologists and the securityscape.

Notes

The opinions expressed in this piece are entirely the author's and do not necessarily express positions of the U.S. Department of State or the United States Government.

1. Clearly, anyone willing to participate in a U.S. government program must be relatively open-minded and willing to engage. The fact that participants often posed very tough questions and did not refrain from subjecting U.S. foreign policy to harsh criticism is a credit to the program.

References

Abramson, David M.

2010 Foreign Religious Education and the Central Asian Islamic Revival: Impact and Prospects for Stability. Available at: http://www.silkroadstudies.org/new/docs/silkroadpapers/1003Abramson.pdf. Accessed July 25, 2010.

Albro, Robert
2009 Ethics and Dual-Identity Professionals: Addressing Anthropology in the Public Sector. *Anthropology News* 50(6):17–18.

Commission on the Engagement of Anthropology with the U.S. Security and Intelligence Communities (CEAUSSIC)
2007 Report of the Commission on Anthropology and the Military and Intelligence Communities. Arlington, VA: American Anthropological Association.

Farr, Thomas
2008 World of Faith and Freedom: Why International Religious Freedom is Vital to American National Security. Oxford, U.K.: Oxford University Press.

Johnston, Douglas, and Cynthia Sampson
1994 Religion: The Missing Dimension of Statecraft. Oxford, U.K.: Oxford University Press.

Weldes, Jutta, Mark Laffey, Hugh Gusterson, et al. (eds.)
1999 Cultures of Insecurity: States, Communities, and the Production of Danger. Minneapolis, MN: University of Minnesota Press.

5

Intelligence Work: The Mundane World of High-Consequence Analysis

Mark Dawson

Mark Dawson has worked in a variety of industries and topic areas over the years in private industry and as a consultant to private corporations and U.S. government contractors. Unlike many of the contributors to this volume, Dawson is a practicing anthropologist with a background in design and software development. He holds an MS.Ed. in Instructional Systems Design from Indiana University and an M.A. in Anthropology from the University of South Carolina. Dawson's research topics have ranged from the social networks of first-time prison inmates to the evolving nature of "entertainment" in different countries, from the changing life of the American Cowboy (and families) to the issues of reintegration of former insurgents.

We first contacted Dawson in 2009, when the Commission on the Engagement of Anthropology with the U.S. Security and Intelligence Communities (CEAUSSIC) was developing its position paper on the Human Terrain Systems (HTS) for the Executive Board of the American Anthropological Association (AAA). At the time, Dawson was a member of a U.S. Army Human Terrain Team (HTT) in Iraq and agreed to be interviewed for the CEAUSSIC report to discuss what his work as an HTT member entailed. Interestingly, thinking that Dawson had probably moved onto other professional work, we did not contact Dawson about participation in this volume until a colleague of McNamara's mentioned an acquaintance who was working as an intelligence analyst. We contacted Dawson, who agreed to write an essay detailing his experience working as a civilian in-theater intelligence analyst for a private contracting company supporting the U.S. Army.

When we received the essay, we were struck by its straightforward, conversational tone. Dawson does not agonize over his career choices, and is quick to emphasize that in his current position, his background in anthropology is "not terribly important."

Dawson recently returned from his one-year deployment to Afghanistan and has returned to private consulting in the United States. He currently has his own consulting firm, Dawson Strategic, which focuses on the military and intelligence communities. When we responded to Dawson's essay, we asked if he would address his HTS experience as well. Dawson declined, explaining that he was reluctant to present himself as an HTS alumnus, given that he was no longer affiliated with the program and believed that his current work deserved focused discussion. We appreciated the point.

I have had the opportunity to speak with anthropology students at several universities in the past about my work with the military. What struck me about those experiences were the kinds of questions I received. Some were about ethics and related issues as I expected, but most of the questions were on the theme of "just WHAT does your day-to-day job look like?" They didn't want to know my theoretical perspective, they wanted to know how I created a research plan; they didn't ask what I learned in nine months of research in Iraq, they wanted to know just how, step by step, I turned field notes into analysis. Their heads were full of theory about their potential profession, but were unsure of the basic skills needed to just get the job done.

This case study is primarily aimed at part of that question: just what does my day-to-day life working with the military in a war zone look like? This is after all written in the spirit of an autoethnography, and a true ethnography of something is not a description of the unusual or exotic parts of a group, but the dozens of terribly ordinary activities and events people engage in on a daily basis. It also bears reminding students that any conversation you have with someone reflects only a moment in time. In this case, I am writing about one job, in one place, that I am doing for a year. It is not reflective of all the work I have done with the military, and has no resemblance to my career as a design anthropologist. It is just one job that I have done out of many, and the invitation to write this case study just happens to have occurred when I am doing a job that is not terribly interesting or challenging. Them's the breaks.

Context Setting

Let's start with just where and who I am: As I write this, it is fall of 2010 and I am working in Kabul, Afghanistan. I am an employee for a small defense contractor that has brought me in as a senior analyst working on a general support contract for the U.S. military at the headquarters compound in Kabul. This means that I am not a direct employee of any part of the U.S. government, but rather an employee of a company that contracts with the government to provide services: the military equivalent of a temporary worker. This also means it is not odd to discover you have been assigned to a job for which you have no background at all. That is normal for a surprising number of military and contractor personnel. I am not here in any kind of cultural analysis role; my current job is to analyze intelligence reports that are generated throughout the country.

How Did I Get Here: My Academic Background

I started my undergraduate studies at age 26 planning for an academic career path that I expected to end with being a teacher at a university. My graduate program in cultural anthropology was fairly typical: classes in methods, theory, gender, identity, etc., and a class that was a small nod that there was such a thing as quantitative research. Rather than going into the business of academics, I chose to join a small but growing field called design anthropology, working with companies on product development and business strategies.

Shifting Careers to the Defense and Intelligence Community

I learned about the Human Terrain System (HTS) at the same time that I was seeking to change my career from design anthropology to working within the defense community. Ironically, it was the outcry from critics that brought the program to my attention. When I heard of the HTS, I was already having conversations with anthropologists in the military and intelligence communities about opportunities for changing my career path. I did not shift to working with the military because of the HTS; rather, I was actively seeking to work with the military at the time and the HTS presented the first opportunity to do so. Although the HTS program was not the direct fit I was looking for, it provided me with important experience in working directly with the military as an embedded researcher on a day-to-day basis. When I left the HTS, I chose to continue working with the Department of Defense (DoD) in different contexts and contracts, which brings me to my current role in Kabul, Afghanistan. As this volume is a collection of case studies of people with anthropological training working with the intelligence community, I am focusing on my most recent work as an intelligence analyst after leaving the HTS program.

What is an "Intelligence Analyst?"

In most cases, with the exception of technical and functional analysts, being an intelligence analyst is a generic term meaning "you read reports, summarize those reports, and you try to examine the contents of those reports in a holistic way that will answer the question asked of you." When you are a work-a-day analyst, you are generally working on a tasking given to you by your boss (and they get it from their boss and so on) such as: "How will the long rainy season affect the peanut harvest in the Eastern region of Pago-Pago?"[1] As the analyst, you primarily derive this information from the Internet, databases, books, by contacting external experts, and, depending on the job, from classified reports and by sending out requests to specialists for additional information. Analysts generally do not engage in fieldwork; your job (my job) is not to go out and interview people or do original work. Everything created is derivative of something else. What's more, you rarely get much context as to just why someone cares about the fictional peanut harvest in Pago-Pago. It is not unlike a writing assignment in graduate school: you are assigned a topic; you go to the library and copy articles out of journals, book chapters, and other sources; you write your introduction, body, analysis, conclusion; include all your references; then hand it in and get your next assignment.

The brief description of my day looks like this: I go to my office in the morning, log in, and quickly scan the report subject lines that come in overnight to see if there is anything worth summarizing for my boss. I cut, paste, and summarize the reports I think will be of most interest to her (and that means of interest to my boss's boss, and so on up the chain). This activity takes a couple of hours. Then for the next 10 or 12 hours I slowly work through a stack of reports assigned to me. At its most mundane description, I look at each detail of an intelligence report and search numerous databases to determine the validity of the content. In the next year, if my job does not change, I will do this over and over again, all day, every day, with hundreds and hundreds of reports.

Why Does Intelligence Analysis Work Look So Mundane?

If this description takes all the mystery out of life, that is because by and large, intelligence work is not mysterious. I don't learn about important state secrets, I don't have the low-down about some big event before anyone else knows it is going to happen. When something big happens, I hear about it on the news just like everyone else. I want to emphasize that I don't think all the analytical jobs in the intelligence world are as mundane as the job I currently have. My job is what it is partly because of the nature of how "soft" analysis is done (as opposed to technical or functional analysis, areas I have no experience with), and partly because I am at the headquarters element, which is largely composed of people doing staff work.

In my observation (and as the "subject" of this autoethnography I am only a single voice and point of view; therefore, reader, do your own homework as well), it all feels so mundane because what is often called "analysis" in intelligence work would not be considered analysis by most people trained in the analytical mindset, methods, and critical thinking skills needed to produce a competent thesis- or dissertation-length work. Reasons for this include an outgrowth of the compartmentalization of jobs, the emphasis on conformity in how analysis is conducted and presented, the sheer volume of questions that someone is tasked to answer, and the very system of the intelligence is designed to reduce the need for critical thought in favor of conformity.

From a system standpoint, the military and intelligence communities are not made up of people, but parts or components. Everyone's job must be dealt with as another part that can be replaced by training, either formally or on the job, with another warm body to put into that particular slot. All of the parts of this massive, lumbering, and ad hoc constructed machine have to fit with as minimal disruption into the rest of the machine as possible. Procedures are more predictable than people, so the procedures often define the parameters of the analysis; from how to access the data you need to how you will present it in the final format right down to mandating the font type, size, and color.

In This Context, My Background in Anthropology is Not Terribly Important

In the context of this particular job, no one I work with or for cares about my background in cultural anthropology other than as an idle curiosity. I don't engage in any of what might be considered "traditional" activities: I don't interact with local populations in any way, I don't engage in any form of cultural analysis (or analysis of any kind in the way that would be considered serious analysis outside of the intelligence community), I don't have a role in providing direction for inquiry, and very rarely interact with the people that consume and use the information I provide. Like many in this business, for me, work flows in and work flows out via "the chain of command" and I receive minimum feedback as to the utility of it. Remember that I am here as a *senior* analyst.

So why I am I here in Kabul, why did they hire me if not as a cultural anthropologist? Four main reasons: I have a security clearance, I have experience working in a war zone with the military, I am willing to leave my life behind and live in a war zone for a year, and as far as contractors and the government are concerned "anthropology" is another general term for a body that is capable of putting various kinds of disparate details together. Analysis, downrange in particular, is treated as something that just about anyone can do, regardless of past experience. So, just what am I adding to the mix here? More from luck than intent, everyone working my shop does have some form of analytic background. Either as career intelligence officers, or like myself, from a career background where analysis and critical thinking is part of the skill set. As an analyst of soft information, unless we are talking of a specific skill such as language training, my years of experience and skill set as an anthropologist are far less important in my job (and in practice, not important at all) than is my ability to adapt to the process and taskings given to me. The result is that intelligence work, frankly, is not very challenging from an intellectual or analytical standpoint.

Why did I take a job that has little bearing on my skill set? As a person changing careers, I have expressly been taking jobs to gain wide exposure to the limits and opportunities available to me in this particular profession, if it is a career path I want to continue. To that end, I have been avoiding positions that focus on cultural analysis or cultural education types of work. I know how to do that; I have not known, however, what being in the intelligence side of the profession is like.

What are the Conflicts between What I Do and the AAA Code of Ethics?

I don't have any ethical issues with my work, and I don't see my work in conflict with the stance of the AAA for a simple reason: I am not a member of the AAA. I have only been a member a few times: when I was in graduate school, when I was invited to give a paper, and when I happened to be in the same city as the conference anyway. But by and large, as a professional association it offers little of interest to me personally, and there are other professional organizations and conferences I attend instead. I think about ethics, and my personal ethics are very important to me, but they are my personal ethics. Discussing ethics is valuable for anyone, not just anthropologists, and the time to do it is long before you get into the job. It is in the conversation about ethics that you start to shape and form your personal views and values.

The military and intelligence communities have a different way of ensuring ethnical compliance: federal law and the Uniform Code of Military Justice. In this community of practice there are a number of laws and regulations that must be followed, and there are significant penalties for not following them: immediate loss of job, loss of clearance, and federal prison. For those in the military, the line they must follow is even narrower as they have obligations to both military and civil laws. The reason most people in the intelligence community are quiet about their work is not because we have some high-level secrets in our heads, it is because we have signed forms saying that we can be prosecuted for talking about it. Even if something is marked at the lowest level of classification and no matter how mundane, it is still classified and therefore someone can be prosecuted for revealing it. It takes a long time to get higher-level classifications, and if you have them revoked, it is difficult to overturn and essentially excommunicates you from the community, leaving you with virtually no job prospects.

If It is All So Dull and Ordinary, Why Is It Such a Big Deal Now?

Part of the reason the conversation about anthropologists working with the military has become a different kind of hot-button issue at this moment is because we are seeing an evolution of practice. More anthropologists, particularly in industry, are applying the lessons learned in cultural anthropology as their basic skill set to provide consulting about broader issues. They have started showing companies how cultural anthropology can be a holistic way of thinking and used to address large complex questions far outside the topic of just "culture." In relation to our current debate, anthropologists are going from writing about the culture of the military as "the alien other" to actively and visibly working with and as a part of the military to accomplish the aims of the military. These applied anthropologists are taking a very active role in a host of areas from shaping directions of inquiry and how the military can approach cultural issues, and in some cases shaping policy. Taking that kind of active role is problematic for some people, no question. In my case, I am currently an intelligence analyst. Even my work, as mundane as it is, has the potential for serious implications someplace in the process. Unlike being in the Human Terrain Program, as an intelligence analyst there is no question that my work could at some point be applied to larger body of analysis that would result in someone being killed or captured, seen as friend or foe, or simply ignored. Do I have evidence that what I have specifically done in the intelligence world has resulted directly in one of these outcomes? None at all. Do I think it has happened to date? I have no idea. But the reality is that as minor as my job is, it feeds into a larger flow of information that has those outcomes as some of the possible results. I think about the potential implications of course. There is no point in getting into this business and trying to rationalize away the reality that doing your job right or wrong could contribute to someone being killed or injured. The primary issue it creates for me is working hard to do as thorough a job in my research of the facts and circumstances surrounding an issue as I can given the tools at hand. I worry if I have uncovered all the facts I need to make a clear and independent assessment of the situation. Is my language clear and to the point? Have I raised all of the red flags that suggest there is a problem with some aspect of the report that warrants further examination? Regardless of the final outcome of the process, did I do my best to ensure the report at hand reflects the facts as I can determine them from my limited arena? In other words, is my minor error—a missed paragraph, name, or date that seems unimportant in the moment—something that could have helped prevent a bomb going off in a marketplace? When I am doing the summaries of reporting for my boss every morning, I have to chose just a small handful of reports out of hundreds that, based solely on my own judgment, I think are of the most immediate relevance for the command to see. I always worry about the reports I don't choose.

Applied anthropology is messy, and doing applied anthropology for the military or a nongovernmental organization (NGO) in a war zone/refugee camp/oppressive regime (choose your wording) is going to be messier still from an ethical standpoint; if you can't deal with that, than perhaps being an applied anthropologist in the military is not for you. You can't take a one-size-fits-all approach to ethics; it is counterproductive, naive, and certainly does not prepare someone for the on-the-fly decisions that have to be made in the field. At some point you have to quit wringing your hands and actually do something, and in turn take the risk of making little or very big awful mistakes. And yes, they have real-world consequences. In the corporate world, if you are working at a higher level, your mistakes can cost people jobs, homes, health insurance. You go someplace where people's lives are teetering on the brink such as a war zone, the stress of your choices is hardly reduced. There is no tenure, no do-overs, no intellectual jousting in journals trading quotes from dead French philosophers. In this case, mistakes can mean people are fired, lose lives, get injured, are accused wrongly, or that resources are put in the wrong place, and all of that has follow-on effects that can last for years—which just might be your fault.

Editorial Commentary

Mark Dawson's entry into the world of security work is intriguing for a few reasons: first, he has no expertise in the geographical regions or cultural domains that interest the military; instead, he is a design anthropologist by training. Second, many of our contributors describe their transition into defense work as secondary (and problematic) feature of a primary career decision—for example, to accept a teaching position that happens to be in a military academy (Clementine Fujimura, Paula Holmes-Eber) or cultural resources management work for a military base (Laurie Rush). Dawson, in contrast, was actually seeking a career shift from design anthropology into defense work. This is such a significant change, and Dawson's tone is so matter-of-fact about this decision, that we wondered what motivated this decision and what he was looking for in terms of a "direct fit" between his career in design and what he encountered in the military.

Dawson mentions that he moved into the defense community via the HTS program, but the reader will quickly notice that he spends only a few sentences on his HTS experience. We actually asked Dawson to comment more extensively on how he became involved with HTS and why he left. He declined to do so, telling us that a great deal of attention had already been paid to HTS, and that he did not want to be known as an "HTS anthropologist" when, in reality, he was no longer affiliated with the program. Instead, he asked us if he could focus his account on his work as an intelligence analyst, which he felt was more current than the HTS experience and a kind of work that few people understand.

This seemed reasonable to us, and we were actually quite intrigued at his description of the "terribly ordinary activities" that constitute intelligence analysis. In fact, all four of us commented on the deliberately mundane tone that Dawson exercises in describing his work environment: getting up in the morning and going to the office, then spending the day reading mountains of intelligence reports, selecting relevant reports for attention, and summarizing these for higher-ups. Dawson's work involves deriving products from documents that are themselves derivative of other documents and sources. His message: the imagined job of intelligence analysis is actually quite different from the reality of intelligence analysis: at least in terms of the day-to-day work, little happens that is troubling or even particularly exciting. Dawson allows that this might be a function of his position in the "headquarters element...doing staff work"—as an aside, this made us wonder what differentiates headquarters from other elements, and staff work from other kinds of work.

Moreover, Dawson is quite blunt in telling us that he is not doing anthropology, nor was he hired for his anthropological training: he had a security clearance and was willing to work in a war zone, which seem to be the primary attributes that got him hired as an intelligence analyst. We wondered what kind of training Dawson had to become an analyst, and what his fellow military and intelligence analysts bring to the table in terms of their own education and training. After all, anthropology is at best a faint background to his work, not as a method (e.g., "ethnography"), so much as a conceptual apparatus and set of interpretive skills (perhaps a kind of holism, insofar as he speaks of an ability to put "various kinds of disparate details together"). This, in turn, raises the question of what anthropology's identity might be outside of the confines of disciplinary departmentalization in the academy, or if anthropology even has an identity in Dawson's world.

In any case, Dawson's account shifts from the mundane to the consequential in a few paragraphs. It begins when he broadens his scope to describe the institutional setting in which intelligence analysis takes place: the military and intelligence communities comprising parts and components, the regulation of work processes and products, the slotting of people into positions and stations. Procedure and process dominate over individualism and creative thinking; Dawson notes that he is a *senior* (emphasis in original) analyst, and we wondered if this was an ironic commentary on the fact that he is ultimately replaceable by another warm body that can shuffle documents and write reports. It is a machine, he seems to be telling us, and he is a cog that will be rotated out and replaced at some point when his contract is up. If the work is so dull and machine-like, we wondered, why bother doing it, particularly given the contrast between Dawson's training in the creative field of design and his current work environment?

Yet Dawson's imagery of the impersonal machine and tedious bureaucratic detail is itself troubling, because as he points out, his work does not bear error, because errors have serious impacts on people. This is the ethical nub: his account of "downrange" intelligence analysis reminded us of Zygmunt Bauman's *Modernity and the Holocaust,* in which he argues that the Holocaust was an event facilitated by modern values and institutions grounded in bureaucratic efficiencies, compartmentalized labor, procedural rationality, and dispersed agency. Although neither Iraq nor Afghanistan represent the wholesale genocidal warfare that occurred during the Holocaust, U.S. military interventions have undoubtedly caused thousands of deaths and even more injuries, as well as profound societal disruptions. The structural parallels between Bauman's critique and Dawson's work environment are striking and somewhat disturbing. Dawson seems to want to have it both ways: his work is simultaneously boring and existentially consequential; he chides anthropologists who belabor the ethics of wartime work, yet he acknowledges that his work has tremendous ethical consequences which he cannot fully understand because, by his own admission, his position in the bureaucratic machine limits his field of vision. He describes the real world as "messy," which is somewhat ironic given that he is unlikely to perceive the messiness in which his work is embedded.

The section on ethics was perhaps the most thought provoking and difficult part of the essay. Dawson is grappling with a typical issue for practicing anthropologists: multiple professional commitments with their respective ethical entailments, which rarely dovetail neatly. Along those lines, we wondered if Dawson really equates professional ethical commitments with membership in particular professional organizations, such as the AAA; certainly there is more to responsibly practicing anthropology than paying dues and adhering to the codes of a particular organization. This raises issue of where anthropological ethics are institutionally and organizationally located, assuming that ethics are more than just personal commitments, despite Dawson's emphasis on the personal nature of ethics.

In any case, Dawson seems to have moved into a different realm of professional ethics, those of the intelligence community: reports must be as complete and free of error as possible, and delivered in clear language and a timely fashion. We wondered if "attention to detail" really represents the limit to the intelligence community's own approach to ethics, and how Dawson has encountered both tacit and explicit discourse on ethics in the domain and intelligence. We were intrigued by his explicit connection between ethical codes and legal codes. For one thing, his description of the penalties and legal ramifications of breaking secrecy regulations is worth deeper consideration in the era of WikiLeaks; we wondered what Dawson thinks of Bradley Manning and Julian Assange. But more importantly, the Uniform Code of Military Justice is not an ethical code. It is a legal code. In conflating the two, we wondered if Dawson was substituting a robust consideration of professional ethics with a particular legal framework and the commitments of a security clearance, both of which define behavioral "dos-and-don'ts" in ways that sometimes intersect with ethics, but that often have little to do with the ethical commitments of particular professions.

We sent Dawson this commentary. We also sent a few questions about the kind of training he received and how he balanced the tension between the mundane and the consequential that we perceived in his work as well as whether he received any feedback on the quality or use of the reports that he was providing his consumers. We also asked for some more detail on the organizational context in which he was embedded as an intelligence analyst. Soon after we sent Dawson our commentary, he provided a response written in much the same, matter-of-fact tone as his original essay, in which he answered our questions and responded to the critique that we offered of his work. This response is included here.

Dawson Response

Headquarters versus Lower Eechelons

My work is primarily used to inform issues that will potentially have a broad impact in-country; the audience includes the General Staff and decision-makers back in the United States. The level behind me in the chain of command is focused on the issues that affect specific Areas of Operation (AO). I work on a strategic level; lower echelons work on more tactical issues.

Training

The short answer is: I have no specific training that anoints me an intelligence analyst. In fact, most of the training I have done is more related to the ethical and legal issues involved with the kind of intelligence analysis I do. My colleagues who work directly for the government tell me how much specialized training you receive is related to the seniority with which you enter the job. Some have never had training; some have had several months. I have personally done online training that was made available to me to better understand the intelligence process. Although I cannot provide examples of specific methods or processes that I use, I would suggest that an individual with the critical thinking skills needed to produce a competent graduate-level thesis and the writing skills to get to a clear and concise "So what?" likely has the skills needed. There are several books publicly available, some published by the agencies such as the Central Intelligence Agency (CIA), that explain in detail the process from collection of information, to the analysis the makes it intelligence, to policy implications. Analysts I work with have a variety of backgrounds: bachelor's, master's, and doctoral degrees in a breadth of academic disciplines. The degree is really more an assumption of some very broad basic skills rather than the importance of the degree itself.

Motivations

Why am I staying in a job that is not all that exciting? I think of the positions I have taken as part of my "apprenticeship" into this field. I went through something similar when I entered the product design world. I have been choosing my jobs to gain broad experience and to determine if I even like the work. My motivation for entering the intelligence field is in fact quite long term. When I was finishing my first master's degree 20 years ago (prior to any involvement in anthropology), I was contacted by a recruiter from a government agency and asked if I would be interesting in applying. I eventually didn't get the job for the most mundane of reasons: budget cuts. My motivations were then as they are now: I wanted to serve and protect my country and its interests, I wanted to stop terrorist and criminal acts before they started and see that the perpetrators where punished, and of course it was a job that I perceived as exciting and that mattered in the world. That interest has never gone away, but when I did not get the position that I had been offered, I assumed that it was a closed door and I took my career into a different path. In conversations a few years ago with other anthropologists that have worked with military and intelligence groups, they suggested that I should look into it again if I wanted to seek a new career path.

Can I Really Understand the Outcomes of My Work? And What About Feedback?

Not knowing the specific outcomes of a specific task is not the same as not knowing what could or is likely to happen. I know the details of the overall work my group is engaged in, and I am aware of the real-world consequences that have occurred at other times. I also know the ethical and legal restrictions placed on others about how information can be used in this process. However, it is also common not to know all the outcomes of my specific work, as it falls under something called "need to know." But that lack of "need to know" does not absolve me of responsibility to be aware of potential outcomes and ensuring the work that I do is with the bounds of my legal and ethical responsibilities. Rarely do I get feedback; mostly, I do not. As a rule, I get feedback when someone disagrees with my conclusions, and hear nothing if people don't. Fortunately, in my working environment, my chain of command believes that you follow the data and the conclusions emerge from that, regardless of any fallout. I have had other units unhappy with my conclusions, but never changed anything because of that. My chain of command sees me as an independent evaluator whose job is to arrive at an independent assessment regardless of other pressures or opinions.

The Personal versus Legal versus Organizational Nature of Ethics

Bottom line: The kind of intelligence work that I personally do, in my view, is not compatible with the AAA Code of Ethics as it is currently written. To use the commenter's phrase, I think the AAA "wants it both ways" when it comes to ethics. The AAA has set itself up as the arbiter, through the Code of Ethics, of what is ethical for individual anthropologists to do, or are sanctioned from doing. I would say that the tenor of the conversation about the AAA ethics is that they are, for lack of a better phrase, the "laws" under which anthropology, primarily cultural anthropology, is undertaken. People can be censured for ethical violations, but what does that mean in reality? The AAA has no authority in any real effective sense. I know many anthropologists that are infrequent members at best; certainly, no one has ever inquired as to my membership status for a job or prior to speaking at a university. However, people seem to argue about the Code of Ethics as if it is some enforceable code, and that it should be the standard by which work should be judged. At the same time, the AAA does not seem to want to commit to the Code of Ethics as much more than guidelines. If that were true, they would not matter to people as much, would they?

For myself, ethics are a very personal commitment; if they are not a personal commitment, then what are they? My sense of meeting my own goals of personal integrity have far more hold over me than an organization. For that matter, the opinions of my family and close colleagues about ethics matter more than an organization. When I have an ethical quandary, I don't write a letter to the director of the AAA; I talk it over with people I respect, who can help me look at the problem from many angles. My ethics, that sense of what I see as wrong or right, is foundation to who I am as a person and not subject to debate by some organization. Of course, some people will see my choices as inherently unethical; some will not. And, importantly, the nuances of those ethics have changed and will continue to change over time as I have been influenced by my education, people I respect, books, and life experiences. This is why that distinction and priority of personal ethics versus organizational ethics matters to me a great deal. Part of personal ethics to me is that I don't make agreements that I can't live up to. I don't agree with the AAA Code of Ethics, not least because they are more and more driven by political ideology and less by science and critical thought; therefore, I cannot be a member of the AAA because that implies I agree with the entirety of the ethical code. I don't.

Laws and Ethics Live Together in the Real World

We all live within a conflation of personal beliefs, ethics, and the law of the land, and that is what makes for Supreme Court cases that do things like strike down segregation or put a woman's legal right to choose what happens to her own body at risk. As I write this, I am a citizen of the United States. This means that regardless of any other ethical issues, I am bound by those laws of the federal/state/local justice systems and the consequences of breaking those laws. You may choose to cast your local police as an "oppressive tool of the state," but it is still advisable that you pull over when you see blinking lights and hear a siren behind you. Your ethics and political opinions don't offer much assistance when you find yourself tagged as a fleeing suspect. If the point arrives that I decide my work and my ethics are in conflict, then I will have little choice but to leave the work. I don't substitute one for the other, but recognize that I have to negotiate both. However, think about how you live your daily life: do you worry constantly that your personal code of conduct, professional ethics, or commitment to the AAA's Code of Ethics is going to land you in jail? You, like me, live your life, go about your job, obey traffic regulations, and don't shout "Fire!" in crowded theaters. Your ethics and the laws of the land are rarely in conflict to the degree that it disrupts your life on a day-to-day basis. The same is true of myself.

Notes

Some of the ideas and opinions I express in this case study I have also written about and taken from postings on my personal blog, http://www.ethnography.com.

1. Any examples of projects or topics are made up to avoid any confidentiality issue, but accurately reflect how mundane questions asked can be.

6

Interdisciplinary Research in the National Laboratories

Laura A. McNamara

When most anthropologists think of national security, institutions like the U.S. Army and the Central Intelligence Agency (CIA) are among the first that spring to mind. However, the U.S. Department of Energy (DOE) has responsibility for perhaps the most existentially threatening technology in the securityscape: the U.S. nuclear arsenal. Its national laboratory system is rooted in the Manhattan Project of World War II, expanded rapidly throughout the Cold War, and continues to steward the United States' nuclear stockpile, even as former nuclear hawks seek a global nuclear zero and the stockpile shrinks in size.

This is a world that is heavily oriented toward engineering, materials chemistry, and physics; but, as both Jessica Glicken Turnley and Laura McNamara's essays illustrate, interest in the social sciences has permeated even these domains. McNamara has been working in the national laboratories since 1997, but has been studying the New Mexico laboratories and their surrounding communities since entering graduate school at the University of New Mexico. A native of New Mexico and daughter of a sociologist, McNamara grew up in the 1980s as the antinuclear movement reached a crescendo, a formative experience that laid the foundation for her long-standing issue in the institutional culture of nuclear weapons laboratories (in fact, her winning eighth-grade science fair project was a survey of attitudes to nuclear disarmament among college students). McNamara wrote a dissertation on knowledge loss among nuclear weapons designers and engineers at Los Alamos National Laboratory (LANL; Ph.D., University of New Mexico, 2001).

Her career since then has been an interdisciplinary one. Upon completing her dissertation, she was hired at Los Alamos to work in the Statistical Sciences group, partnering with Bayesian statisticians to develop methods for eliciting engineering judgments for statistical models. Later, she moved to nearby Sandia National Laboratories, where her current work focuses on the organizational dynamics of informatics software tools, visual analytics, and high-performance computing research and development in the United States' intelligence and military communities.

We put McNamara's essay after Dawson's and Abramson's because her current work focuses on organizational studies of intelligence analysts in the U.S. Intelligence Community (IC). McNamara is a member of Sandia National Laboratories' Human Studies Board, and recently served on the National Research Council's Committee on Improving the Decision Making Abilities of Small Unit Leaders (2010–2011). Most of her publications are in computing and engineering journals, but she is coeditor (with Robert Rubinstein) of the forthcoming book Dangerous Liaisons: Anthropologists and the National Security State, *to be published by SAR Press in 2011. In addition to her work on the American Anthropological Assocation's (AAA) Commission on the Engagement of Anthropology with the U.S. Security and Intelligence Communities (CEAUSSIC), she served as an at-large member of the board the National Association of Practicing Anthropologists (2009–2010) and is a member of the AAA Executive Board's Task Force on Ethics (2009–2011).*

My career and workplace are complicated. I'll begin with the workplace: I work for a DOE laboratory that is a hybrid research-industrial-government workplace. Officially, I am Principal Member of Technical Staff in the Computing Research Center at Sandia National Laboratories. Unofficially, I am the lone anthropologist in a nuclear weapons and national security laboratory of about 7,000 staff members. Many anthropologists these days pursue both academic and industrial careers in computing and software development, so that's not very unusual. What is unusual is the place where I work: Sandia National Laboratories is at once very much like a university and completely different than a university; it is very much like a corporate workplace and completely different than a corporate workplace; it is both a government facility and a private corporation; and we do both highly classified and completely open scientific research. The same was true at Los Alamos National Laboratory, where I began my career in the national laboratories as a graduate research assistant about 14 years ago; and as far as I know, this category mixing is common across all of the DOE's national laboratories and associated facilities (actually, historian Peter J. Westwick explains all of this quite nicely in *The National Laboratories: An American System* [2003]).

In any case, the DOE "complex" consists of about 20 sites and facilities around the country, in addition to several DOE headquarters facilities in the Washington area. DOE employs more than 30,000 scientists and engineers, making it one of the largest science and technology employers in the country. However, most of the people that work in the DOE complex are technically not government workers. Confusingly, many of the DOE's sites are government-owned, contractor-operated (GOCO) facilities. This means that the DOE—the U.S. government—owns the physical plant and sites for the purpose of carrying out various aspects of DOE's mission, which encompasses both civilian energy research and civilian control and management of the U.S. nuclear stockpile. However, at most of these sites, a contractor manages day-to-day workforce and operational issues. Historically, these contractors have been either universities or a large military-industrial corporation: for example, for many years, the University of California ran several DOE labs, whereas Bell Laboratories (and later AT&T) held the contract for managing Sandia National Laboratories. Periodically these contracts are rebid; right now, for example, a university-industry consortium now manages LANL and Lawrence Livermore National Laboratories (LLNL) in the wake of two fierce bidding wars that pitted several large industrial contractors against each other in pursuit of LANL and LLNL management contracts. Because I work at Sandia National Laboratories, I am formally an employee of the Sandia Corporation, a subsidiary of the Lockheed Martin Corporation, which won the contract to manage Sandia back in the 1990s.

I came to Sandia after six years at LANL, where I was fortunate to have gotten a position that allowed me to write a dissertation on culture-of-science issues. LANL had a generous student research program, if you could find a staff member willing to hire you to help out with their projects. I found one: I was hired to "assist" a project examining the role of mentoring in career development for underrepresented populations—namely women and nonwhite, non-Asian minorities—in the LANL technical workforce. I figured it would make a good dissertation topic, but soon found something much more interesting.

When I arrived at LANL in August of 1997, the United States had recently signed the Comprehensive Test Ban Treaty, and the DOE's national laboratories were adopting Science Based Stockpile Stewardship as an alternative suite of methods and facilities to certifying the stockpile in the absence of full-scale testing, something that Hugh Gusterson has written about as well (Gusterson 1998, 2004). Given that the weapons programs had for decades relied on the testing program to train and socialize newcomers in the practices of weapons physics and engineering, many weapons experts were profoundly concerned about the potential disappearance of knowledge. I remember the day a senior engineer invited me to his office and told me he hoped that an anthropologist could help him and his colleagues save "this culture." That was when I decided to write a dissertation on the impact of the Cold War's end on the training and socialization of novice weapons physicists and engineers. I managed to find a sponsor for this idea, moved to LANL's Archives and History Programs, and spent two and a half years interviewing weapons experts, observing a variety of weapons science and engineering activities, and traveling to the Nevada Test Site. It was incredibly fun and fascinating.

At the same time, I remember feeling completely overwhelmed. As a 27-year-old graduate student with heavy training in social theory and qualitative research, a smattering of statistics, and no physics, I was utterly lost in the math-and-physics world of Los Alamos. Fortunately, I was not the only disciplinary "outsider" at LANL, and others had developed good career paths and were willing to help me. In particular, I met a cultural anthropologist, Mary Meyer, who had spent her career in the statistics group at LANL developing methods for expert knowledge elicitation; she kindly took me under her wing and helped me get oriented to the laboratories. The laboratory historian, Roger Meade, gave me free run of his library and helped me understand how the weapons programs worked. He also put me in the queue to get a security clearance, which was absolutely necessary if I was going to study weapons physicists and engineers. For the first year that I was an uncleared staff member, I literally couldn't go to the bathroom or grab a glass of water without having someone escort me. Once I got my clearance, just being able to walk around freely in the building where I worked was a tremendous relief.

Although I was acutely aware of my outsider status, there was also an odd, comfortable familiarity about LANL. I couldn't put my finger on it until one spring day in 1998, when I was sitting in the sun in front of the cafeteria. As I watched a group of researchers and students walk out to lunch, I realized that LANL felt as much like a university campus as a nuclear weapons laboratory. People wrote proposals, attended conferences, served on committees, and published papers; had offices filled with books and articles; dressed casually in jeans and t-shirts; covered their office doors with witty cartoons; and spent a lot of time hiking, biking, and skiing. They saw me as a student. As Ph.D. researchers, their responsibility was to mentor and to help me. When I arrived at LANL in August of 1997, I knew no one in the weapons programs. By December, I had no fewer than four weapons staff members, including a senior nuclear weapons physicist, helping me pull together my fieldwork project. I remember commenting to one of my engineer mentors, "Bet you've never mentored an anthropologist before." He looked a bit puzzled. "Well, that's true. But you're a student, and I've mentored a lot of students." I don't think he felt the difference in disciplines was particularly important, even though I was acutely self-conscious about my lack of knowledge in physics and engineering.

LANL hired me as a full-time staff member in April of 2001. I'd just finished my dissertation and was offered a job working alongside my anthropologist mentor, Mary Meyer, in the Statistical Sciences group. In retrospect, this was a difficult transition, because it was where I ceased being a doctoral student pursuing a project under my own control and direction, and became a staff member. This meant I would be performing project work as part of an interdisciplinary team, which is the normal working arrangement for the national laboratories—indeed, since then, all the laboratory projects I've worked on have been intensely interdisciplinary, favoring math- and physics-oriented disciplines but with a wide range of application areas, from engineered systems to computer software interfaces.

My new workplace consisted primarily of statisticians, many of them Bayesians (as opposed to frequentists), which is important because Bayesians are open to the use of subjective probability assessments in the form of "expert knowledge" or "expert judgment" to both formulate and populate statistical models. This meant they were open to methodological research about how to interact with communities of experts—hence, my friend Mary's tremendous success in that environment; her creative application of ethnographic observation and interviewing techniques for statistical modeling made her a highly respected and sought-after staff member, though she had little training in statistics.

My first official postdissertation project involved working with a very distributed team of Department of Defense (DoD) test engineers, university researchers, and private contractors to map the distribution of knowledge about propulsion and guidance systems for space launch vehicles. My work would contribute to structuring a Bayesian statistical model of reliability for these systems. If this sounds overwhelmingly technical, that's because it was—and it was terrifying. I ended up traveling all over the country, doing interviews, taking field notes, and drawing diagrams, iterating among the different communities to make sure that I was capturing what was important, and that I was representing it correctly. I made a lot of stupid mistakes, but they were all very patient with me. To support my learning, I not only read a lot about propulsion systems and space launch vehicles, I also read copiously in decision theory, where there's an extensive history of research on how people form and express subjective judgments. Eighteen months later, I remember my statistician colleagues and I literally rolling out a 35-foot graphical representation of the model—it had more than 700 elements to it. And to make it readable, we had to use a plotter to print it. Unfortunately, the modeling techniques were never adopted by the communities we were working with; as I discuss later, experimental interdisciplinary research and development (R&D) projects like this often struggle with issues of adoptability, usability, and utility, themes that are a main focus of my career interests now.

I left LANL in July of 2003, mostly because I was tired of commuting between Albuquerque and Los Alamos—it's a 90-mile drive each way, and my husband and I wanted to continue living in Albuquerque. So I applied for a job at Sandia National Laboratories, was hired as a staff member in the summer 2003, and have been there ever since.

Sandia is very much like LANL in that it's a national laboratory. However, LANL is known as a "physics" laboratory because its weapons and academic research have been focused on high-energy physics (although Sandia does have a major experimental physics facility, the Z-Machine, and employs many theoretical and experimental physicists). Sandia has historically identified as the DOE's engineering laboratory. In layman's terms, Sandia's historic weapons mission involved designing and developing all the parts that connect the nuclear explosive or "physics package" to the delivery vehicle—a missile or a bomb. It's all interconnected, of course, but the difference matters because Sandia is, in some ways, a much more diverse institution than LANL. If you believe that organizations reflect the technologies that they develop, then Sandia is responsible for a dizzying array of engineered parts, and has a diversity of technical experts focused on small systems and subsystems. This makes for a highly fractionated organization. Also, my purely subjective sense is that Sandia seems to have moved more rapidly than LANL did to diversify its mission at the end of the Cold War; when I arrived, there were actually a number of sociologists, political scientists, and even a historian working in policy areas related to international security and nuclear nonproliferation. As fellow contributor Jessica Glicken Turnley writes in her essay, Sandia's leadership had become attuned to the 1990's discourse about "economic security" and was orienting itself to fit that mission, which is how she came to be hired at Sandia.

I had expected moving to an engineering laboratory to be difficult. I thought that LANL, with its academic orientation, would be a more welcoming place for a social scientist than an engineering laboratory focused on problems like tolerances and reliability. However, I soon had more work than I could handle, and on problems with explicit social science components like developing models to assess the impacts of water rights transfers on hydrological resources in water-scarce New Mexico.

It's worth pointing out that many of the DOE's national laboratories do hire social scientists, but they tend to have backgrounds in psychology and work on human factors types of problems. I did meet several archaeologists when I worked at LANL, and I expect that there are others scattered throughout the DOE's 21 sites and research facilities, since DOE is responsible for maintaining the historic and environmental integrity of the sites it owns. However, there are far fewer cultural anthropologists. Off the top of my head, I can think of five Ph.D. cultural anthropologists who have worked for a DOE site, including Turnley.

Most of my work is oriented toward the human and organizational aspects of science and engineering at the national laboratories, such as studying technology adoption among intelligence analysts, examining how funding models and project timelines influence research partnerships across organizational boundaries within Sandia, working with statisticians to develop Bayesian models that capture expertise distributed across multiple organizations, or examining how discourse about "valuable work" shapes individual approaches to particular tasks in a workplace. In this work, I do get to perform some ethnography. This year, for example, I will likely spend time observing engineering analysts as they work with computational models. I also spend great deal of time studying how intelligence analysts in a number of workplaces interact with classified information to form judgments about their topical assignments. However, I tend to rely less on indirect observational methods, and more heavily on interviewing and cognitive task analysis, to understand what people are doing and how they perceive their individual work in relation to the projects and programs to which they are contributing.

My research and work does have a strong "national security" component. I have studied analysts of varying stripes in the Defense Intelligence Agency and the National Geospatial Intelligence Agency, for example. The fact that an anthropologist is gainfully employed as a member of Sandia's technical staff, and can get support for qualitative field research among intelligence analysts, speaks to rapid evolution of the national laboratories' collective mission space over the past three decades. One of the reasons I plan to remain at the laboratories is precisely because of the proximity to the national security community that my workplace affords. I am not a national security hawk, but I am fascinated by the rapid evolution of what constitutes "national security" in the post–Cold War era. I encounter it on a daily basis in my work. For example, until the early 1990s, the DOE laboratories were primarily physics, engineering, and materials science research facilities oriented primarily (though not exclusively) toward nuclear weapons and nuclear power. When the Cold war ended, the DOE reorganized the nuclear weapons complex, and its national laboratories sought new ways to make their research and development capabilities and facilities relevant to problems beyond nuclear weapons. My dissertation research coincided with this trend. I think that LANL was in the midst of an identity crisis that made it possible for a social scientist to make productive connections with weapons experts who were suddenly faced with a tremendous organizational problem of knowledge management, transfer, and loss.

But there's no question that interest in social science, and particularly in anthropology, has skyrocketed since the 9/11 attacks in a much more direct way. The United States has spent the past decade rather frantically seeking new ways of making sense of radical terrorism, and we are also engaged in two counterinsurgency ground wars. "Hearts and minds" campaigns seem to have cued military decision makers into the importance of understanding "culture" on complex battlefields, and anthropology is one of several social science disciplines perceived as having potential for making sense of the non-Western "others" whose activities we are seeking to mitigate (terrorism) or whose countries we would like to reform in some strategically desirable fashion (Afghanistan, Iraq).

Within the national laboratories, and across the DoD and in many areas of the IC, the methodology of choice for examining these issues seems to be the computational modeling and simulation project: agent-based, systems dynamics, and various mixed-methods techniques imported from fields as distant from the social sciences as control theory and statistical mechanics. My introduction to this methodology occurred at LANL. In January 2002, a physicist colleague called me and said he wanted to discuss a "computational model." When I walked into his office, I was surprised to see a stack of ethnographies on his desk. He explained to me that he'd been awarded a contract to develop a computational model of religious violence, and that the ethnographies were part of a literature review he was conducting. When he asked if I had any experience identifying general principles of human behavior from ethnographies, I explained that this was not normal practice for anthropologists. How one would begin distilling a single ethnography, much less a stack of ethnographies, into a set of abstractions suitable for coding a computational simulation, was so foreign as to be mystifying.

Although much of of my work deals with human-computer interaction, and I work closely with computer scientists, I don't usually contribute to computational modeling and simulation projects as a cultural "subject matter expert." In fact, it drives me crazy when people ask me to participate in computational modeling and simulation efforts that are oriented toward understanding the dynamics of other countries. When I decline, I explain that I am an anthropologist, but I have no expertise in working with foreign populations. Moreover, I am always hesitant about contributing to projects whose intended applications and outcomes aren't specified enough for me to address them responsibly (not to mention that I have no research experience at all in areas like insurgency and terrorism, which are frequently the topics of these models).

Instead, I have been partnering for the past six years with a mathematician, Timothy Trucano, whose work in experimental physics drew him to critiquing computational modeling and simulation as a source of evaluative knowledge for assessing the performance of engineered systems. I came to him expressing concern about the proliferation of computational social science models and simulations for national security decision-making, and we began a years-long partnership to bring the extensive work on computational physics and engineering methodologies to bear productively and often quite critically on so-called "predictive" computational modeling and simulation.

I think this is one of the most important forms of critique I can do: he and I have been interacting with a range of federal agencies that are trying to figure out whether computational models of cultural and social phenomena can be used to forecast emerging "national security" issues. We have also drawn a lot on organizational and ethnographic studies of technology, computing, modeling, and simulation to raise issues related to the communities of "decision makers" that are the ostensible users of these technologies. It is exciting that our work is getting a lot of attention; last year, we organized a critical workshop for the Defense Threat Reduction Agency (in which coeditor Robert Albro participated), and we have been asked to assist in several other policy-oriented workshops addressing the intersection of computational methodologies and national security policy- and decision-making.

One of the reasons I love working for the national laboratories is because I am always forced to articulate how my training in ethnography can intersect with and bring nuance to problems that are quite far afield from cultural anthropology—high-performance scientific computing, Bayesian statistical modeling and simulation, and computer model verification and validation. I like working with mathematical and physical scientists. Their training is so profoundly different from mine; I have to listen and think hard to understand the conceptual foundations from which they are working, and figuring out ways to bridge between my training and theirs is difficult and exhilarating. Similarly, they have worked to understand my background and identify ways in which I can support their research and development goals. My activities in the broader anthropology community also have won consistent management support because, as one manager told me several years ago, "You're a scientist and a professional."

Editorial Commentary

McNamara's identity as an anthropologist becomes salient in some work contexts, while it recedes in others. Calling forth the image of the anthropologist as defender of vanishing ways of life, a senior engineer beseeches McNamara to help him save "this culture," as the Comprehensive Test Ban Treaty ended decades-old ways of introducing new practitioners to weapons physics and engineering. Other disciplinary "outsiders"—a historian and a cultural anthropologist—help orient McNamara during her early days at LANL, incorporating her into the larger fold of "social" scientists. During McNamara's dissertation fieldwork, an engineer advising her downplays McNamara's anthropological identity, stressing instead her status as a student and his as a mentor. Her value as a "cultural" anthropologist becomes reaffirmed in the post-9/11 era, as a few computational modeling colleagues reach out, assuming McNamara to be the stereotypical expert on "other" peoples. McNamara bristles at such requests, just as Turnley hates to be the "pet anthropologist" on similar projects.

McNamara is at ease working in interdisciplinary teams, and she notes the satisfaction she gets in having to articulate how her ethnographic training bears productively on issues quite distant from cultural anthropology. Reading McNamara's account alongside Simons', in which we learn that the Naval Postgraduate School's Department of Defense Analysis also has a very interdisciplinary faculty, we are curious about the extent to which certain work settings (national security ones, especially) put a high value on "problem solving" that throws as many different smart minds as possible at an issue. Knowledge production is not tied to the reproduction of clear disciplinary boundaries or the "purity" of one kind of information over another—as it might be in a traditional academic setting. Anthropologists (well, an anthropologist, in the case of Sandia National Laboratories) seem to specialize in moderating the more hyperrational knowledge forms that are the currency of doctrine and discourse in matters of national security. This makes them at least one kind of arbiter of "common sense" and practical reason in contexts where that function might seem a little exotic as an expert contribution.

McNamara recounts the emergence of computational modeling and simulation as the methodology embraced by the national laboratories in tackling issues related to radical terrorism and counterinsurgency—prevailing security concerns in the post-9/11 era. She relates her concern about the proliferation of computational social science models and simulations for national security decision-making, in particular their use at forecasting developments. This is a subject of key importance to which her informed critical thinking and role as an anthropologist are highly relevant. We wanted to know more about why questioning predictive modeling and simulation is, as she says, "one of the most important forms of critique I can do." How has she been able to rally financial support for this kind of work? We discussed whether her critique has been well received among the national security sponsors that she hints at, and if she has created controversy among her colleagues. We also wondered about the extent to which she has effectively informed other coworkers or other practitioners outside the national laboratories. Given her proximity to these projects, we also wondered if she puts any faith in computational models of cultural and social phenomena that policy and decision makers would like to use in discerning the national security horizon.

Finally, while we get an excellent portrait of McNamara's work situations and their satisfactions and possibilities for an anthropologist, we get much less information about the kinds of articulations that her "local" work at Sandia entails as she moves among the other operations and institutions of the defense/security sphere. Those employed by Sandia do studies and consult in many other arenas, which involve circuits of travel that must be very interesting to an anthropological curiosity. As McNamara's colleagues, we commented that she is constantly traveling to meetings, conferences, and national security sites to do field studies and present papers and such. She also frequently mentions working with "customers," a term we associated with industrial contractors rather than government agencies. This, then, hints at complications in the way the national laboratories fit into the security and defense worlds. Along those lines, McNamara does not tell us how she actually works with the intelligence analysts that she studies.

In addition, we wondered whether it is her position in the national laboratories that gives her access to such a broad range of institutions, or if her security clearance—which we assume she still has—is the real "ticket," so to speak, that gives her entrée. In other words, would her institutional affiliation matter so much if she did not have the badges that designate her as a trustworthy member of a massive classified community? In addition, McNamara does not explain the mechanisms through which she produces knowledge, or the channels through which it is distributed and consumed. Given the AAA's recent discussions about the importance of transparency in dissemination, the limitations that McNamara faces in publishing her studies and, perhaps more important, her critiques of major investments in computational modeling, are striking omissions from her essay. We asked her to address these issues in her response, which is below.

McNamara Response

A few years ago, I quite visibly irritated a senior figure at one of the DOE's national laboratories when I commented that our increasing use of "customers" as a framing metaphor for laboratory relationships with its federal sponsors was a problematic one. In the view of this manager, the laboratories' emphasis on "customers" was valuable because it instilled in staff an ethos of quality, service, responsiveness, and timely delivery, and he did not see how these traits could be a problem for the laboratories. I took a deep breath and responded that most of the laboratories have many different sponsors, both civilian and military, each of which brings somewhat different goals, priorities, drivers, and restrictions to the programs they fund at the laboratories. This occurs even when those sponsoring elements are inside the same federal agency: for example, the DOE's Office of Science emphasizes the national laboratories' impact on academic and industrial research, whereas the National Nuclear Security Administration—the office that oversees the nuclear weapons programs—is far less comfortable (to put it mildly) with open publication. Funding carries expectations that can be difficult to resolve in practice. At Sandia, I see that my coworkers are remarkably creative in working around these things. For example, researchers are adept at finding ways to describe their work in ways that are technically transparent but programmatically opaque. However, the dynamics can become quite complicated.

Our exchange carried on for a while (and ended amicably), but I use this vignette to illustrate a salient theme in most of the national laboratories' organizational cultures, one that also permeates Sandia's organizational culture: our status as a GOCO facility that straddles the boundaries among academic, industrial, and government research, and our ongoing attempts to manage the dynamics that attend our hybrid institutional status. Sandia's articulations with "national security" occur along all these boundaries (e.g., when we receive DoD funding as part of a partnership with a team of university researchers). As the Cold War has been transformed into the post-9/11 era, the dynamics of those articulations have changed, too. For example, both Sandia and LANL historically received most of their funding from the DOE's nuclear weapons programs. Slowly, however, the balance has shifted so that so-called "Work for Others" programs—meaning programs that are not funded through the DOE but through programs like the Defense Advanced Research Projects Agency (DARPA; interestingly, the Intelligence Community now has its own version of DARPA in the form of the Intelligence Advanced Research Projects Agency, or IARPA) or any of the so-called "three-letter agencies" that comprise the U.S. Intelligence Community—have come to represent extremely important funding sources for all the national laboratories, not just Sandia.

In my own world, this plays out in the number and type of "projects" that I either lead or in which I am involved. As the commentary astutely observes, most of my work emphasizes a practical kind of research output. In my projects, which usually last anywhere from six months to three years, I am responsible for using my research skills to incorporate what are often called "human factors" issues into a project, either as a lone researcher or as part of a team seeking to solve a problem for a "customer." The interesting part occurs during negotiations to identify what that problem actually *is*: for example, the "customer" might be an upper-level manager in a three-letter agency, and she is concerned about the massive amounts of information that her analysts are dealing with on a daily basis. She has come to Sandia hoping that computer scientists can develop informatics software for the analysts. The computer science team sees an opportunity to develop algorithms that address a certain class of "big data" problems. The team and the customer perceive like purpose.

But this is often not quite the case. In my experience, the intended users of new analytics technologies—the analysts themselves—are very rarely involved in discussions about what, precisely, might be wrong with the way they do their work. The problems tend to be defined *for* the analysts, not *with* the analysts, usually by well-meaning managers or enthusiastic technology proponents who want to improve the overall agency's performance by developing "solutions" to information "problems." Although it's a cliché, a certain "If we build it and it's faster, they will use it" mentality permeates these discussions, which I think ethnography is ideally positioned to break down. Hence, my articulations involve a lot of traveling, spending long days with intelligence analysts in their workspaces, taking copious notes as I observe their interactions, interviewing them about the work they do, or performing a structured task analysis. I use my data to explain how organizational dynamics in the analytic workplace strongly condition whether new software is perceived as "useful," above and beyond algorithmic efficiency or scalability.

My research products take the form of presentations to sponsors (a lot of Microsoft PowerPoint) and so-called SAND reports, which is the term for a publication issued by Sandia, as well as presentations and conference papers in venues like the Institute of Electronics and Electrical Engineers (IEEE) and the Association of Computing Machinery (ACM). Like my other research colleagues at Sandia, I have learned how to represent my work in ways that enable publication without compromising any sensitive information that might attend my fieldwork. I realize that statement might raise anthropological eyebrows—you might be thinking, "What is she holding back?"—but I can honestly say that I have never encountered a situation in which I felt I had to disguise a controversial finding or a program that deserved public scrutiny or critique. What I am holding back are details that influence decisions about classification: it's a matter of describing one's work in ways that are general enough to be publishable, while retaining enough descriptive specificity to be informative. For example, although I am currently working on a project in which I am studying how imagery analysts interact with imagery intelligence, such as satellite imagery. I will not write about the satellite systems, nor can I identify the specific geographic regions on which the analysts are focused. However, I can write extensively and openly about the organizational challenges that attend this kind of work, and the strategies that different analytic workgroups employ to balance competing demands on their time and attention.

In many ways, I think my raison d'etre workwise is to challenge the technological determinism that permeates so much of the national security community. In the case of computational social modeling and simulation, the technological determinism is particularly annoying since so much computational social science writes social scientists straight out of the picture. I'm not sure which is worse: when social scientists, including anthropologists, throw their own disciplines under the bus insofar as they uncritically present computational modeling and simulation as a useful way for national security experts to assess phenomena; or when computer scientists and engineers tell me that the mathematical formulations they've developed are generalizations that will shed light on the social processes in ways that social science does not. As far as what I think of computational modeling and simulation, it depends very much on the research design in which it plays a role. The context of development is what makes a model or a simulation good, not the technology itself; as far as I'm concerned, computational modeling is method, not answer. I think Scott Atran is an example of someone who does a tremendously good job incorporating modeling into a broader research agenda around radicalization and terrorism.

I've been pleasantly surprised to discover that I'm not the only scientist in the national security community, social or otherwise, who is skeptical of both the envisioned benefits of, and the particular projects that constitute, the broader "computational modeling and simulation" revolution that continues to be promoted in the intelligence and military sectors. In June of 2011, LLNL organized a workshop on high-performance computing for policy-making, and asked if I'd lead a discussion session on computational social science. When I told the organizers that I was extremely skeptical of how these technologies were being framed and sold, they told me, "That's why we asked you to do it." It would be wonderful if more social scientists would take the time to learn about computational simulation methodologies, so that we can develop a public and judicious position on technology trend in which we are implicated, but weakly engaged.

7

Standing at the Crossroads of Anthropology, Public Health, and National Security

Monica Schoch-Spana

What happens when ethnographic knowledge about peoples abroad is applied in military settings has been the key issue to trigger current anthropological debates about security sector engagements. Monica Schoch-Spana's case broadens our perspective to consider the profound changes in governmental institutions and everyday life occurring in the name of U.S. homeland security and the issues of identity, ethics, and practice emerging for an anthropologist enmeshed in these domestic reconfigurations. Schoch-Spana is a Senior Associate with the Center for Biosecurity of the University of Pittsburgh Medical Center (UPMC) and an Assistant Professor in the School of Medicine's Division of Infectious Diseases. The Center for Biosecurity works at the intersection of public health and national security to affect policy and practice in ways that improve the country's ability to withstand biological attacks, large-scale epidemics, and other events with extreme health impacts. Indeed, Schoch-Spana was invited to participate in the second generation of the Commission on the Engagement of Anthropology with the U.S. Security and Intelligence Communities (CEAUSSIC) to help leaven discussions about the full range of ways in which anthropological and security realms now overlap.

Since 1998, Schoch-Spana has briefed numerous federal, state, and local officials as well as medical, public health, and public safety professionals on key issues in biosecurity and public health emergency preparedness. National advisory roles include serving on the Steering Committee of the Disaster Roundtable of the National Research Council (NRC; an entity considered in greater length in the Albro essay), the Institute of Medicine Standing Committee on Health Threats Resilience, and the NRC Committee on Increasing National Resilience to Hazards and Disasters. She also serves on the faculty of the National Consortium for the Study of Terrorism and Responses to Terrorism (START), one of more than 10 university-based "centers of excellence" supported by the U.S. Department of Homeland Security (DHS) and tasked with generating basic and applied research to help ensure the country's safety and security. Schoch-Spana's research has focused on community resilience to disasters, public engagement in emergency planning, and stigma in the context of epidemics. She has also collaborated with multidisciplinary teams on social and organizational challenges faced by hospitals and health departments in managing public health emergencies.

Schoch-Spana has had a long-standing interest in promoting public dialogue on a professional ethics framework suited to today's security environment. At the 2002 American Anthropological Association (AAA) annual meetings, she organized and chaired an invited session titled "Defending the Nation? Ethics and Anthropology after 9/11," in which contributors Rubinstein and Simons also participated. In parallel that same year, she organized the AAA panel "Emerging Diseases, Bioweapons and Other Anticipated Microbial Horrors." Schoch-Spana has attempted to leverage her experience with bio- and homeland security policy makers while serving on (2008–2010) and then co-chairing (2010–2011) the AAA's Committee on Public Policy, hopeful that the discipline can become better positioned and practiced at influencing public policy. Schoch-Spana received her Ph.D. in cultural anthropology from The Johns Hopkins University (JHU) in 1998. Prior to coming to the University of Pittsburgh, she held faculty positions in the JHU Bloomberg School of Public Health's Department of Epidemiology and Department of Health, Policy and Management.

For some people, "What do you do for a living?" is a question with an easy, one-word answer like "teacher" or "doctor." When faced with this polite question, I typically have to pause, assess the social situation, and take a stab at labeling a complex professional identity. Cultural anthropologist, medical anthropologist, social scientist, policy analyst, public health practitioner, disaster expert, preparedness practitioner, biodefense professional, biosecurity expert? Part of the messiness comes from having multiple disciplinary affiliations; part of it comes from the politically charged nature of my work. Is concern over a possible biological weapons attack reasonable in today's political and biotech contexts, or is it a trumped-up threat for inducing the American public's consent for dubious foreign policies?

My formal biosketch introduces me as a Senior Associate with the Center for Biosecurity of the UPMC and a faculty member in the School of Medicine's Division of Infectious Diseases. The Center for Biosecurity is an independent, nonprofit organization of UPMC whose formal mission is "to strengthen national security by reducing the risks posed by biological attacks, epidemics, and other destabilizing events, and to improve the nation's resilience in the face of such events." We are an interdisciplinary academic center that conducts policy analysis and offers advice on matters where national security and public health intersect. The bulk of our funding comes from a UPMC endowment and from major foundations such as Alfred P. Sloan and Robert Wood Johnson. On occasion, we may take on a government-funded project (as in the case of a Department of Health and Human Services contract to assess the impact of their hospital preparedness program), but we keep such arrangements to a minimum to maintain our independence.

Affiliated with UPMC since 2003, our organization nonetheless had its start as the JHU Center for Civilian Biodefense Strategies. The Biodefense Center was founded in 1998 by D. A. Henderson, the former dean of the JHU School of Public Health, and the former head of the World Health Organization's Smallpox Eradication Campaign. The Center began with the assumption that a covert biological attack resulting in mass casualties among U.S. civilians was a likely event and that the nation—and the world—were unprepared for a deliberate outbreak of infectious disease. The Center maintained that appropriate preparations could mitigate the death and suffering possible with such an event, and that raising awareness about biological weapons might arguably lead to measures that could prevent their development and use. Our principal program areas included preventing the research, development, and use of biological weapons; preparing the health care system for mass casualty scenarios; strengthening public health system capabilities to track and treat an epidemic; and articulating biomedical research and development strategies to enhance diagnostics and therapeutics to manage an intentional outbreak of disease.

Deeply disturbing developments in the 1990s spurred Henderson to found the Biodefense Center: new revelations about the existence and scope of covert offensive bioweapons programs within the former Soviet Union and Iraq (both signatories to the Biological Weapons Convention); the Aum Shinrykio gas attack upon the Tokyo subway, whose subsequent investigation revealed an active though not yet successful bioweapons program; the potential for bioweapons proliferation (comparable to the "loose nukes" phenomenon) with former Soviet bioweaponeers put out of work during a period of profound economic stagnation; and mass casualty attacks upon U.S. civilians by individuals and groups characterized as "terrorist" (i.e., the bombings of the Murrah Building in Oklahoma City and the World Trade Center Tower in New York City).

How I ended up working at the Biodefense Center was serendipitous. I was a fresh Ph.D. on the market in 1998 when I came upon a job posting within the JHU system about a newly forming academic center. Disbelief was my first reaction, followed by curiosity. My interest was piqued for several reasons: my graduate training had been in the anthropology of science, technology, and medicine, and my doctoral dissertation focused on the U.S. nuclear weapons complex at the end of the Cold War as it shifted from producing fissile materials and nuclear weapons to addressing the environmental and health legacies of the earlier production. I had also worked with Emily Martin on her Flexible Bodies project examining the immune system as a prevailing metaphor in U.S. culture, and I had consulted on several applied public health projects on HIV/AIDS. Work at the Center offered a unique opportunity to meld my interest and expertise in two very disparate fields: nukes/national security and infectious disease/public health. I was also hooked as an ethnographer interested in understanding how and why biological weapons were emerging as a central problem in national security.

Initially, then, I conceived of the Center as a "field site" to explore U.S. national security institutions and concepts further. This distanced observer position, however, eventually gave way to a growing insider perspective: I came to learn more about the history of biological weapon programs, the developments in the life sciences (e.g., genomics and the explosion of computational power) that could lead to more potent weapons, and the decrepit state of the public health infrastructure both domestically and internationally. Biological weapons as a global health threat became, in my mind, a contemporary social problem on which I could reasonably focus as a principal concern in my own professional life (rather than a second-order or indirect concern worthy of anthropological analysis).

At the outset of my tenure at the Biodefense Center, I first approached biological weapons as an intellectual problem. This stance contrasted with my more impassioned sense of the danger posed by nuclear weapons—in prior work, I had seen the actual reactors and engineers that made the destructive materials of plutonium and tritium. The prospect of both mass-casualty terrorism and a bioweapons attack, nonetheless, shifted from the abstract to the concrete in the fall of 2001. The 9/11 attacks provoked my own realization that a small group of people could have the motivation and the organizational sophistication to inflict mass casualties. I had the chance to see the heaping, smoking pile of rubble that was the World Trade Center Towers when, in the two weeks following the 9/11 attacks, I led a small research team up to New York City to study self-organizing groups of volunteers. Very soon after that, the anthrax crisis demonstrated the fragility of the nation's public health system when only 20 or so cases of anthrax infection and five deaths overwhelmed it. These events were transformative for me in that they solidified otherwise abstract dangers and helped me appreciate the value of the Center's work in a very sobering way.

As an anthropologist working in the science, technology, and medicine realm, I have worked on projects both socially critical and practically applied in nature, from studying the disciplining of the nuclear weapons complex workforce to chronicling the dilemmas faced by HIV-positive women in making reproductive decisions. Aligning myself with the Biodefense Center has managed to activate and sustain both dimensions of my professional anthropological experiences, and they have remained in creative tension throughout my tenure with the group. I have felt like an anthropological insider-outsider: at once in the thick of things, helping shape biodefense policy and practice, and at the sidelines, reflecting on the direction of the field and the country. This tension plays out in myriad ways at the office, from discussions and hopefully productive arguments with colleagues, to the types of research projects I tend to initiate, to the advice I pass on to leaders in government and public health regarding best practices and principles for building what we in the field call "preparedness and response systems."

One of my earliest interventions, and one that has shaped the contours of most projects I have directed since then, was to challenge a pernicious image that dominated much of the bioterrorism preparedness and response literature, policy discussions, and training exercises—that of the panic-stricken, socially volatile masses who quickly resort to violence to gain access to scarce hospital beds, vaccines, or antibiotics, thus prompting the arrival of the National Guard to quell the unrest. The "problem" as articulated in early dominant bioterrorism discourse was not only the irrational, emotionally consumed terrorist (whether the fundamentalist or millennialist) who would resort to repugnant bioweapons to kill large numbers of peoples, but an irrational, hysterical public who would produce social chaos in the aftermath of an attack. This, of course, left government leaders and response professionals as the only levelheaded ones in the room! This assumption was best captured in the words of former U.S. Secretary of Health and Human Services Tommy Thompson, who asserted in the fall of 2001, "The role of the federal government is to prevent panic."

Contrary to the scary stories authorities may tell each other, however, panic is the exception and creative coping is the norm during extreme events, according to extensive social research into disasters, terrorist attacks, and even novel disease outbreaks. Communicating this extant body of knowledge artfully to policy makers has been a continuing task. In 2001, a sociology colleague and I prepared an article for preparedness professionals that criticized the tendency within bioterrorism policy and response planning to assume the public to be "irrational, uncoordinated, and uncooperative in emergencies—not to mention prone to panic" and that outlined officials' obligations to foster circumstances in which people can readily cope with extreme health events (Glass and Schoch-Spana 2002). To upend the prevailing image of a hysterical public during biological attacks, we wrote of the public's temperate response during the anthrax letter crisis. What was described in news reports as rampant "panic-buying" of gas masks and antibiotics was a behavior in which few people actually engaged, according to academic polls. Moreover, mass testing and antibiotic distribution at affected work sites was an orderly process, as hundreds and even thousands of people waited in line for their turn.

That article is now widely cited in the newly emerging field of "public health preparedness" and even featured in a textbook on homeland security—an achievement not likely to help land me an academic anthropology position, but one that I believe is significant nonetheless. In taking on the panicked public ideal, colleagues and I have tried to undermine biodefense discourse that legitimates the use of force against U.S. residents and the trampling of their freedoms in the name of security against the dual threats of terrorism and disease outbreaks. I have also tried to undermine the notion of the public as a mere bystander to health emergency policies, offering instead a more nuanced and comprehensive picture of how community members—not just emergency professionals—can help mitigate health disasters. Elsewhere I have detailed other notional publics within the dominant biodefense discourse that I have critically examined: the anxious audience, the self-sufficient stockpiler, and the resilient survivor (Schoch-Spana 2009). Each warrants close review not simply because they may reflect poor reasoning, but because they represent different political possibilities harnessed to the biodefense project.

Some anthropological readers at this point may be wondering whether such socially critical efforts might better take place "outside" biosecurity circles and institutions. Or, perhaps another way to state the issue is: why would I want to work in such a "questionable" venture in the first place? There have certainly been times when I have weighed the possibility of leaving my position. As noted earlier, I am convinced of the importance of developing effective policies and practices that can avert the development and use of biological weapons, and, should prevention fail, reduce the human suffering and social disruption that could result. This was and is the central draw of my position. The other draw to the job—another reason for staying—is a sense of obligation and commitment to help articulate forms of government that can effectively and humanely address the problem of extreme health events, including intentional epidemics. Such forms of government do not simply happen on their own, and in fact, many poor and some disastrous policies have evolved around the prospect of a biological attack on U.S. civilians.

Keeping me in my job, then, have been ill-conceived government ideas about how to manage what are called "public health emergencies." I have consciously shaped my research agenda, policy analysis, and soapbox interventions in politically significant venues to counter harmful, ineffective approaches. As a member of the leading academic center on biosecurity matters, I have had the chance and the credibility to be heard by decision makers in positions of authority when presenting a counterbalancing argument. Of course, there certainly have been low points in U.S. biodefense policy where I have felt that the "threat" to the nation was less about a biological attack or large-scale epidemic than about the government policies developing around these scenarios. When H5N1 was the influenza strain of concern, the medical director for DHS expressed deep worry over the potential for "insurrection" and the president in October 2005 advocated military-enforced quarantines in the context of an evolving pandemic. I presented evidence before a congressional panel that a panicked population was an unfounded fear by authorities, and I joined the American Civil Liberties Union (ACLU) in arguing about the detrimental public health impacts of pandemic response plans that treated "sick people" as the "enemy."

Public health, like anthropology, has had strenuous public debates about the potential pitfalls of engaging with the security sector. Where anthropology has been concerned about the misapplication of ethnographic knowledge and potential harm to inhabitants in geographic areas of strategic importance to U.S. national security, public health has grappled with concern about the militarizing effects of a counter-biosecurity agenda and the field's taking on a preparedness mindset. Among the principal concerns are the possibility for distortions in public funding, with resources siphoned away from health and social welfare toward military and national security purposes (Sidel et al. 2001), and newly emerging collaborations and information-sharing arrangements among public health, national security, and law enforcement practitioners that could drive people from the care they need (Annas 2002; Goldman 2003). The caution against the militarization of public health is worth heeding (and a lengthier argument than can be covered here).

Yet, the question remains as to whether the policy turn toward public health preparedness can be reduced to an unfettered process of militarization. Some public health leaders, notably from within state and local health departments, have embraced the opportunity to develop new capabilities and to shore up a woefully neglected public health infrastructure. Some proponents of the need to develop better public health emergency policies and practices argue that having to side with a preparedness agenda or not is a false choice; society needs public health and health care systems responsive to both routine and emergent needs. I agree with this perspective. Moreover, while convinced of the potency and seductiveness of militaristic frameworks and investments, theorists such as Catherine

Lutz (2002), Laura McEnaney (2000), and Cynthia Enloe (2004) have also argued that a society's embrace of war-making and bellicose ideals is neither preordained nor unstoppable. I am hopeful in this regard as well.

Future historical accounts may delve into our current records and conclude that public health and medicine formed an ill-conceived alliance with national defense objectives. Such a rendering of today's complex workings would be inadequate, I argue, for its failure to explore the intricate conflicts over the very meaning of "security" occurring within health emergency policy and the struggles to envision and build social institutions by which to bring that collective well-being about. I hope that colleagues in both public health and anthropology come to see security not simply as a homogeneous, static sector with "obvious" ethical and political pitfalls, but more as something in the making that can be redirected in more beneficial ways.

Editorial Commentary

In the United States, professional identity is one of the most important cues through which we categorize ourselves and each other. Schoch-Spana's essay opens with a dilemma of identity: describing what she does. Anthropologists reading this essay can probably sympathize with Schoch-Spana, since people who are external to the discipline tend to be curious about what "being an anthropologist" actually involves. For Schoch-Spana, the question is perhaps trickier because her work entails such a complex intersection of workplaces, professional activities, and problem areas. She is both faculty member and research associate at an institution with roots in two well-regarded universities; she is an anthropologist, but works in medicine and public policy; and she is working in biodefense, a field that conjures images of virulent diseases, bursting hospitals, and—as she points out—panicked masses. What does it mean to "be an anthropologist" in such a complicated space?

Schoch-Spana tells us that initially she viewed her association with the Biosecurity Center as if it were a "field site." Fujimura, Holmes-Eber, and Simons all make comparable points in this volume, with each treating their professional military education (PME) affiliation and work teaching and training military personnel as at times like "fieldwork." This is particularly clear for Holmes-Eber. In different ways, these anthropologists have conducted initial fieldwork at some other geographic point on the compass and then trained an ethnographer's gaze upon their institutional contexts of employment. This is offered as a way to maintain continuity with an "anthropological" orientation to their professional identity while working in an environment others might consider well outside that of traditional academia. But for Schoch-Spana, matters are the inverse. Rather than coming to think of her work in ethnographic terms, she starts out that way but moves steadily away from such a stance toward "insider"-dom, while not altogether setting aside an ethnographic stance.

It appears that at least one reason for this is that she finds her work in "public health" to be in many ways anthropological, as a regular part of the job. She notes the creative tension she experiences between the more "critical" and "applied" moments of her work. But, interestingly, much of her work, as she describes it, takes a deconstructivist aim, if you will, at prevailing policy assumptions built into the discourse of preparedness and response planning regarding likely public responses to a bioterror attack. In other words, she engages the epistemological horizon of the assumptions underwriting public policy in ways Albro describes as particularly difficult in his dialogues with counterparts in the security sector.

As Schoch-Spana observes, policy maker understandings of public behavior are largely shaped by the media's attention to public hysteria during terrorist attacks, natural disasters, and other mass injury/casualty events. Even when the majority of an affected population is calmly taking care of business, the media is likely to focus on the minority who are purchasing gas masks and stockpiling antibiotics. Unfortunately, such media images become the distorted lens through which policy makers view the broader public. In the policy imagination, the disorderly "masses" become a self-interested population whose demands for government assistance threaten to overwhelm state resources. In her critiques—effectively presented for policy makers—of the misguided assumption of an "irrational, hysterical public," Schoch-Spana, in other words, is effectively doing a recognized kind of anthropology: cultural critique, but in an applied form that is accessible to the policy community.

Schoch-Spana's work in the arena of public health policy is also a model for a different kind of public anthropology, where "public" most often corresponds to "public policy." This is, of course, a kind of engagement, but not of the activist or advocacy sort. As such, it broadens the parameters of how we might understand a public anthropology that is properly concerned with important social questions. For Schoch-Spana, this takes the form of a critical examination of the "notional publics" of the biodefense field, including of political decision makers.

Schoch-Spana's work is also literary: she describes a kind of Canterbury Tale of a response to a biological event in which anxious audiences, sufficient stockpilers, and resilient survivors make their way through a disaster without collapsing into hysteria. In this way, Schoch-Spana has created an alternative imaginary that prods policy makers to rethink their assumptions about the public so that they are better enabled to think about the public in a different role: as "resourceful ally."

What also stands out is the way that Schoch-Spana describes her changing investments in her work on bioterror: from interesting if abstract intellectual problem to more urgent, concrete, and real. As others have reported in this volume, 9/11—in Schoch-Spana's case together with the anthrax scare—was transformative and upped the ante of her professional commitment to public health as a question of security. She poses this threshold as a contrast between abstract problems and concrete realities.

For her counterpart editors, Schoch-Spana's essay caused us to wonder how her deconstructivist critical discourse and cultural critique might forcefully make its way in these policy spaces, since it trucks more in the arena of knowledge production and the influence of ideas, particularly given the concrete urgency she ascribes to likely security threats and given the relatively more direct access her job affords her to the ears of policy makers. Just how willing, in other words, are her policy interlocutors to pay attention to the implications derived from critiques of merely "notional publics"?

Second, Schoch-Spana also notes that her Center minimizes the amount of federal funding that they receive so as to "maintain independence." One question this raises is what "independence" entails: is distance from federal, state, and local policy makers necessary for the Center to maintain the credibility of its work? Or are there concrete (if subtle) ways that federal funding shapes the work of the Center? It would be interesting to learn more about the influence of funding sources on the practice of research. One assumes that private organizations attach fewer strings to their monies than the federal government might. In particular, what kind of requirements do different private foundations attach to work, if any, and how do these differ from the expectations attached to public funding? This assumption may be neither fair nor generalizable across the heterogeneous world of private foundation funding.

Schoch-Spana Response

More on Professional Identity

To draw out the messiness (in a Mary Douglas sense of "matter out of place") of my professional identify and that of the Center even further, I should comment on the issue of formal titles. When the JHU Biodefense Center was coming into being, the issue arose as to what employees should call themselves. We were/are a university-based center whose principals hold formal academic titles (professor, etc.) in either a medical or public health school department. Yet, our directors also envisioned us operating in the sphere populated by think tanks such as the Brookings Institute and the Center for Strategic and International Studies. To be legible "inside the Beltway," we required a comparable naming system. Hence, we were Fellows and Senior Fellows when we were at JHU, and now with UPMC, we are Associates and Senior Associates—the "senior" title being reserved for individuals with terminal degrees and significant experience in either policy or practice. At the outset, then, we desired to be seen as "more than" an academic outfit, in the traditional sense.

We hold the status of an academic endeavor, with associations of intellectual independence, in-depth analysis, and scientific rigor, and at the same time, convey our interest in engaging with public authorities on current, complex matters. But there are also negative associations in being seen as "academic" in the public policy arena. One implication is that one's writing is jargon filled, opaque, and not meaningful, except to a handful of specialists. Another is that one's analysis is naive in that it ignores or underestimates the practical and political dilemmas that people in positions of authority routinely face. Still invested in the idea that being academic is a good thing, I cringe at those times when I receive feedback from colleagues that my writing in certain cases is academic and needs further polishing. On the other hand, I admit cringing when listening to certain talks at the annual AAA meetings, wondering why writing and speaking obtusely can be rewarded behaviors.

Betwixt and between, in certain contexts I am seen as too academic and in others, as not academic enough. I recall the time when a favorite colleague referred to me as a "practicing" anthropologist, and I wondered then why I wasn't just an "anthropologist anthropologist." Why did I have to be in the marked category, signifying something as other or less than?

Bringing the issue of social categories and social hierarchies back to the securityscape, while working in the biodefense policy arena, I have had to acquire a certain lexicon to be intelligible to others. One speaks in terms of "policy makers and practitioners," "decision makers and operators"—crudely, people who work at the strategic level (sometimes called the "30,000 foot" perspective) setting a high-level vision and making influential decisions, in contrast to people who carry out the everyday task of implementing (sometimes called "boots on the ground" or "where the rubber meets the road") that vision and those decisions. (The military goes even further, slicing the worlds into strategic, operational, and tactical levels.) I remember being taken aback initially by the very idea that only some people were considered "decision makers"—as if being in the world wasn't itself a series of conscious and unconscious decisions that we were all constantly having to make? The valuation of people via the mind/body dichotomy is constant, across multiple sectors in the United States.

More on Cultural Critique

I have often approached my work as an act of "studying up," seeking to understand how and why policy makers in national security and public health think about "the public" in particular ways. What goes on in the imaginations of these agents of the state? Why, for instance, has the image of panicked mobs on the verge of violence been so central to early bioterrorist narratives? In my mind, my "research subjects" are the policy makers rather than the publics they intend to protect. Yet, from the perspective of many of my colleagues, associates, and acquaintances in biodefense, I am the specialist on population behavior in disasters, the psychosocial dimensions of epidemics, disaster mental health, and risk communication.

The operating assumption is that I study "the people," not the policy maker. I am called upon as the expert witness on all things social and behavioral in relation to extreme events. Certainly, I have become familiar with what anthropologists as well as sociologists and psychologists have written about communities facing catastrophe. I have used these various literatures as well as my own ethnographic and archival studies to refute harmful, unfounded assumptions held by policy makers and practitioners in relation to public health emergencies. What this all boils down to personally—in terms of my expertise—is that I feel like a critical cultural anthropologist playing the television role of an expert on human behavior in disaster.

Joking aside, to work effectively in the public policy arena, one does not have the option to culturally deconstruct and walk away. To challenge deeply held beliefs about mass behavior in epidemics and disasters, I have needed to provide a compelling counter narrative, backed by empirical evidence (and, in the case of the myth about public panic, data do exist). Policy makers and practitioners in public safety and health have a genuine desire to know how people in crisis are likely to behave so that they can apply the resources at their disposal to manage the event. Working in biodefense since 1998, I have seen policies shift away from images of disorderly mobs and hapless victims; today, the prevailing idea is that of hardy and helpful survivors. Based on feedback from associates in biosecurity, I understand that my writings and briefings have had some influence in altering assumptions held at higher levels of government.

We are not, however, at a moment when we can breathe a sigh of relief and express self-satisfaction that officials in biosecurity and homeland security have finally gotten things "right" about mass behaviors in disasters and epidemics and they can now plan accordingly. I still wonder what larger "political" work the new assumption about community resilience is doing and what critical analysis is needed now. Federal discourse includes a strong message to local communities that they should be prepared to "be on their own" for 72 hours, as it will take time for federal assets to arrive after a disaster. The resilient survivor ideal is reaching ascendance at a time when officials at all levels of government are trying to scale back public expectations about what the public sector can do in relation to large-scale emergencies. Yet, in my mind, vital public health and public safety institutions are an important part of what makes local communities and the nation resilience; essential, too, are governmental endeavors focused on prevention such as improved zoning and building codes in the case of earthquake and hurricane safety. The disaster resilience ideal deserves as much scrutiny as public panic.

More on Funding

The Center for Biosecurity is interested in preserving its reputation as a credible and neutral entity that provides effective guidance to policy makers and practitioners on the best course of action in relation to public health emergencies. Depending exclusively or primarily on government funding would compromise our credibility (in that people might see us merely as a mouthpiece for the current biodefense agenda) and/or reduce our degrees of freedom in conducting the analyses that we consider vital to national biosecurity and global health. Nonetheless, we have done contracted federal work for specific tasks that clearly fall in our realm of expertise (e.g., overview of biosurveillance systems; review of the federal program for local hospital preparedness). Federal projects have clear scopes of work, timelines, and deliverables; thus, the institutional arrangements feel more constraining for the analysts than those in play with foundation support. We have been lucky in securing significant support from the Alfred P. Sloan Foundation, which has given the Center great latitude in setting research and analytic priorities. Whereas the government has been interested in discrete deliverables, the foundations have been interested in evidence of overall influence and impact for the public good, as has the UPMC.

References

Annas, George J.
2002 Bioterrorism, Public Health and Civil Liberties. *New England Journal of Medicine* 346(17):1337–42.

Enloe, Cynthia
2004 Demilitarization—or More of the Same: Feminist Questions to Ask in the Postwar Moment. *In* The Curious Feminist: Searching for Women in a New Age of Empire. Pp. 145–47. Berkeley: University of California Press.

Glass, Thomas, and Monica Schoch-Spana
2002 Bioterrorism and the People: How to Vaccinate a City Against Panic. *Clinical Infectious Diseases* 34:217–23.
Goldman, Janlori
2003 Balancing in a Crisis? Bioterrorism, Public Health and Privacy. *In* Lost Liberties: Ashcroft and the Assault on Personal Freedom, C. Brown, ed. Pp. 161–83. New York: New Press.
Lutz, Catherine
2002 War at Home in the United States: Militarization and the Current Crisis. *American Anthropologist* 104(3):723–35.
McEnaney, Laura
2000 Civil Defense Begins at Home: Militarization Meets Everyday Life in the Fifties. Princeton, NJ: Princeton University Press.
Schoch-Spana, Monica
2009 Anthropology, Public Health and National Security—An Eyewitness Account of Colliding Worlds. August 21, 2009. Available at: http://blog.aaanet.org/2009/08/21/ceaussic-anthropology-public-health-and-national-security/. Accessed August 5, 2011.
Sidel, Victor W., Hillel W. Gould, and Robert M. Gould
2001 Good Intentions and the Road to Bioterrorism Preparedness. *American Journal of Public Health* 91(5):716–18.

8

Culture in/Culture of the United States Naval Academy

Clementine Fujimura

The editors' participation in several years of Commission on the Engagement of Anthropology with the U.S. Security and Intelligence Communities (CEAUSSIC) activity taught us a great deal about the ways in which anthropologists assume professional roles in a range of private and public institutions. In particular, we came into contact with several anthropologists holding faculty positions in the professional military education (PME) colleges and universities. In its PME system, the Department of Defense (DoD) maintains an extensive network of institutions of higher learning that provide both graduate and undergraduate instruction, and that comprise a kind of parallel universe to the academic one in which anthropology is practiced and taught. Holmes-Eber, Simons, and Fujimura are all members of this professional sector.

Considered in this exchange is the U.S. Naval Academy (USNA), founded in 1845 as the U.S. Navy's undergraduate college and charged with the academic and professional training of future naval and marine officers. The essay's author, Clementine Fujimura, is a Professor in the USNA's Languages and Cultures Department, who first came to the institution in 1993 after receiving her Ph.D. in cultural anthropology from The University of Chicago. Fujimura has taught courses at USNA in Russian and German languages, cultures, and literatures as well as in cultural anthropology and intercultural communication.

Fujimura's ties to others in this volume are multiple and diverse. Interestingly, she and Albro overlap in their doctoral program and advisors. This web of connections indicates that a larger dialogue about anthropology and the securityscape has been going on for a while, and takes place in the social networks traversing different institutional terrains. In addition, Fujimura has been an active contributor to discussions about how anthropology is located and practiced in the securityscape. For example,

Laura McNamara and Robert Rubinstein (who also contributed essays for this volume) invited Fujimura to participate in a School for Advanced Research seminar on anthropologists and the national security state in 2008. Fujimura and Schoch-Spana participated in a similarly themed panel at a meeting of the Society for Applied Anthropology. Last, Albro and Fujimura are working on an interagency workshop at the Woodrow Wilson Center—a site where academic, government, and military personnel frequently intersect and connect, and which also figures in the accounts by Miller and Abramson. Fujimura's narrative examines the intersection of her career as an anthropologist with the world of PME in ways that both parallel and challenge the accounts of Holmes-Eber and Simons.

Fujimura published her dissertation, Childhood in Russia: Representation and Reality *(Creuziger 1996), for which she studied child abandonment, children's rights, and ethnic marginalization in Russia and former Soviet republics. From 1999 to 2001, she conducted fieldwork on the subject of homeless children, the basis for her second book,* Russia's Abandoned Children: An Intimate Understanding *(Fujimura et al. 2005). The study of culture in the military context, however, is the subject of Fujimura's present research and publication, and she has examined the role of anthropology in military education as well as the teaching of culture and language in a military environment. Rubinstein and Fujimura are working on an edited reader to aid in the instruction of anthropology in the U.S. military. Fujimura has presented her work across diverse venues, including the Chief of Naval Operations Strategic Studies Group, The Elliott School of International Relations, and the Watson Institute.*

"You got a job where? That'll be interesting. How in the world are you going to teach about culture in a place that is about learning to kill others, not understand them? Of course, you won't be there for long. You need a real teaching job."

Such were the questions, comments, and implicit judgments of many peers and mentors as I packed my belongings to move to Annapolis to take a tenure-track position teaching Russian and German languages and cultures at the U.S. Naval Academy in 1993. Although I had received a classical graduate education in anthropology at the University of Chicago, I had chosen to accept a positing at the USNA teaching language and culture courses because of my love for teaching about cultures and languages and of course, the rather competitive job market. That being said, I was not sure how long I would remain at this position, given the peer pressure to leave and my thoughts about teaching in a military environment at the time. However, throughout my time at USNA, I would come to learn that even though military students were motivated in different ways than my previous civilian college students, they were just as complex, just as talented and eager to learn about cultural matters, and profoundly motivated precisely because of their professional calling, which would inevitably lead to interactions with foreign communities and societies. I also came to realize via various comments from my students and military officers that just as I had wrongly assumed certain characteristics about the military, they had likewise stereotyped my field and what it meant to study cultures. The discovery of these mutual ethnocentrisms became apparent over time to both my students and me through self-reflection on both our parts, an outcome of interactions within and outside class. What follows is the story of the beginning of this discovery.

In my former teaching positions, I had entered college classrooms as familiar places, having myself achieved degrees in liberal arts institutions. Entering a military classroom was different. I had been told I would teach undergraduates, but that they had motivations unlike my own for studying my subjects. I needed to scrutinize the implicit assumption that finishing my doctorate made me ready to teach at "any" undergraduate institution in the United States because it is presumed that there is a world view shared by my students and me (see Marcus and Fischer 1986:23). Nonetheless, I prepared as any academic might, packing all the books that had served me and would no doubt continue to serve me well: texts on the theoretical grounding of my discipline, examples of traditional and more radical approaches to conducting fieldwork and to thinking about culture, cutting-edge works in public culture including the latest in gender studies, for example. Surely this collection combined with my latest personal experiences in the field would inspire even academy students to pursue similar work in their graduate studies. Or so I believed. Yet, all the while, in the back of my mind, a voice kept questioning my every step in preparing to teach at USNA: Could I really expect the same enthusiasm for my subject matter when these particular students are being prepared to fight and possibly kill those about whom I am teaching? How could my teaching convey the basis of anthropology and convince such students that there is value in studying others as cultural beings who possess "specific ideas about what is true, good, beautiful and efficient" (Schweder in Borofsky 2001:437), while developing in them a broad appreciation of cultural life? Although I understood that such questions were based on assumptions I held, initial warnings about the military conveyed to me by my fellow anthropologists did not help to dismantle my biases.

Nevertheless, always aware that everything I think I "know" about groups of people needs to be questioned as I enter a new place, I tried not to let that inner voice deter me from my new job. Instead of accepting as true my personal notions (and fears) of why students signed up for my classes, on the first day of Russian Language and Culture in August 1993,

I asked that each student answer on a note card why they chose my class. I have always done this, in part to see if I can address individual students' interests throughout the semester but also in part, to get to know them better. Usually there are no surprises and, for the most part, the midshipmen came up with answers similar to those of civilian students such as: "Always thought it might be cool to know more about Russia, to speak the language, to challenge myself…". But then there were some new ones which had me reading them over and over again to be sure I had read correctly: "To understand the enemy, to beat them, to find their weaknesses." Mind you, this was in 1993: perestroika and glasnost had happened, the Cold War was supposed to be over. Surely, I thought a couple of years later, students would not have the same motivations for my Introduction to Cultural Anthropology Class? But there too, I found disturbing comments: "to know how culture works so I can understand the enemy…" and, much to my dismay, "Anthropology is a soft science, I took it for an easy A," and of course the inevitable: "I thought I would be digging for bones. I must be in the wrong class."

Indeed, I quickly realized: this was no ordinary teaching job; in effect, I was facing a new student culture; if I was to be successful in teaching, not only would I have to change some classroom goals, but I would also have to study and understand my new students and their aspirations on a deeper level. I had to do what I had been trained to do: become a participant-observer. As a faculty member I was expected to participate beyond the classroom, completely, to embrace their mission, to support not only academic goals but training goals, to help "shape" and "transform," even "indoctrinate" midshipmen into becoming the ideal naval officer. This new vocabulary offered keys to understanding my new surroundings and seemed to feed rather than dispel the preconceived ideas I held of the military.

Beginning with my interview for the position and continuing until I received tenure, I was reminded verbally: "Remember always: this is not your average college. You are part of a system to educate, indoctrinate, and mold midshipmen into fighters, warriors, and leaders." I was expected to reflect my membership in this system in my style and by upholding rituals and rules that seemed completely foreign to me at times. Such rituals include demanding that midshipmen call "attention on deck" both before and after class (that is, having a section leader call midshipmen to stand at attention "on deck," as if we were on a ship), that midshipmen stand at the back of the classroom if they feel tired during a lecture, expecting to be called "Ma'am" and maintaining formality in our interactions. Furthermore, in evaluating my classes, colleagues are required to comment on the extent to which I maintain military decorum.

The problem: I was being asked to become part of the military community beyond my role as that of a teacher, but as a member, one who, to teach well, must also speak their language, a language that seemed to convey underlying meanings to which I was averse. Although I might admit that "shaping" my students was a nice thought, "transforming" or, indeed, "indoctrinating" them was never my intention as a teacher. The situation was problematic in that, as a participant-observer, I felt the need to establish a good rapport with my community, and to question or judge their goals, aspirations, or even the language they spoke was not a great place to start. The most challenging part of my participant-observation experience in research and teaching at the academy is that it urged me to question not only the stereotypes I held of military culture, but also the moral principles I hold to be true for myself. In participating in the daily lives of a community with whom I believed I disagreed with fundamentally, I found that I was questioning myself as an anthropologist.

Acknowledging the dilemmas involved in my role as both anthropologist and participant in a naval education and training facility was at the very least a first step in uncovering the motivations, contradictions, and complexity of the U.S. military and simultaneously challenging the stereotyping of anthropologists by the military. Just as quickly as certain surface interpretations of language and symbolism seemed to reinforce my superficial notions of the military, comments and discussions made me pause and reconsider what I thought I was seeing. Was the U.S. military really the homogeneous killing machine even some of its members were claiming it to be? As my peers reinforced this stereotype of the military, the stereotype was dislodged by those who had returned from the first Gulf War, those who had participated in military exercises abroad, and by my students, the midshipmen. As the story unfolds here, it will become clear that mutual ethnocentrisms, when confronted through open conversation, can lead to mutual motivations and understandings, thereby opening doors to both communities.

From 1993 until the attacks on the United States on 9/11, my career at USNA was characterized by a lack of support for my field of teaching and research by the leadership, yet encouragement by my immediate colleagues at the academy, especially those who had fought overseas. So great was the tension that between 1994 and 2001, I was asked to teach an introduction to anthropology course under a different title, thereby masking the contents. Since psychology was just being accepted as potentially helpful in the military and anthropology was not, I was advised to and ultimately did teach the course under the title "The Psychology of World Cultures." It was only with the failing missions after 9/11 that the leadership began to notice my work, albeit skeptically.

In 2004, a colleague at the Watson Institute at Brown University invited me to participate in a meeting that would bring Marines and anthropologists together to discuss how anthropology could aid in mission accomplishment. The Watson Institute worked to find anthropologists who were already working in education in the military. I cannot deny that the invitation caused a wave of hope and enthusiasm in me. I truly believed that finally the U.S. military had come around to valuing both the importance of cultural studies and cultural integrity. However, after the opening discussion, my heart sank as an officer reminded us: "Look, we don't have time to truly understand in all its complexity what culture is, what makes our enemy who they are. What we need to know is facts we can learn quickly. And mind you, this is not about becoming overly sensitive. Remember, we are trained to kill. Those people are our targets! We need your information to kill more effectively" (Marine major, unpublished observation, 2004). As this Marine major saw it, anthropology was an aid in accomplishing effective killing and fewer U.S. casualties. I returned to my classroom less hopeful that my decision to teach at USNA had been a sound one. Morally I felt torn. It was hard to imagine that part of my work was to feed the Marine major's understanding of purpose in cultural learning. On the teaching/participant side, I halfheartedly returned to the classroom. On the observation side, I became more vigilant.

Not making my work any easier were the grumblings among anthropologists who were taking note of a new interest by the military to employ them, worried about the damage such work could do to anthropology as a field. I no longer received urgings by my peers to leave; instead, contact between myself and those peers seemed to fade completely. One colleague wrote in a brief email: "Given your work, we can never be friends." A mentor let it be known via a colleague that he worried about me and my work, adding that perhaps this would be the time for me to leave the USNA. And he wondered: did I even realize the problematic situation I was in?

My professional vigilance threw me into a whirlwind of taking note of everything I heard or saw. I desperately tried to understand the meaning my students and peers at USNA attributed to their behaviors and symbolism that at first glance seemed to feed negative stereotypes. As a result, while my academic colleagues were urging to me to run away, I felt more committed than ever that this was exactly where I needed to be: if I ran, if we all run, how could the message of cultural worth ever be conveyed? A final note of caution from the Marines begging anthropological engagement was the deciding factor: "If you anthropologists don't give us what we need, we'll teach culture anyway, our own way. We'll figure culture out ourselves."

The words of the Marine major made it all the more clear why I was at USNA. After all, educating academy midshipmen is different from training Marines at other institutions with less time. At the Naval Academy, a four-year program, I have the opportunity to help, in their own words, "shape" thinkers and ultimately leaders. The USNA's goal is not about abuse of cultural knowledge, but about the benefits of cultural understanding to avoid bloodshed and mission failure. As I write these paragraphs, I am reminded of a recent correspondence with one of my outstanding former midshipmen who went on to fight in Afghanistan and lost both lower legs in an improvised explosive device (IED) explosion. His strength of character and soul moves him forward; after all he has been through, he writes: "Your classes, your time and your counsel are a particularly fond source of strength for me since leaving school. Speaking pidgin Russian to an Afghan commando Brigade commander won me great points during a particularly tense meeting months ago and I could fill dozens of emails with culture lessons from working with Afghan government forces and local people. You helped open me up to that world and I thank you for it" (Marine, unpublished observation, 2010). Could cultural education lead to abuse of information? Certainly. Is it a risk worth taking? For me, the answer is, "Certainly." My students have shown me this time and time again.

Challenging Tradition at USNA with Anthropology

Traditional goals of the Academy are continuously challenged and adapting to meet the demands of the times. The dynamic student body finds creative outlets and ways to question the structure and content dictated from above and forces the academy as a system to remain in touch with a changing world. It is this changing world that has led to the infusion of the study of languages and cultures in the curriculum, a development that can no longer be ignored or denied by either the academy or by those practicing in the field of anthropology.

The USNA is proud to graduate engineers and works hard to continue to increase student numbers in science and technical majors. This has proven to be a difficult task, since most midshipmen for various reasons choose the humanities and social sciences, and the mandated increase seems rather forced. In fact, during a convocation in 2006, the Dean addressed the faculty and in particular those covering the social sciences: "You are doing a superb job. In fact, you are doing your job too well! We need you to not do such a good job and bring midshipmen back to majoring in the more technical departments." However, a mandate from the DoD prompted academy administrators to urge faculty to expand offerings in language, regional, and culture courses. Still, the tradition of USNA as an engineering institution endures and culture, even after a mandate, remains a peripheral yet vital subject.

Why, I had to ask again in 2009, were students still signing up for my courses? Whereas in the 1990s answers to this question had invoked the notion of anthropology as a "soft" and easy course, new answers read: "I want to be a Marine and the Marine Corps seems to be pushing cultural understanding" or "I have heard that this is important for me in my future as an officer" or "I did not have room in my schedule to take a series of language classes, but I know it's important to learn about other cultures...". The list went on to make one thing clear: times were changing. Recognition by the academy and its students of the new mission was the first step in anthropology's acceptance.

In adopting anthropology, the academy also inevitably changes as midshipmen and officers come to discover its potential vitality in the military context. The result of midshipmen studying and reflecting on the cultural dynamics that motivate their own and others' behavior has already had an impact on midshipmen, some of whom are now officers leading the Navy. In giving military officers the opportunity to use the tools offered by anthropology, we equip them to make more nuanced decisions. As one midshipman described in his conclusion to a paper for my class titled "Macho Mini Men: Masculinity, Competition, and the Sprint Football Subculture":

> Who is the Brigade of Midshipmen? Before my anthro class, I would have been able to give a confident answer to this question in under thirty seconds. Now I know the truth: I cannot give a complete answer in thirty years. Underneath the trappings of uniformity and homogeneity, a complex jumble of diverse subcultures thrives with unique sets of behaviors, ideas, and identities. Through the window of the Sprint Football team, I was granted a glimpse into the intricacies of this blended reality. The microcosmic example of the Naval Academy demonstrates just how diverse a single, apparently uniform society can be and just how much we misunderstand each other, as fellow Midshipmen and as fellow human beings" (Midshipman Baird, unpublished manuscript, 2010).

As midshipmen are given the opportunity to see what the discipline of anthropology is really about, their understanding of the world around them changes, challenging them to know when and how to humanize their "targets" and to better understand themselves as individuals, as part of the Navy and the U.S. military in the process.

Risks of Engagement

Until I was able to dispel some of the stereotypes I held of the military and the academy, it was difficult to acknowledge that the military represented a part of my own society and that the "other" was no other than a part of who I was and am. Embracing this other seemed dirty and immoral. As I corresponded with my peers back in more traditional universities, I was challenged to consider their urging me to leave: "Don't you realize that by signing on to teach 'them' you are also accepting a political policy of invasion and colonialism that we as anthropologists have been fighting?"

The dangers of engagement implied by my colleagues in regards to teaching military professionals seem to ignore risks of nonengagement. As I was told over the years, whether or not anthropologists aid in the education of future officers and enlisted soldiers, the role of "culture" is taken seriously. Entire education and training facilities have sprung up and center around "cultural sensitivity training and preparedness" whether or not anthropologists are involved. Needless to say, this is a frightening thought: the subject of our entire field and identity as anthropologists risks being diluted and misunderstood as we inadvertently nurture the stereotype of anthropologists who live in a vacuum disengaged from our own society, devoid of rigor, and ultimately, unhelpful.

In the end, we share in our motivations. The U.S. military needs anthropologists to do a better job, to seek out ways in which to avoid bloodshed. We as anthropologists need to help to avoid misunderstanding, misuse, and abuse of the idea of culture and cultures. Both communities fear the potential risks involved in not engaging one another, but also in engaging: from the military perspective, such time and energy might not be well spent if the results are not helpful. For us, the fear is that we may be engaging in something dirty, thereby sullying the field of anthropology and denying our most basic values, including that of cultural preservation. Not engaging, however, could be more damaging to the people of cultures for whom we work and on whom we base our livelihood. We engage then, with the hope for a positive outcome: a better future for ourselves as either military professionals or anthropologists, as citizens of a global community, and for the global community itself, which ultimately would mean to avoid suffering.

Editorial Commentary

Crafting an entrance narrative, Fujimura relates and reflects on how she came to be faculty at the USNA in 1993—or, in her words, "a participant in a naval education and training facility." Unlike the 9/11 mobilization, Fujimura is brought into the defense world not by a crisis of conscience or identity, but because of "the rather competitive job market" and the continued opportunity to pursue her "love for teaching." Her essay reminded us very much of Holmes-Eber's account later in this volume: the uncertainty about going to work in a military educational institution, then the tentative entry, the culture shock, the decision to fall back on ethnography, and a growing appreciation for the military personnel she is encountering, as well as a sense of being disenfranchised or disconnected from the anthropology community.

Many peers and mentors, for instance, met Fujimura's decision to accept a USNA faculty position with scorn and words of caution, implying that it was not a "real teaching job" and asking how students "learning to kill others" could actually appreciate culture and its study. Fujimura admits nagging doubts "in the back of [her] mind" about the new job. Developments early on also helped raise the pitch of this "inner voice": some students expressed interest in her language and culture classes as a way to "understand the enemy." Institutional expectations of Fujimura included participating in the larger military community and exercising a training function through which she would "'shape' and 'transform,' even 'indoctrinate' midshipmen into becoming the ideal naval officer." (We were curious to learn more about how such expectations were set, by whom, and in what contexts.)

Striking to us was how Fujimura initially dampened her apprehensions and adapted to an uncomfortable situation by "anthropologizing" her predicament. That is, she confronted the strangeness and ethically challenging aspects of her situation by assuming the pose of the distanced participant/observer. Her students double for her as research subjects. This stance pays certain dividends for Fujimura. She is able to confront her own ethnocentrisms and dispel stereotypes about the military (which turns out to be "less homogeneous" and more "complex" than assumed) and to examine the "behaviors" and "symbolism" of the Navy (e.g., implications of an institutional emphasis on engineering). Fujimura's narrative echoes similar self-discoveries and commentaries by Goolsby, Milliken, Holmes-Eber, and Rush, particularly their respective epiphanies about the heterogeneity of the military and the security sector, and the perceived humanity of the people employed there.

Fujimura approaches her job as a case of navigating a series of "cross-cultural encounters" with midshipmen and other Navy personnel, which she describes as an internal "other" of U.S. society. The ethnographic stance helps her define her ethical predicament. She realizes that her job is not just a job but involves her in a coded way of life: doctrines, becoming part of the military community. As distinct from the typical dilemmas of practicing anthropologists, a question posed by Fujimura's narrative is thus the extent to which these several roles—academic faculty, trainer, participant in the Navy's mission, and ethnographer—are in fact mutually compatible. She is aware of the tensions built into them. And one wonders to what extent Fujimura can maintain the balancing act between teacher, trainer, and ethnographer in this context.

Fujimura's USNA career spans from the early 1990s—a time of U.S. military operations in Iraq, Somalia, and former Yugoslavia—to today.

The account jumps from her early years to 2004, and we wondered about the intervening period. Nonetheless, we learn that she underwent another round of peer pressure to abandon her position following 9/11, but that such entreaties also became less frequent due to receding contact with anthropological peers. We were struck by the vignette of the anthropology colleague who cast disapproval of the U.S. military (and larger national security policy) in terms of friendship denied to Fujimura. We reacted to this policing of disciplinary boundaries in intimate kinship terms, and one of us posed the question of whether an anthropologist who passes judgment on in-the-flesh colleagues in the security sector may be engaged in a personal political act of resistance to U.S. foreign and defense policies that they may be otherwise unable to oppose directly.

Fujimura briefly recounts attending a workshop in 2004 to bring anthropologists into conversation with Marines about how cultural expertise can aid overseas missions. (We were curious about who convened the meeting, how anthropologists were recruited, and what outcomes were expected.) There, a Marine major bluntly remarks that anthropology is a tool with which to target the enemy more effectively and reduce U.S. casualties; this bleak appraisal throws Fujimura back to the fundamental moral dilemma about her work at USNA. As a result of the jarring episode, she redoubles her commitment to teach midshipmen so that they can avoid the abuses and misuses of culture, make more nuanced decisions as future officers, humanize potential "targets," provide more ways of avoiding bloodshed, and build greater appreciation of diversity into the Navy. Absent the cultural sense-making that she can help provide, she feels that more harm is possible once these young officers are deployed on behalf of U.S. military objectives.

Defending "the message of cultural worth" in a military context is how Fujimura ultimately frames the purpose of her work at USNA. She notes that her students time and again have reinforced her appraisal (her hope?) that conveying this message to aspiring officers has transformed their perceptions and helped them to avoid bloodshed and mission failure once deployed. She does not tell us, however, how exactly she has drawn this conclusion, and we wished for were more details about what her students were doing in the field that could more fully represent the positive consequences of her anthropological interventions. The anecdote about her midshipmen student reflecting internally on his own cultural setting and writing an essay on masculinity in USNA culture, however, provides a small glimpse of the kind of impact that Fujimura intends.

Given the length of her teaching career, Fujimura is able to chart changes in the broader curriculum at the USNA. She notes a recent DoD mandate prompting academy administrators to "urge faculty to expand offerings in language, regional, and culture courses." Fujimura's essay conveys her own rationale for teaching about culture, but we are left wondering about what the military "wants" in adopting a cultural framework. Anthropology today is way beyond simple training about culture; contemporary cultural analysis is framed by critique, politics, and values. It is not apparent from Fujimura's account whether there is room in the academy's curriculum for these elements. Last, we questioned whether Fujimura experiences any sense of restraint or censorship in her job, given that the cognitive frame for thinking in the military is "doctrine" and that training requires "technologized" knowledge.

Fujimura responded to most of our questions and comments in a revised version of her initial draft essay. This revised version is the one published in this essay. However, she also wrote an addendum in which she described how she conceptualizes what it means to teach anthropology well in a military academy, and how this differs from teaching anthropology in a civilian university.

Fujimura Response

Understanding anthropology and certainly teaching anthropology means much more than training about culture. Anthropology has developed into a field that examines the complex dynamics and interrelations between culture, history, literary criticism, sociology, psychology, and ethnic and gender studies, to mention a few. If one claims to be a scholar of anthropology and cultural studies, a study of these connections are of the utmost importance. These levels of cultural analysis get the most pragmatic treatment in training environments and only get introduced at the undergraduate level. Furthermore, subjects within anthropology such as the poetics of culture, ethnolinguistics, ethnomusicology, or commodification and the like, are realms that are important but present themselves as difficult subjects to study on a meaningful level in a military classroom, even at the academy level. A fear that anthropology may get watered down or even misrepresented as it is geared toward more practical application is valid among scholars in the field.

However, many of these themes are touched on in introductory anthropology courses throughout the United States at liberal arts colleges, and many students end their study of anthropology with a glancing familiarity. Still, these undergraduates leave with a better understanding of the field and its significance, often opening doors to better understanding and communication between these students and the people they will come to meet later in life. Likewise, a solid introductory course in a military educational institution such as at the service academies is within reach if the academies choose to have the courses taught by anthropologists and if anthropologists are willing to teach at the academies. At the USNA there is at least one such course. Unfortunately, at the U.S. Military Academy and the U.S. Air Force Academy as of 2011, there are no anthropologists teaching such courses.

The concern then is about the possibility of good anthropology existing in a military educational context, which would allow for cultural analysis "framed by critique, politics, and values." Success in this endeavor depends on the military recognizing that this must be done and making it a priority, and can only be done by those who receive solid academic preparation in the relevant field of study. It also depends on anthropologists acknowledging that more harm can be done by not engaging. By neglecting to help the military develop its cultural studies, the field of anthropology will be misrepresented and the cultures we study could fall into harm's way. Unfortunately, those who impede the progress of a worthy military cultural education are those that cannot see beyond what they see as "right" or correct training for the military, which involves a definition of the military as an unchanging entity. This perspective confuses a timeless ethos with innovation and changing perspectives. In fact, the constraints I have experienced comes from leadership in the military who fear that such a new subject as anthropology may take away from the more traditional offerings in engineering or western history. Other hurdles for me have proven to be colleagues in anthropology who do not understand the changes the U.S. military is inevitably experiencing and actively developing with or without anthropologists' support.

References

Borofsky, Robert, et al.
2001 When: A Conversation about Culture. *American Anthropologist* 103(2):432–46.

Creuziger, Clementine C. K.
1996 Childhood in Russia: Representation and Reality. Lanham, MD: University Press of America.

Fujimura, Clementine, Sally W. Stoecker, and Tanya Sudakova
2005 Russia's Abandoned Children: An Intimate Understanding. Westport, CT: Praeger.

Marcus, George E., and Michael M. J. Fischer
1986 Anthropology as Cultural Critique: An Experimental Moment in the Human Sciences. Chicago: University of Chicago Press.

9

Teaching Culture at Marine Corps University

Paula Holmes-Eber

Paula Holmes-Eber currently is Professor of Advanced Operational Culture at Marine Corps University. She also advises staff at the Center for Advanced Operational Culture Learning (CAOCL) on academic matters concerning culture, Islam, Arab society, and North Africa. Holmes-Eber completed her M.A. and Ph.D. in anthropology from Northwestern University. She holds a B.A. (magna cum laude) from Dartmouth College, a Certificate in African Studies from Northwestern University, and a Certificate in Tunisian Arabic from the Ecole Bourguiba des Langues Vivantes in Tunis, Tunisia. Her research and expertise focus on kinship and social networks in Arab and Muslim culture in North Africa.

Prior to her current position, Holmes-Eber was an Assistant Professor of Anthropology at the University of Wisconsin–Milwaukee and a Visiting Scholar in the Middle East Center at the Jackson School of International Studies at the University of Washington. She is fluent in French, Arabic, German, and Italian and has lived and traveled in more than 40 countries, including Tunisia, Morocco, Turkey, Israel, Mongolia, China, Taiwan, Japan, Russia, and Tonga.

Holmes-Eber is the author of three books: Applying Operational Culture: Perspectives from the Field, *coauthored with Patrice Scanlon and Andrea Hamlen (Marine Corps University Press, 2009);* Operational Culture for the Warfighter: Principles and Applications, *coauthored with Barak Salmoni (Marine Corps University Press, 2008) and* Daughters of Tunis: Women, Family and Networks in a Muslim City *(Westview Press, 2003). She is also the author of several entries in the* Encyclopedia of Women and Islam *and multiple articles addressing the incorporation of culture into Marine Corps planning as well as teaching and training with respect to culture in the Marine Corps.*

The editors have known Holmes-Eber for some time. As a colleague of one of the commission members, Kerry Fosher, she was interviewed by McNamara as part of the preparation for the Commission on

Anthropology's Engagement with the Security and Intelligence Communities' (CEAUSSIC) 2007 report to the American Anthropological Association (AAA). In addition to her career teaching Marines, Holmes-Eber's work is particularly interesting in the ways it helps us to consider the similarities and differences between traditional kinds of academic knowledge production, such as her ethnography of Tunisian women and their families, and the kinds of scholarship carried out within the Professional Military Education (PME) setting represented by Operational Culture for the Warfighter *(Salmoni and Holmes-Eber 2011), which is at once scholarship, training manual, and even quasi-doctrine for the Marine Corps. Given the occasional debates about how to identify the academic sources of military knowledge production (e.g., the 2006 Army* Counterinsurgency Manual*), Holmes-Eber offers an illuminating point of view about questions of situatedness and the proprietary control over knowledge production in the securityscape.*

Teaching culture to the U.S. military was the last thing on my mind when I completed my Ph.D. in sociocultural anthropology at Northwestern University. I had selected Northwestern for its outstanding reputation in African studies, hoping to follow in the legacy of such great anthropological great minds as James Bohannan and Melville Herskovits. As an undergraduate at Dartmouth College, I had traveled to Morocco and became fascinated with North African Muslim culture. So, it had been my dream in graduate school to study Arabic, Islam, and African and Middle Eastern anthropology; conduct fieldwork in some exotic North African Arab community a la Lila Abu Lughod, Victor Crapanzano, or Dale Eickelman; and return to spend the rest of my years teaching and publishing monographs on North African women's hospitality and wedding rituals as a professor at a traditional scholarly university.

A conventional career path seemed to shine brightly on the horizon as I completed my fieldwork in Tunisia under a Fulbright grant; accepted a tenure-track position as Assistant Professor of Anthropology at the University of Wisconsin–Milwaukee; and proceeded to publish the appropriate books, journal articles, and encyclopedia entries on Arab Muslim women's social networks in North Africa. Four years later, I moved on to a position as Visiting Scholar at the Middle East Center, Jackson School of International Studies at the University of Washington (UW). As I pedaled to work under snowcapped mountains, I could not imagine how I could ever want to do anything more than conduct research, publish, and teach classes on such topics as "Peoples and Cultures of the Middle East," "Anthropology of Islam," or "Women and the Family in the Muslim World."

Overnight, September 11, 2001, changed all that. Suddenly, my colleagues at the Middle East Center and I were thrust into the political limelight. For days, the telephone at the Center would not stop ringing with requests for one or more of us to speak to the newspapers, radio, or television about the latest event. Local universities and community and political organizations all desired immediate lectures and roundtables from the UW faculty about Islam, the Middle East, and the current political situation. And on campus, my classes on the Middle East were overflowing with students who were desperately seeking to understand the issues surrounding Islam and the United States' role in Afghanistan and then Iraq.

At first, I suppose my colleagues and I viewed this barrage of interest in our hitherto esoteric region of the world as exciting, even gratifying. (While it is hard to believe today, prior to September 11, 2001, few people thought that understanding the Middle East or Islam was an important scholarly pursuit.) However, as requests for talks and interviews continued for months after the terrorist events without any seeming effect, many of us began to feel frustration and exhaustion. The growing racism and attacks against Muslims and "Arabs" (sadly to include any dark-skinned person wearing a turban, such as Sikhs) indicated a depressing ignorance of the social, cultural, religious, and political context of events by the general public. And daily reports of a war in Afghanistan and a looming war in Iraq only deepened our sense of discouragement that our government's policies reflected a similar dearth of cultural understanding of the political and religious environment into which the United States was marching headlong. For most of my colleagues, their response was to withdraw back into the ivory tower, to ignore (with an occasional witty critique of the latest U.S. political or military gaffe) the ongoing political events, and to return to "life as usual" back in the safe world of the academy.

I could not. Two months after the attacks of September 11, 2001, I stood in front of a standing-room-only audience of more than 3,000 people from the Seattle community giving a televised talk titled, "Conceptions and Misconceptions of Muslim Women" as part of a Jackson School Series on "Understanding 9/11." As I gazed out over a sea of faces desperate to make sense of a changed world, it occurred to me that, somewhere, I had crossed the line between scholarship and policy, between academic detachment and political engagement. Whether I wanted to or not, my research and work had ceased being simply an academic discussion on scholarly issues: my very presence in that room was a political statement. The topic I had chosen to speak on—Western prejudices about Muslim women—reflected an intellectual alignment. And the role of the media had shifted the lecture from a scholarly presentation to a social and political commentary (albeit academically based).

Perhaps it was then that I began to question the ethics—and illusion—of scholarly nonparticipation. Although ideally and theoretically, anthropologists and other scholars simply conduct research and publish the results, as my own experiences interacting with the media were teaching me, there is always the possibility—even likelihood—that these results will have political and policy implications.

Even more troubling to me, however, was a growing realization over the ensuing months that my background and knowledge of the region was desperately needed, not only by the Seattle community, but by a U.S. government fumbling with a culture radically different from ours. When the United States invaded Afghanistan, and then Iraq, I wondered whether withholding my knowledge of the culture and region was fair, given the struggles the Afghans, Iraqis, and U.S. military faced as they each learned bitter (in fact, fatal) lessons about working with each other. Nonparticipation provided the illusion of safely avoiding the ethical questions of cooperating with questionable government policies. Yet refusing to offer needed cultural understanding—which could help prevent unnecessary misinterpretation, conflict, and deaths—was also ethically problematic.

Indeed, it seemed that in my case, nonparticipation was not actually an option. For by remaining silent and allowing the conflict to escalate, I was tacitly supporting, even encouraging, the current devastating trajectory by the U.S government and military. I could not help comparing my situation to that of a medical doctor walking past a severely injured accident victim without offering assistance. If I chose to walk away and let others suffer and die, knowing that I had the cultural skills and knowledge to help, was I not also guilty of carrying blood on my own hands?

Admittedly, I was slow to respond. It's not easy to go against the conventional wisdom of one's scholarly discipline, or to toss out a comfortable life with a predictable trajectory. But ultimately, it is harder to wake up each morning with a nagging sense of moral responsibility, knowing that the reason I was doing nothing was that I was afraid: afraid of losing my status within the academic world; afraid of facing the criticism, prejudice, and even hatred (not that I could ever have imagined its extent) of my colleagues; afraid of the unknown world ahead.

I took a year and a half off to travel and work for a nonprofit foundation. Upon my return, it became clear that I would have to choose between being true to my conscience or continuing a life of false safety: hiding behind excuses that avoidance of action was somehow less problematic than conscious action. Finally, I began to check around with my friends for other career possibilities, thinking that perhaps I could work for a nongovernmental organization (NGO) or the U.S. State Department.

The opportunity that appeared was not what I expected. I received a call from the assistant director of a military culture program. He was on the search committee to find a professor who would develop a cultural curriculum and teach courses on anthropology and the Middle East for the Marine Corps University.

At first, I was not particularly interested. I was all too keenly aware of the conflict that existed within the AAA regarding anthropologists who worked for the military. Looking back, I was also incredibly uninformed and prejudiced about the roles and functions of the U.S. military. I assumed that all military members carried rifles and killed people. (Actually, only a tiny percentage ever engages in combat; most provide logistical and operational support). And, I believed that the only role of the U.S. military was to conduct war. (Not until later did I understand the immensely significant role the Marine Corps plays in international peacekeeping and humanitarian operations. Indeed, in most conflict and disaster areas, most NGOs are unwilling to enter an area until the U.S. military has first provided some level of stability and security).[1]

Despite my reservations, the assistant director of the Marine Corps culture center was persistent. He faxed me reports from officers who were working on humanitarian aid projects and stabilization and reconstruction programs in the Horn of Africa. I was surprised to discover that the Marine Corps did much more than shoot people. The officers' reports discussed building wells and roads, inoculating animals, offering medical care to children and women, and providing training to local police. Perhaps I have been mistaken in ignoring the military, I wondered. For if Marines were undertaking many of the tasks of NGOs and other aid organizations, shouldn't they be receiving cultural education to help them better understand and communicate with the people they were assisting?

Out of curiosity, I went out for the job interview. I was intrigued, but not convinced. The position as the Professor of Operational Culture at Marine Corps University seemed reasonable enough: I would be teaching graduate-level university classes to senior Marine officers, and conducting research and publishing, just as in my current position in civilian academia. Although the university curriculum heavily emphasized military history, I was also pleased to discover that the various programs included courses on leadership, ethics, negotiation, regional studies, and even Arabic. My job would be to incorporate additional classes on anthropology, Islam, and the Middle East in the curriculum, providing cultural knowledge and perspectives to the future military planners and decision makers of our country.

However, I would also be supporting the culture center's Middle East cultural and language training program—a job that seemed closer to the current military operations and more potentially ethically challenging. The assistant director was clear that I would *not* be expected to provide the predeployment cultural training itself. Instead, I would assist in overseeing the materials that were taught to ensure their accuracy and appropriateness. My role would be to teach and mentor the instructors and course-developers as well as assist in the development of a larger Marine Corps policy on culture and language. This curriculum would be based on "open source" materials—nonclassified literature (scholarly books, articles, and Internet sites) that I had always used in my normal civilian classrooms.

My initial position description included a requirement to obtain a secret clearance. I was told that this was standard procedure for the faculty positions, but I was very uncomfortable with this expectation. First, I felt that if I had a secret clearance, sooner or later I might be expected to be familiar with the secret documents relating to my region, and then asked to apply that knowledge to my work. I was aware that, historically, anthropological knowledge has sometimes been used by the military for intelligence purposes: to seek out and destroy individuals and communities. Overseeing a culture curriculum that used only open source materials seemed a fairly clear way to avoid providing instruction that would intentionally harm others. But I feared the ethical lines could become blurred if I became familiar with classified documents that targeted specific individuals or groups.

A second concern was that a secret clearance would damage my future ability to conduct ethnographic research in Middle Eastern and Muslim countries. I knew that most of the countries in the region required researchers to submit an extensive application for permission to conduct their fieldwork. I believed that holding a secret or top secret status with the U.S. government would lead the Middle Eastern governments to suspect I was a spy. After explaining my issues with the vice president of the university, the requirement for a clearance was dropped.

Ultimately, I accepted the position. Although not the career that I had imagined, this job offered the chance to apply my knowledge to alleviate cultural misunderstanding in contemporary military conflicts. The job was also an exciting opportunity to build a long-term innovative program on a sound theoretical and conceptual basis. Perhaps most important, from a personal point of view, I quickly began to see the immediate relevance of my own classes to current military operations and decision-making.

Within a few months after my students graduated from my first year of teaching, former officers from my courses started to send emails expressing the value of my classes as they deployed around the world to Iraq, Afghanistan, the Horn of Africa, the Philippines, and elsewhere upon graduation. By my second year of teaching, my former students—now battalion commanders and senior planners—thought my courses important enough that they started asking me to give classes on cultural principles to their own units around the United States. Due to the joint efforts led by myself and a handful of other brave anthropology colleagues, in the following years, key Marine Corps and sister military organizations began incorporating cultural principles into U.S. military doctrine, training, and policy. But perhaps the most powerful measure of the success of our work has been the results of a recent survey on attitudes to culture and language learning in the Marine Corps (Homes-Eber et al. in press). According to the responses from 2,406 career Marines, cultural and language skills were ranked "important" to "very important,"[2] 81 percent of Marines who had received cultural training prior to deployment reported that this training had made them more operationally effective,[3] and those Marines who worked in ground combat positions (infantry, artillery, tank operators, and engineers) stated that, on the average, they used cultural knowledge of the area "often" to "very often" in their previous deployment.[4]

It is difficult to believe that I have now been in my position as a Professor of Operational Culture at the Marine Corps University for four years. The position has been one of the most challenging, demanding, frustrating, and interesting jobs I have ever held. Ethical issues do form part of the challenging nature of the job—although not the ones I expected.

Even though my decision to abstain from holding a security clearance has not affected my ability to conduct my work as a professor and scholar, it has limited some of my opportunities to engage in additional projects. For the most part, this has been fine, since these projects are frequently ones that are ethically problematic for me. However, my decision not to hold a security clearance recently led to a very difficult personal dilemma—forcing me to choose between assisting my former students (now deployed) in developing a culturally appropriate plan for transitioning out of Afghanistan or continuing to work without a clearance. In the end, I decided that holding a clearance even for a "good cause" would involve me in decisions that could harm at least some of the local population. So after much personal agony and numerous sleepless nights over the issue, I chose to remain without a clearance and let someone else participate in the project.

Sadly, a field trip to my original research area revealed that conducting fieldwork in North Africa while working for the U.S. military caused great suspicion—with or without a clearance. The reality is that foreign governments and people tend to view all research conducted by military personnel (including civilian military professors) as intelligence. Given that the research data and any subsequent publications do belong to the U.S. military and government, this is probably not an unreasonable expectation. As a result, I have shifted my work from "outside" to "inside" the culture of the Marine Corps where I work.

Another ethical challenge has been negotiating the awkward boundary between academic freedom and government property. As a government employee, everything that I write belongs to the government. On the other hand, as a scholar and professor, I am permitted the same freedom to write and publish my work as my colleagues at civilian universities. The apparent contradictions in the situation have led to a number of legal and ethical questions, particularly regarding the legal ownership of and right to publish the two books I have cowritten since arriving at the university (Holmes-Eber et al. 2009; Salmoni and Holmes-Eber 2011).

Although some of my colleagues at Marine Corps University have been permitted to publish books with scholarly presses, in these cases, the subject of their research has been esoteric and not in high demand by the Marine Corps. Fortunately, or unfortunately, in my case, both of my coauthored books seem to have great value to the Marine Corps—connecting basic anthropological concepts to the practical challenges of militaries working with foreign peoples. As a result, I have produced two unexpected "bestsellers" for the Marine Corps University Press, distributing more than 10,000 hard copies and an unnamed number of electronic copies of *Operational Culture for the Warfighter* in just two years. I do not, however, retain copyright of the books, do not receive royalties, and only one of the books has been permitted to receive an ISBN.

This issue of scholarly ownership of books written by military university professors is currently under debate in Congress today. One of the greatest problems, of course, is that the objectivity of any work produced for and approved by a government organization is suspect. However, similar issues apply to any scholar who conducts research while working for a private, nonprofit, or governmental organization.

Yet, surprisingly, the greatest problem I have faced in my work has not been solving ethical issues. It has been time. Due to the fear most anthropologists have of the military, I am only one of a handful of doctoral anthropologists working for the military services. As a result, the amount of work to be done to develop this enormous cultural initiative is far more than can be accomplished by the very select few scholars available. Disappointingly, there seem to be plenty of unqualified, unskilled individuals who are willing to fill in the gaps, leading to shoddy, unprofessional work that undermines the integrity, validity, and quality of these exciting cultural programs.

Despite these challenges, I do not regret the unexpected direction my career has taken. Every now and then one of my former students—now a major or lieutenant colonel in command of an infantry battalion in Iraq, or a civil affairs unit in Afghanistan, or a senior planner for the Haiti emergency relief regimental staff—writes back to me from the field. Consistently, their emails express the importance and relevance of my courses and books in helping them to work successfully with the local cultures to achieve stability and peace in their area. The direct impact and relevance of my work in alleviating the suffering of the current conflicts is, ultimately, the one reward I know I will never find in conventional academia.

Editorial Commentary

If the 9/11 attacks mobilized us all for a while in their aftermath, only relatively few ruptured the continuity of their lives in response, especially when they were satisfying professional lives. Of these the most commonly shared stories are those who have enlisted in the military (most famously, the Pat Tillman story). But here we have a rather dramatic turning from an anthropological career that had already moved from comfortable and promising academic employment toward policy analysis and research on the Middle East at the University of Washington.

After 9/11, Holmes-Eber took on a public educative role in her Seattle community, but her strong commitment to taking action meant a decisive movement away from her academic career first toward NGO work and then recruitment to the military's parallel to an academic institution—the Marine Corps University. After 9/11, she seems most bothered by "a life of false safety." In discussing her narrative, we wondered why Holmes-Eber felt it necessary to make such a complete break from the world of mainstream, civilian academic practice where she had established a viable career. Many anthropologists find avenues and opportunities to pursue outreach, activism, and to participate in the public sphere while located in a university department. We wondered if Homes-Eber's decision indicates that perhaps anthropology itself has become a particularly rigorous case of a self-policing discipline sensitive to past association with lending its expertise to government in times of war. Along those lines, Holmes-Eber indicates that the Marine Corps actively and persistently recruited her, and that their search committee apparently anticipated encountering problems in attracting qualified anthropologists. We wondered how they represented the institution to Holmes-Eber, as well as the role that they expected anthropology to play in its work.

We have the sense that the role Holmes-Eber expected was aligned with the Marines' humanitarian, stabilization, and reconstruction activities. Indeed, the extent to which Marines are involved in humanitarian operations alongside combat operations is a revelation to Holmes-Eber, and she comes to invest the ethical virtue of her choice in this side of the military. It seems to have been one of strong selling points in her recruitment. However, this also raises the question about the reconciliation of humanitarian operations with combat operations, a theme raised in multiple later essays in this volume, most notably Omidian's, but also Rubinstein's and Van Arsdale's.

At the same time, we had the sense that Holmes-Eber's movement into the Marine Corps University involved ongoing negotiations with herself, her employers, and perhaps with family and colleagues. How she has established a career and life with which she feels comfortable becomes a core and interesting aspect of her experience, particularly given the tremendous impact that her work on operational culture appears to be having in the Marine Corps. How did she establish a career and life with which she could be comfortable? Her negotiations and possible costs that she has paid are the core and most interesting aspects of the experience that she relates.

To situate herself in a position that is satisfactory to her personal ethics, and as an adherent to the ethics of professional anthropology, she refuses any sort of security clearance; she agrees to work only with open source materials; and she refuses to directly train personnel scheduled for deployment. The majority of her time is spent teaching in the university classroom and writing and publishing, similar to professors in civilian universities, with additional time reviewing training, policy, or doctrinal materials. She also has time to develop research projects, including the design and implementation of the survey she describes. Yet, we wondered if her refusal to get a security clearance presents any limitations to what she can pursue in the Marine Corps. It seems as if she spends most of her time teaching, writing, and publishing, not unlike a mainstream academic university professor.

So far, many of the satisfactions in her job seem to parallel those in a standard academic career: the ability to do research and publish, the gratitude of students. At the same time, one expects that life in a military university does differ from life in a civilian one, such as in formal structure and atmosphere. Her essay indicates that the institutional conditions in which Holmes-Eber creates and/or articulates anthropological knowledge are different from what one expects to find in a civilian academic environment. She is involved in the design, writing, and publication of manuals and training curricula for Marines, often in interaction with high-ranking officers. This is work that she has found deeply involving and satisfying, but this is not the kind of work that mainstream academic university professors engage in on a regular basis.

Moreover, Holmes-Eber mentions that as a military university professor, she does not have ownership of her publications, but that they belong to the U.S. government. Perhaps most notably, many of her colleagues have security clearances, but may lack appropriate qualifications for teaching students. Holmes-Eber brings unique expertise, but we wondered how different levels of expertise and experience affect a sense of collegiality across faculty, particularly if the less-qualified are treated as experts in the same way that Holmes-Eber is, or if they are moving through these positions on a rotational basis.

We were also intrigued by the concept of "operational culture" as an incarnation of anthropology's culture concept into the domain of military pedagogy. As Albro discusses in his essay, the "culture concept" has become a vehicle though which institutions in the securityscape both label and claim a stake in certain forms of social science knowledge. In

Holmes-Eber's account, the idea of operational culture seems to be an instantiation of this process in the context of the Marine Corps. As is true for most anthropologists, the concept of "culture" is a core element of Holmes-Eber's professional identity, and in her position in the Marine Corps University, her work seems to be organized around the deployment (so to speak) of this concept. Not only does it become a medium through which certain forms of area knowledge relevant to military activities on the ground can be represented and communicated to students, but Holmes-Eber's work involves the translation of anthropology's core concepts across institutional worlds, and perhaps their reification into new forms, in ways that probably parallel and diverge from these representations and communications in mainstream civilian academia.

In academic life, scholarly expertise is sustained by an active research career. However, Holmes-Eber found that she can no longer feed her expertise by active field research in North Africa and the Middle East because of her employment. It must be a challenge to maintain the area expertise of the sort that she is expected to apply in her designing of cultural training. We thought that this is perhaps the greatest personal cost Holmes-Eber has paid. To adapt, she describes shifting her research from "outside" to "inside" the culture of the Marine Corps. In other words, her personal ethnographic research is refocusing on a community to which she has access by virtue of her career change. Studying one's students is not something we see in mainstream academia, despite the old graduate student joke that someone, somewhere, ought to write a dissertation on the culture of academic anthropology. In any case, such a significant shift in orientation could be quite difficult in a civilian institution, which made us wonder about the formal and informal conditions that must be met if she is to pursue this research in accordance with the Marine Corps University's institutional requirements. The outlet for her anthropological curiosity is now her ability to make what she can observe and experience an object of study, and this is now a personal project.

Last, we asked if Holmes-Eber could provide an example that traces granularly the direct impact of her work "on alleviating the suffering of the current conflicts." After all, this direct connection, or sense of connection, is what seems to have tipped the balance in favor of a move that seems to entail a dramatic reorientation of Homes-Eber's professional identity.

Holmes-Eber Response

Invariably, whenever I hear such questions as "Why the military and not some (nicer, less harmful) organization?" or "What a sacrifice for your career!" my thoughts turn to Mary Douglas' book, *Purity and Danger*

(Douglas 1966). Douglas was one of the first to recognize the cultural dichotomy and tension between those objects, acts, and people that are considered pure, clean, sacred, good, and safe and those that are defined as dirty, unclean, polluting, taboo, forbidden, evil, and dangerous.

We do not need to go far from home to observe such cultural oppositions. I would argue that in the anthropological academy, scholarly theoretical work is considered the sacred, pure world into which a lucky few are admitted, whereas work with the military is defined as so polluting that once an anthropologist has had contact with this dangerous and unclean group, he or she is permanently shunned from the anthropological community.

In this worldview, it is understandable that my fellow anthropologists would be puzzled that a member of the anthropological community would voluntarily elect to become an outcast by associating with the untouchable military and, indeed, wonder why she would not, at least, have chosen a middle ground—for example by seeking applied work with a "less polluting" organization such as an NGO or the State Department. Yet, in many ways, these organizations are no less "tools of empire" than the military in furthering U.S. government values, policy, and strategy. Many of the astute Marines in my classes question the ethical right of U.S. government and nonprofit organizations to impose democracy, gender equality, Western education, or even modern technology on cultures that do not seem to value or want these changes.

More important, given their tiny budgets and manpower relative to the enormous size of the military, civilian agencies often find that whether they like it or not, the military dictates what is possible and how it is done in a particular area. Although anthropology has a long history of working with and for powerless, marginalized groups and organizations, as Laura Nader pointed out 40 years ago (Nader 1972), by failing to "study up" within those powerful institutions (such as the military) that have the potential to radically effect change, the discipline as a whole risks becoming irrelevant and ineffective. Although perhaps in the anthropological worldview it would be "more pure" to lead "sit-ins" (as one commentator suggested in a blog about a National Public Radio [NPR] interview on my work [NPR 2010]), the best one can hope is that such efforts force an earlier end to a current conflict. However, in the long run, the military as an organization will not change from such demonstrations, and will enter the next conflict (which there will always be) no wiser or better from the experience. It is my personal belief that to effect lasting change one must work from the inside, rather than the outside, of any cultural group—the military included.

Interestingly, this anthropological worldview that the military is a polluting, dangerous organization is not held by most of the other social science academic communities. The discipline of psychology, for example, has many respected applied practitioners who work for the military. Historians actually have a subfield called military history and teach happily on the faculty of the West Point Military Academy and the U.S. Naval Academy. Likewise, scholars with Ph.D.s in international affairs and political science often use their experience in the many national security think tanks around Washington, D.C., as a footstool to move on to prestigious positions at the Harvard Kennedy School, or Johns Hopkins' School of Advanced International Studies.

Hence, I do not see my decision to teach at the Marine Corps University as a break from the academic world at all—it is simply a break from the anthropological world. It is true that I do not publish in anthropological journals, but I continue to publish and present in journals and at conferences in other fields: international studies, security studies, psychology, and even education. Although I have moved away from the topic of my original fieldwork, I continue to conduct ethnographic research by "studying up" to understand the culture of a taboo organization (for anthropologists): the Marine Corps. In fact, my research on culture policy and the Marine Corps has led to a number of publications that are at least as important for developing a successful military cultural program as any of my classes on the Middle East. It is not that I have ceased to be a scholar or member of the larger academic community, nor have I sacrificed my professional and personal development; rather, I have switched my scholarly focus, community, and audience.

Are there costs to my decision? Of course, just as there are costs to any career choice. I sleep less, see my family less, work significantly harder and longer, and worry more about my work and students than I ever did in classic academia. It is lonely out here sometimes. In many ways I feel as if I have been in the field for four years—the lone anthropologist in a foreign land—and I hunger occasionally for a conversation about symbols and taboos and Mary Douglas without facing blank stares. On the other hand, I never question whether what I do is actually relevant or useful to anyone or that I have a role in fundamentally changing the way the military solves conflict, especially when I receive messages like this:

> Understanding the culture is what makes us money on the ground. It goes without saying that people fear the Marine Corps or worse hate the Marines for being in their country. Our ability to have the smallest possible impact on daily life and their culture helps them to open up and trust us. When they trust us the biggest battle of all has been won. When they call us friend is when long term change has taken place and we have made a measurable difference in their way of life. None of this is possible without cultural training. —26-year-old infantry Marine Gunnery Sergeant

Notes

The opinions expressed in this paper are the author's own and do not represent those of the Marine Corps University, the Center for Advanced Operational Culture Learning, the U.S. Marine Corps, or any other U.S. government organization.

1. According to Adam Siegal (1994), from 1990 to 1992, the Marine Corps conducted 108 humanitarian aid and disaster relief efforts. These figures do not include the past two decades during which the U.S. Marine Corps provided major relief efforts to the tsunami victims in Indonesia, the earthquake victims of Haiti, and the flood victims of Pakistan.
2. Mean response was 3.25 for culture and 3.09 for language on a scale from 1 (not important) to 4 (very important). N = 2,385 for culture and N = 2,405 for language.
3. N = 1338 for Marines who received culture training.
4. Mean response was 3.11 on a scale from 1 (never) to 4 (very often). N = 297 ground combat arms responses.

References

Douglas, Mary
1966 Purity and Danger. London: Routledge and Kegan-Paul.

Holmes-Eber, Paula, Basma Maki, and Erika Tarzi
In press Attitudes to Culture and Language Training in the U.S. Marine Corps: A Survey of Career Marines. Quantico, VA: Marine Corps Center for Advanced Operational Culture Learning.

Homes-Eber, Paula, Patrice Scanlon, and Andrea Hamlen
2009 Applications in Operational Culture: Perspectives from the Field. Quantico, VA: Marine Corps University Press.

Nader, Laura
1972 Up the Anthropologist! Perspectives Gained from Studying Up. *In* Reinventing Anthropology, D. Hymes, ed. Pp. 284–311. New York: Pantheon Press.

National Public Radio (NPR)
2010 In Class, Marines Learn Cultural Cost of Conflict. January 9. Available at http://www.npr.org/templates/story/story.php?storyId=122362543. Accessed September 26, 2011.

Salmoni, Barak, and Paula Holmes-Eber
2011 Operational Culture for the Warfighter: Principles and Applications. 2nd edition Quantico, VA: Marine Corps University Press.

Siegal, Adam
1994 A Chronology of the United States Marine Corps Humanitarian Assistance and Peace Operations. Alexandria, VA: Center for Naval Analysis.

10

Protecting the Past to Secure the Future: An Archaeologist Working for the Army

Laurie Rush

Cultural anthropology has dominated debates about anthropological engagements in the national security arena, as embodied in concerns about ethnography in support of frontline military operations. By spotlighting military archaeology, the following essay broadens the discipline's discussion and self-reflection about its presence in the securityscape. Featured here is Laurie Rush, a civilian archaeologist who has worked with the military since the early 1990s, primarily on issues of cultural resources management (CRM). She was also part of the second iteration of the Commission on the Engagement of Anthropology with the U.S. Security and Intelligence Communities (CEAUSSIC), when an effort was made to more fully represent the range of anthropological disciplines.

Rush's professional activities are a reminder that the Department of Defense (DoD), and the federal government more broadly, is the owner of vast tracts of land whose management has long required archaeological support. After a tenure in museum and archaeological work in northern New York in the 1980s, Rush entered the military sector, first to establish an archaeology curation facility at Fort Drum, New York, in 1992 and then to assume management of the installation's cultural resources program in 1998. More than 150 Native American archaeological sites on Fort Drum have been uncovered by teams working with Rush, and she has established consultation partnerships between the military installation and three Haudenosaunee Nations, the Oneida Indian Nation, the Onondaga Nation, and the St. Regis Mohawk Tribe.

Rush's occupational pursuits have since shifted, revealing how the job description of a DoD employee can change radically once war breaks out. Rush now plays a principal role in cultural preservation efforts as part of the larger U.S. military presence, as well as diplomatic and development endeavors, in Iraq and Afghanistan. In 2009, Rush served as military liaison for the successful return of the ancient city of Ur to Iraqi stewardship; in 2010, she met with the Deputy Minister of Culture and the Director General of Heritage for the Islamic Republic of Afghanistan in Kabul, with the goal of increasing awareness and military partnership for preservation projects in Kabul and in Mes Aynek. In collaboration with the Archaeological Institute of America and Colorado State University, she has also produced a comprehensive awareness-raising and training initiative on cultural heritage preservation for soldiers deployed to Iraq, Afghanistan, and Egypt. In recognition of her efforts to protect cultural heritage in conflict zones, Rush was the 2010–2011 Booth Family Rome Prize Winner in Historic Preservation.

In 1984, when I completed my Ph.D. at Northwestern University, there were perhaps five academic jobs available in anthropology nationwide. My husband, a family practice physician, was completing his public health service obligation in a remote part of northern New York, and we had a young family. There did not seem to be any point in my attempting to compete in such a discouraging job market, so we decided to wait until his service was complete before I even began looking for work as an anthropologist. We had, and still do have, an agreement that we would move to wherever I found employment. My very first job was at the Antique Boat Museum in Clayton, New York, where I wrote grants and did research for exhibits in exchange for money for a babysitter. The Museum was also gracious enough to send me to a Smithsonian "crash course" for outside professionals entering the museum field. My four years at the Museum offered experience in collections management, museum administration, object conservation, and institutional planning. The highlight, though, was a National Endowment for the Humanities (NEH) grant that enabled me to study social class relationships as expressed in the design and construction of small boats indigenous to the region, St. Lawrence Skiffs.

After the Antique Boat Museum, I shifted my professional life to working from a home office, consulting for a variety of museums in the region, and expanding into compliance archaeology for small construction and water projects. It was during this time period (1992–1994) that the U.S. Army approached me for the first time and asked if I would be willing to accept a two-year contract with the U.S. Army Corps of Engineers Construction and Engineering Laboratory to set up a curation facility and inventory Native American collections at Fort Drum, New York. The Army's interest in this project was to bring Fort Drum into compliance with the Native American Graves Protection and Repatriation Act (NAGPRA). I did and still do share the goals of repatriating Native

American human remains for proper burial. The United States was not involved in any form of armed conflict at the time, and the tasks at hand did not seem to challenge any of my beliefs about the military and nonviolence that had formed as I came of age during the Vietnam era. To be honest, at that time, I never thought twice about working for the military in my capacity as an anthropologist and museum professional. Once the curation facility was up and running on its own, the federal archaeologist for Fort Drum took over responsibility, and I returned to consulting for other agencies on a project-by-project basis.

In 1998, the federal archaeologist at Fort Drum approached me to ask if I would consider taking on the writing of a long-range plan for the Fort Drum program. I think that it is at this point where my story becomes of interest in terms of anthropology careers and ethical decision-making. At first, it was supposed to be another project contract for a year, but it evolved into a career with the U.S. Army. Here was the situation at the Fort at the time:

- Only 10 percent of the acreage (more than 100,000 acres) had been properly inventoried for Native American ancestral places (prehistoric archaeological sites).
- Military training involving substantial amounts of ground disturbance was taking place on the installation and in areas that had potential for archaeological sites.
- The installation has been unable to retain qualified archaeologists for its staff.
- Due to the turnover in expertise and lack of proper inventory, military commanders responsible for compliance with federal law concerning archaeological sites on military land at Fort Drum had not been provided either with accurate information about the site potential or their stewardship responsibilities.
- Due to the lack of continuity in qualified expertise, installation leadership had been unable to establish any form of consultation relationship with representatives of Native American Nations who were concerned about the ancestral places on the installation.
- The Native Americans were becoming increasingly anxious about the situation and were concerned about the possibility that the continued military training would disturb ancestral remains.

When the federal archaeologist and the director of the field survey abruptly departed, representatives of the installation offered me a permanent position with a generous salary and benefits and agreed to support me in addressing these issues. The position actually made me an employee of a major university that had a contract with the DoD, so I was not a military employee. From my perspective, it was at this point that I made my first major decision in terms of working permanently in a military setting.

At that point, I began to work year-round full-time in an office on the military base. Many of the people around me were DoD employees. It is often difficult to tell the difference between university, contract, and DoD personnel in a work setting like this one. As I began to work, it became increasingly clear that the installation had many highly significant ancestral places. Some were at risk of damage and destruction from further training and from proposed construction. I became an advocate for site preservation and was tasked to educate a succession of base commanders. I also discovered that at least two of the ancestral places were potentially sacred to the Native Americans. I began to establish contact with representatives of the Native American Nations who were anxious to establish formal consultation relationships with the military leadership on Fort Drum. As I worked on these issues, I discovered that, by law and DoD policy, the person who represents the installation in formal consultation has to be an employee of the federal government. I was the only person currently working on the base that had any qualifications for establishing a Native American consultation program. I knew that if the federal position as a DoD employee was offered to me, my university contract position at the Fort would no longer exist. The only way that I could continue my work would be to become a military civilian employee. I think that it is important to note that the federal position required me to swear to uphold the U.S. Constitution, which to be honest, I had never read carefully.

This offer became another critical decision point for me. I did accept the job and found myself formally working for the DoD. I was successful in my efforts to preserve important ancestral places on the installation, and had the support of the installation leadership for my stewardship efforts. In fact, I think that it is important to note that this work gave me the opportunity to work with outstanding military officers who were willing to make difficult decisions to save Native American ancestral places, even when it meant redesigning major construction projects and the Installation Master Plan. One of the sites we saved is so important that Native Americans have brought their children there for special celebrations and to teach about the wisdom of the ancestors. I began to realize that my work was having a positive impact on the members of the Native American Nations with whom I was working. It also became extremely personally and professionally fulfilling.

Over the course of these few years, my family, which now included college-age children, was also becoming increasingly dependent upon my income and benefits. Then September 11, 2001, came. The installation where I was working mobilized to prepare personnel to deploy to fight the global war on terror. My work became part of a process that made more training land available and improved training opportunities to soldiers and airmen. The idea of military training at this point was no longer an abstraction, and military service in the United States took on much more serious implications. For the purpose of this case study, these realities could indicate another job decision point. I chose to stay in my job; we moved on to 2003, and the United States initiated war in Iraq. Fort Drum was preparing soldiers and airmen to deploy to this conflict. As with the global war on terror, my efforts and the efforts of the cultural resources program continued to support the training and deployment process. In addition, my teams were continuing to find additional significant ancestral places, and we were being asked to take a more proactive role in protecting the known sites on the installation as training intensified. 2003 could also be considered another decision point, and I continued in my job.

In the fall of 2004, I was on my way to work when I heard the news that U.S. military personnel had caused damage at Babylon. I realized that because of my experience with the military, including an understanding of military bureaucracy, I was in a position to act as an interlocutor between the archaeologists who were expressing anger over the damage and the military organizations responsible for preparing deploying personnel. I also realized that my program had failed to prepare the military personnel who trained on Fort Drum to anticipate the archaeological challenges that they would face in places like Iraq and Afghanistan. Becoming directly engaged in these issues was not a requirement of my position, but I chose to engage anyway. I also knew that there was a possibility that I might be asked to travel to a war zone as a result.

I also knew that this decision would involve me even more directly in deployment training. I thought about my responsibility as an American citizen to engage and the fact that when I took the job, I had already sworn to uphold the Constitution. To me making promises is very important, and I want my word or oath to be able to be respected as a word of honor. I also found that the more time I spent working in a military setting, the more my preconceived and stereotyped ideas about the military that had been formed during my youth in the Vietnam era were being challenged. As I had worked on military land management issues, I had met distinguished officers who had led peacekeeping missions, who had brought water and food to starving refugees, who had completed water projects in sub-Saharan villages. I began to learn that military service is far more complex than the average person realizes. I also gave more thought to the fact that I think it is a privilege to be a U.S. citizen and that I genuinely appreciate the fact that my family and I live in a relatively stable and orderly society.

As I began to learn more about damage to archaeological property in Iraq and Afghanistan, I began to discuss the issue with soldiers who had returned from the war zones. They told me that the opposition was using archaeological sites, cemeteries, and sacred places as positions for attacking U.S. personnel. They wanted to know if it was okay to shoot back in these situations. They explained that if a professional archaeologist told them it was okay to return fire in these situations, it would lessen the possibility that they might hesitate. It was at that point that I realized that the issues surrounding cultural property were far more complex than just teaching about identification and preservation. I also continued to engage in discussions and preparation with military personnel given that I had a much more sophisticated understanding of the true nature of the issues at stake.

It is also critical that an anthropologist considering employment with the military be aware of the very powerful acculturation practices in the military environment. Ceremonies like retirements, changes of command, welcome home, and memorials are extremely powerful in this respect. It is also critical to remember that individuals create strong personal bonds in any workplace. Anthropologists on military installations may use government daycare, for example. The experience of picking up your child on a weekday afternoon and discovering that your child's best friend has just lost their parent in battle will have an effect on your life and on your decision-making.

One reason why I decided to share my "case" with the AAA casebook project is that I wanted to challenge the reader with the fact that the question of "Should I take this job?" may be more nuanced than one might expect. It is also critical to remember that once an individual accepts a full-time position with full benefits, especially if this individual is supporting or helping to support a family, it may be very difficult to resign. A military job raises questions of personal identity as an individual, a family member, a member of a community, a citizen of the United States, and a member of the international community. In my case, it was a series of decisions that became increasingly complex as the situation became increasingly complex. I think that it is critical that any anthropologist considering a job with the military be fully aware that one job may lead to another, or that one set of responsibilities can become tied to a related set of responsibilities, and that this process raises ethical considerations all along the way.

Editorial Commentary

Rather than a singular event, the decision to pursue a career in archaeology with the Army is a gradual one for Rush. A series of choices bring her into a closer, more formal affiliation with the DoD. She begins as a consultant on CRM at a military base that is populated with ancestral sites of great significance to Native American Nations. Rush then assumes a university post, continuing her site preservation work on contract to the installation. Stymied in her role as base liaison to the Nations, however, she agrees to become a military civilian employee, knowing that this affords her the legal authority to establish a Native American consultation program and more fully meet her stewardship commitments.

Reading Rush's essay, we noticed that she was careful to mark these gradations of affiliation, each with their attendant legal and institutional obligations. She is a consultant, a contractor; she is part-time, then she is in a full-time position with the military performing CRM work whose ethical purpose and goals she strongly supports. We wondered why this was important for Rush to mark out in this way. Would others maintain the same degrees of affiliation, or would they collapse the distinctions as irrelevant as it relates to engagement with the military/national security state? How does Rush's entry into the defense world compare with that of other anthropologists?

At first, Rush's military connection seems hardly controversial; her CRM duties differ little from the occupational pursuits of many of her peers. In fact, Rush's account reveals that the responsible operation of a military base shares many of the same management challenges as any other large federal installation. Military bases are not exempt from NAGPRA, which stipulates the inventorying of sites of cultural significance to Native Americans, which might involve human remains, and which mandates consultation and cooperation with nearby Nations on these matters. Rush signs her original consultant agreement "with almost no second thoughts"—it is peacetime and she shares NAGPRA's goals. Moreover, her position affords her strong opportunities for advocacy on behalf of marginalized populations.

Rush, like Holmes-Eber, Dawson, and other contributors, attempts to carve out a work environment within the military that does not conflict with personal values and/or professional ethics of doing no harm. Other anthropologists who have contributed to this volume have also worked to set up comfortable "safe" spaces within national security institutions, where they are pursuing their anthropological practice in ways that are consonant with their perceived professional and personal ethics. This raises interesting questions about the degree to which an individual controls the content and application of her or his work, as well as the extent to which institutional mission inevitably shapes one's work. We expect this varies tremendously across contexts; certainly it seems as though Rush has managed to align multiple levels of goals in her career, from the Native American communities with which she partners, to those of the Army at Fort Drum, to her own interests and commitments as a practicing archaeologist. Does the specific content of an individual's work and career matter more, we ask, or does the larger institutional mission always override that? How and why might other anthropologists set the same or different boundaries?

Circumstances shift radically around Rush after 9/11, upending the ethical terms that she first set for herself in working at the base: no compromise with her "strongly held beliefs in nonviolence." Still preserving sacred ancestral sites, her work now facilitates the release of more installation land for training purposes as the base prepares soldiers and airmen to deploy. Two moral imperatives for Rush are now at odds: protecting the cultural heritage of marginalized populations and preserving a stance of nonviolence. Given her strong commitment to nonviolence, we wondered what prevented her from resigning her position at this point. Perhaps the positive impacts of her CRM work outweighed the possibility of the indirect support of wartime operations; in many ways, Rush's account reveals the special challenges that archaeology faces when professional practice intersects with warfighting and stability and reconstruction operations.

In any case, Rush maintains her position at the base. However, her moral landscape shifts abruptly again when she learns of the damage caused by U.S. military personnel at Babylon. Her professional expertise and understanding of military bureaucracy put her in a unique position possibly to prevent future harm to archaeological sites in war zones. These events also put into relief an often-neglected backdrop to the U.S. presence in these countries: the increasing global significance of "cultural heritage" as a national but also multilateral concept and subject of policy, development, and humanitarian assistance, as well as source of international debate over ownership of cultural property (see Brown 2003)—a set of developments reflected in the global outcry against the Taliban's destruction of the Bamiyan Buddhas in Afghanistan, the ransacking of the Baghdad Museum, and the bombing of the Samarra mosque in Iraq. Compelled by a personal sense of obligation, Rush is also in part responding to a dynamic and changing global political environment with respect to cultural heritage, patrimony, and property.

Cognizant of becoming more entrenched in warfighting operations, Rush nonetheless decides to shape pre-deployment training actively, so that military personnel are in a better position to value and protect culturally significant sites and artifacts. The stark realities of wartime assert themselves, as returning soldiers then look to her for guidance on returning fire to opposing forces who position themselves in archaeological sites and cemeteries. We expect that Rush was cognizant of dilemmas engendered by her professional and personal positions of "do not harm." Rush's account of her unfolding career as an Army archaeologist reveals an ongoing process of self-reflection, moral stock-taking, and negotiation of ethical boundaries as the larger context for her work evolves and competing obligations emerge. Her essay hints, too, at how her movement into full participation in DoD has changed her sense of self vis-á-vis the military. Strong personal bonds in the workplace; acculturation practices such as ceremonies to welcome home troops, mark changes in command, and memorialize fallen comrades; and economic dependence in the form of full-time employment with full benefits are all forces that bear upon Rush's relationship to and perspectives on the military and the people who populate it.

In the end, we wondered if she ever regrets having made that first decision to consult for the Army, given the long series of choices it seems to have generated. On the other hand, the tone of Rush's essay indicates that she values the opportunities that the military has presented for applying her skills and achieving cultural preservation at home and abroad.

Rush Response

The editors asked me, "Knowing what you know now, would you have taken that first step? Have the opportunities that the military has presented for achieving cultural preservation at home and abroad been worth it?"

My first thought is to answer the question with a question, worth what? I suspect that the volume's editors are referring to compromise in terms of my personal beliefs in nonviolence. However, engagement with the military has taught me that damage to cultural property prolongs conflict and results in increased violence. The tremendous complexity of these issues means that the more education that we can provide to our deploying personnel, the greater potential for stability, common ground, and peacemaking. So I have found that I have an opportunity to work toward peace from a completely unexpected context.

The editors also asked if I should involve myself in tactical conversations. It is true that soldiers asked me whether it was permissible to return fire coming from a cemetery and that I answered yes. I don't really consider that to be a tactical conversation. Are there individuals who would honestly advise a U.S. soldier not to defend him or herself when under fire? I have provided informational presentations to soldiers of all levels concerning the culture and heritage of Iraq and Afghanistan and the importance of showing respect, but I have neither the background nor the expertise to provide tactical advice to anyone. I have also had the opportunity to discuss the importance of heritage preservation with international military personnel from across the Middle East, but again, those conversations are not of a tactical nature.

I really do not feel like I have made any significant personal sacrifices. I did risk my life to go to Kabul as an advocate for historic preservation, but that effort resulted in a million-dollar project to construct a building to help the Afghans save Buddhist sculptures at Mes Aynek. My family has made huge sacrifices in terms of my absence and worry. There were the angry archaeologists at the World Archaeological Congress in Dublin, and from time to time I encounter someone who is completely appalled to meet an individual who is on the U.S. Army payroll. However, those individuals are far outnumbered by people from all different kinds of backgrounds who feel that my work is vitally important. My position as a social scientist working for the Army also added tremendous credibility to my criticisms of the Human Terrain System. Many young anthropologists and archaeologists express tremendous interest in my work.

My willingness to engage in preservation issues at the international level has resulted in opportunities for travel and personal growth that are so amazing that it is embarrassing to describe them. As of this writing, I have traveled to the Middle East more than 10 times, including Iraq. I had the privilege of flying in a tiny helicopter from Baghdad to Ur, and all of the reading I had done in graduate school unfolded beneath me. I saw Iraqi people tending their animals, driving camel caravans, and growing date palms. Those scenes filled me with hope. I have had conversations with Egyptians that portended the recent change in government there and travel that has offered me insight into world events that would have been impossible to gain in any other way. I have been to Jordan, Abu Dhabi, Dubai, and Qatar. I have visited museums and sites of Islamic art, Egyptian archaeology, desert oases, ancient Roman cities, and Nabitean tombs. I have bargained for souvenirs in Middle Eastern marketplaces and Bedouin caves. I have had a chance to ride on camels and in the jump seats of military cargo planes. I have crossed a military airfield in the dark of the night on an old school bus and followed a human chain to safety in fog so thick that I could only see the person in front of me. I have met heroes who risked their lives to provide medical care in Sadr City, to start recycling programs in Afghanistan, and to clean up U.S. garbage in Iraq. I have been invited to speak at international conferences throughout Europe, and now I write this response from the American Academy in Rome as the Booth Family Rome Prize Winner. I wake up every day to the sun rising over Monte Cavo.

I have also had extraordinary opportunities for professional accomplishment. There are at least two archaeological sites in Iraq where my efforts prevented and stopped damage by the U.S. military. I played a role in returning stewardship of the ancient city of Ur to the Iraqi people.

I have had the opportunity to travel to Afghanistan to meet their heroes of heritage preservation, and was able to offer them substantive assistance.

This essay will end with my admission to a bit of sophomoric behavior at a military environmental conference a few years ago. A small group of us snuck out of a hotel through the back stairs of a parking garage to avoid two prominent colleagues who wanted to join us for dinner. We had not invited them to join us. However, they positioned themselves with a view of the front door of the hotel to catch us on the way out. The reason we did not want to share our evening with them was simple: one of the individuals had advanced his career by "telling the military what they wanted to hear," and this resulted in decreased funding and damage to programs that we cared deeply about.

That evening, I spent a lot of time thinking about how we evaluate ourselves and each other. I try to be hard on myself in terms of evaluating my own behavior, but I also care what valued colleagues think of me. That night I decided that, for me, a very important form of evaluation would be whether people I respect are willing to share a meal. I am happy to say that since that time, my opportunities to dine with colleagues have exceeded my wildest dreams, and I am fortunate in the extreme.

Knowing what I know now, would I have taken that first step? In a heartbeat!

Reference

Brown, Michael
2003 Who Owns Native Culture? Cambridge, MA: Harvard University Press.

11

Staying Safe: Aid Work and Security in Afghanistan

Patricia Omidian

Patricia Omidian received her Ph.D. in medical anthropology from the University of California–San Francisco and Berkeley joint program (1992). She has taught in the areas of medical anthropology, research methods, and community wellness in the United States, Pakistan, and Afghanistan. She went to Pakistan in 1997 on a Senior Fulbright Award to conduct research on mental health and to teach at Peshawar University. Omidian has 25 years of experience as an applied medical anthropologist in the area of war trauma and community wellness. She has consulted for a range of agencies (Save the Children US, Save the Children UK, Save the Children Sweden, and the International Rescue Committee [IRC], donors [Novib], and United Nations agencies (UN Development Fund for Women [UNIFEM], UN Children's Fund [UNICEF], Joint UN Programme on HIV/AIDS [UNAIDS], and World Food Programme [WFP]). She has written many reports and published extensively on Afghanistan and Pakistan. She uses anthropological approaches to community wellness and community psychology, program design and implementation, and psychosocial wellness training. She has also worked on gender issues, including violence against women and family violence. She continues to live and work in Pakistan.

Omidian's own research is in the area of mental wellness and resiliency. In 2004 and 2005, she collaborated with Dr. Ken Miller (a psychologist) on a project to understand posttraumatic stress disorder (PTSD) and Afghan categories of mental health and illness/distress. The first tool to be developed was the Afghan Symptoms Checklist (ASCL), measuring perceived stress in relation to day-to-day stressors. This checklist has been used by researchers in Afghanistan, and the methodology has been tested in Iraq and Sri Lanka.

In December of 2001, she moved to Kabul where she worked for five years, including three years as Country Representative for the American Friends

Service Committee (AFSC). Since her return to Pakistan in 2007, she has conducted numerous trainings on culturally based approaches to psychosocial wellness, partnering with local mental health projects in Karachi and Multan. Based on understandings gained from similar projects in Afghanistan, her work addresses depression and trauma through a nonclinical, culturally relevant peer approach. Omidian currently trains staff of local nongovernmental organizations (NGOs) as mental health peer counseling trainers.

Omidian's work in Afghanistan and Pakistan stood out to the editors, given her long experience in these countries as well the extent and variety of her work in the NGO and multilateral context, and given the attention she has paid to what it means to work in conflict zones while not working for the military. We have been interested in, and are convinced that more attention should be paid to, the parallels and differences of anthropological practice in and with the security sector versus such NGO work. Omidian's is a good example of the work of a practicing anthropologist that geographically overlaps with that of the U.S. military, and/or is plugged into many humanitarian or development objectives either directly or indirectly implicated in the securitized contexts created by the coalition presence in Afghanistan or the security-driven policy priorities prevailing in these countries.

Omidian has been an advocate of the possibility that to work in such conflict zones does not mean one necessarily needs to work with the military. She aired these views in the context of discussions of the Human Terrain System program while attending the American Anthropological Association (AAA) annual meeting in 2007. Omidian has explored alternatives to so-called military anthropology. In this essay, nevertheless, she addresses some of the ways in which even NGO work is shaped by the broadest implications and extent of "security," where multilateral agencies find their work in unavoidable proximity to the exigencies of the securityscape, broadly conceived.

When I consider the issue of security in Afghanistan, I don't see it as an issue of national or military importance ("Security" with a capital "S"). Rather, as an applied anthropologist who has worked in Afghanistan for a number of years, I use the term to designate more personal and immediate ("security" with a little "s") concerns revolving around safety in a country that continues to be burdened by war. During the time I worked in Afghanistan—from 1998 to 2009, traveling in and out of the country from my base in Pakistan between 1998 and 2001 (Omidian 2011) and living in Kabul from 2002 to 2007 (Omidian 2009), with short trips each year after that—I had to pay attention to security issues for myself, my colleagues (both expatriates and Afghans), and any beneficiaries of projects which engaged my services as a researcher or program developer.

Trained as a medical anthropologist, I worked as a consultant for various national and international NGOs, and for the two UN agencies. In this case study, I discuss security concerns I faced when I was based in Kabul from 2002 to 2007, highlighting the way security and personal safety shaped my experience and my work, as well as possible ethical ramifications that could result. During this period I watched security rules, as defined by international organizations like the UN, shift from being almost casual to becoming stringent, with greater fortifications and ever increasing vigilance. As an aid worker whose work placed me within local communities, I had to balance security issues (and how each agency approached security for their international staff) with the need to complete the projects for which I was hired. Whether I was working as a consultant, independent researcher, or head of agency I had to consider safety for myself, as well as for those with whom I worked. Then, as the Country Representative for the AFSC for three years (2004–2007), the issue of safety expanded to encompass deeper levels of concern—my responsibility for the safety of my program and office staff. During this period of time, we worked through the Ministry of Education to build schools, conduct various levels of teacher training, and train university students in community mental health programs for schools.

Throughout most of my time in Afghanistan, the Taliban and other antigovernment groups (insurgents that include warlords, druglords, private militias, and armed robbers) targeted various Afghan government and coalition forces (including North American Treaty Organization [NATO] forces, the International Security Assistance Force [ISAF], and various Western armies, such as those from the United States or United Kingdom). These insurgents and others initially attacked major projects such as road building or power supply but also, and from the beginning, attacked aid workers. They seemed to target health clinics and schools, killing doctors, clinic staff, and teachers. Because of the insecurity in the south and in remote areas, military groups worked on projects that usually were left to civilians in the development and health sectors. These Provincial Reconstruction Teams (PRTs; often engineers and other "professionals" hired by the military) brought programs and projects to local populations without consideration for existing activities, and were part of the "hearts and minds" campaign by the U.S. military. As these projects gained in prominence, the lines between civilian aid workers (like myself) and the military became blurred. This blurring meant that insurgents would attack anyone, and locals could not know who to trust, who was neutral. My colleagues and I at AFSC found that the best way to avoid trouble was to avoid working where the military had one of their hearts and minds projects, because these areas were more likely to be targeted by insurgents.

The PRTs did not use standard models of participatory development, nor did they try to enlist the support of local groups. Their model, to buy their way in by building something big, tended to increase local expectations for handouts. Our avoidance of these areas, therefore, had two purposes. One was to avoid areas where insurgents might be active, as it was hard to see which came first to an area, the PRTs or the insurgents. The other was the problem of increased community expectations for handouts. For this reason, our work was easiest if we did not have to compete with PRTs or deal with their militarized aid. By avoiding PRTs, we also avoided militarized areas.

In Afghanistan, one was most vulnerable when traveling. During my time there, I watched security concerns grow and the areas where we could move easily steadily shrink. In 2002, I traveled in many areas of the country, including by road from Kabul to Kandahar. By 2003, this road was not safe. Over the next five years, the spread of the power of the various warlords and the changing character of the insurgency forced most people in the aid community to change how they traveled, both within Kabul and between the various regions. By 2007, there were few safe roads in the country, and improvised explosive devices (IEDs) were a ubiquitous hazard, even in areas close to Kabul. Our office drivers took courses in how to avoid assaults, how to escape being boxed in during an attack on the vehicle, and where to look for bombs that might be planted on the car. Most aid staff stayed in touch with their offices by radio or through text messaging on cell phones.

Within the urban areas, one could be at risk by following military convoys too closely or by being at the wrong place at the wrong time—as when an IED might detonate. In Kabul, insurgents tended to target Afghan military and government transports as well as ISAF vehicles. We were warned by security advisors to avoid traffic jams, which were frequent in Kabul, as they gave thieves or insurgents opportunities to target those who were essentially trapped in their cars. Most problems would not be dissimilar to those one would experience in some U.S. cities, although here one would not be given a lecture on what to do if a hand grenade is lobbed through an open window of one's car.

The areas that posed the greatest threat to personal security were those with ongoing military action—usually in the southern and eastern portions of the country. Eventually, we closed an AFSC project in Ghazni Province because it was far too dangerous to go there. This was an area with a heavy NATO presence, numerous antigovernment actors, and extensive drug trafficking. None of our Afghan staff felt safe there. In fact, an Italian woman who worked for the UN, and who was well known in the area, was killed as she traveled through the main market city of Ghazni. Yet, this province was one of the closest places for us to work—within an hour's drive from Kabul. As we were a Quaker organization, it was important for us to maintain neutrality. Because of the heavy military presence and the large number of insurgents, we could not move safely without armed guards, and the presence of armed guards could have compromised our neutrality.

Most NGO, UN, and other official vehicles were marked by logos or special license plates, and could be targeted. I always felt these cars were easy targets as they were easily identified and tended to travel in groups of two or more. In contrast, my staff and I often traveled in a local taxi hired on a contract basis. In fact, my driver in the early years owned his own taxi and was the son of one of my surveyors. Once he became our agency's logistics officer, he hired our next driver, another man from his community. The driver needed to be someone we could trust and who also trusted us. I felt safer in cars that looked like every other car on the street. Safety of the Afghan staff was as important as for the internationals at the office. By hiring people from the same community where we worked, we ensured another level of safety and security.

When we traveled to the rural areas, we were most at risk. Before traveling to an area, we always called our partner NGOs in those areas to assess the best time and route for the journey. For our trips to Bamyan, in the first few years we drove like we were on a picnic. The car needed to be four-wheel drive to get to many of our destinations, but we worried about accidents caused by the rough road, not from roadside bombs or robbers. Over time, more Afghan aid workers were being targeted and fewer roads were safe for travel. Some, such as the shortest route from Kabul to Bamyan by way of Wardak, became so risky that we stopped going that way. By 2006, we had an NGO send their car from Bamyan to Kabul to pick up our staff for their work in that province. The province of Bamyan was still safe and the route from Kabul through Parwan generally remained open, though the road needed repair. Sadly, other places I visited in 2004 were off-limits by 2006. And by 2007, it was recommended that international staff fly to the nearest airports within the country, instead of traveling by road.

As my colleagues and I worked with local partners in five provinces, we found that security was best in the smaller communities where we worked, because the local people got to know us and knew why we were there. I felt that the more remote the location, the safer, because no group seemed to want to be there. U.S. or NATO forces would not be in evidence. But mostly, communities in these areas still honored local traditions that demanded the protection of guests. For example, on one trip, we flew from Kabul to Mazar-e-Sharif, where we were met by the local NGO staff, who drove us to a remote area of Faryab province. Our local escorts were able to move us through some areas that were considered unsafe because of the level of drug-trafficking there. Once in the area where we planned to build schools, we were so safe that we traveled to the various sites by horseback. One day, we visited so many places and were out so late that we had to wait for moonrise before we could see well enough to return to our village, giving us the luxury of a moonlight ride on some very energetic horses.

In a country with so much strife, international organizations tried to keep their international staff safe by having them live in well-known areas of Kabul, and usually with three or more staff per house. Most agencies maintain guesthouses for their international staff, where everyone lives and works together for months on end. Insurance requirements for staff in high-risk areas, and the need to know where staff are at all times, makes this the easiest solution. This reduced the cost for the agency in support staff and guards. In contrast, the various jobs I had required me to find my own housing. I liked it this way, and I depended on my Afghan friends to help me find the safest place. My home for three years was in an apartment block that included a number of families who had been refugees in Iran. I fit in nicely with my slight Iranian accent, which served me well. Once, a group of police (although we were never sure who they were) came to the market near my home and asked for information on any foreigners living there. My neighbors told them there were none, but that one woman had lived abroad for so long that she often forgot how to speak properly. They meant me. I never lied about my background but I was careful. If a stranger asked me, I always told them I had lived in Iran but left there 30 years ago. My gray hair allowed me a lot of latitude, and people would then laugh at my linguistic failures.

Unlike many who came to Afghanistan to work, the Quaker model was to live locally and to share the lives of those with whom we worked. I saw my security as tied to that of my staff, who felt like members of my own family. They worked hard to keep me safe. But I also listened to them and tried to give them the same level of support. They let me know when I needed to stay out of certain areas or to take greater care. Risk was a shared responsibility. By 2004, it was harder to remain independent because foreigners were being targeted more and more often. The reaction to these attacks by most international agencies was to reduce the number of international staff or to increase the number of people per house. At one point, there was talk of creating a fortified "green zone" like that in Baghdad, Iraq. But such enclaves also increased the ability of insurgents to target the aid community. Because these areas were targeted, living in another district of Kabul meant that I was less likely to be in the midst of such an attack.

In the early days (2001–2003) some agencies had bifurcated policies: internationals lived by one set of rules, locals by another. Such rules often left local staff at greater risk. At one NGO coordination meeting, shortly after Médecins Sans Frontières (MSF; Doctors without Borders) pulled out of Afghanistan when their medical staff at a remote clinic was killed, we discussed the problem of local staff being asked to return to dangerous areas before they felt it was safe to do so. I knew of several cases where Afghan staff were told they had to return to their post or lose their job. In one case, a man (born and raised in Kabul) was asked to return to the same town where the MSF clinic had been attacked in the north of the country. Because he had no family or supporters there, he felt particularly at risk and refused to return. Even though international staff were not allowed to return to work there at that point, he was fired when he refused. Those of us who advocated on his behalf were criticized and were unable to help him get reinstated.

Conclusion

At any time in the years I lived there I am not sure I was every really afraid. There were times when my colleagues and I had to be ultra-cautious, and we acted accordingly, like the time of a major riot in Kabul, when many international NGOs were attacked. But such events were rare. I was never personally threatened or attacked. As long as violence was random, it was easy to manage a sense of safety. In general, I am a cautious person. I dressed in local styles and managed to look like I belonged in Kabul. I spoke broken Persian with a mix of Kabul and Tehran dialects, confusing most into thinking I was a local who moved away from Afghanistan when I was young, and only returning when the Taliban were forced out of the country. Thus, safety and security were best maintained when I stayed "under the radar" to avoid drawing attention to myself.

I think one of the reasons I left Afghanistan in 2007 was that I no longer felt I could tell what was safe and what wasn't. I knew my coworkers, who treated me like a member of their family, would protect me as best they could (and I had a few examples of that over the course of my work there). Afghans are famous for protecting their guests. At that time there were many warnings from Taliban that Afghans who worked with foreigners could be killed. My presence could have endangered my friends, and I knew I never wanted that to happen. That is the nature of terrorism, to create insecurity and uncertainty.

I continue to visit Kabul and maintain a connection to several projects there. Friends and former colleagues, who welcome me into their homes, always meet me at the airport. I know of other anthropologists who do the same. Yet the situation changes very quickly. I was chatting on the

Internet with the 15-year-old daughter of a close friend. She begged me to let her come live with me in Pakistan. She asked me: "Auntie Pat, are you scared like me?" When I answered no, she said: "Kabul has become a city of death and we have holidays from our courses because of the attacks on the city center hotel. All I say is that I am waiting to die by a bomb in my school or when I come home."

Editorial Commentary

Omidian offers a glimpse of the several ways constant attention to security—understood as personal and immediate—shaped her professional conduct as a consultant, researcher, and project manager working for various national, international, and multilateral NGOs and agencies in Afghanistan. If Omidian understands security as primarily "personal," it is also clear that, after 2001, security—for her, for her colleagues, and for beneficiaries—was fundamentally bound up with the presence of the United States–led military coalition. While working for a Quaker organization (2004–2007), Omidian was engaged in tasks that included building schools, training teachers, and developing mental health programs for Afghans. These goals were complicated by the presence of U.S. PRTs, joint civil-military units under U.S. command dedicated to improving security, increasing Afghan government authority, and undertaking development projects often similar to those of nonmilitary NGOs. Omidian identifies two major problems: Taliban attacks on aid workers and the blurring of lines between military and civilian aid workers, caused in significant degree by the presence of PRTs.

Much of what Omidian discusses with respect to security is in response to this "blurring." The position of the Quaker NGO for which she worked was to avoid operating "where the military had one of their hearts and minds projects" so as not to be targeted. And even when not working in proximity to military counterparts, Omidian describes having to manage the counterproductive expectations for handouts generated by ongoing PRT efforts. In short, even when not working for or collaborating with military actors, their presence has drastically altered the modus operandi of civilian NGOs of all sorts working in Afghanistan, circumscribing the art of the possible for the humanitarian aid community by drawing it into the mix of nonlocal actors composing the securityscape—beyond personal security—in Afghanistan.

But Omidian also emphasizes the efforts of her Quaker organization to maintain "neutrality" with respect to the conflict. Though she does not explain it this way, neutrality appears to be entangled with the question of security in many ways, including the NGO's decision not to use armed guards, their use of unmarked cars and local drivers, opting to work in more remote locations where U.S. and NATO forces are not present, and opting not to live in well-marked safe houses. Omidian also stresses the Quaker model of living "locally and to share in the lives of those with whom we worked," which sounds an ethnographic note. For Omidian, this meant dressing in local clothing styles and allowing herself to be thought of as a family member recently returned after many years from Iran. Omidian describes treating risk as a "shared responsibility," leaving Afghanistan only when she could no longer tell "what was safe and what wasn't." Of course, her Afghan counterparts do not appear to have the same choices. A question this raises is whether humanitarian NGOs can in fact maintain neutrality in conflict zones such as Afghanistan, particularly when risk is not ultimately shared in the same ways, and where it is almost impossible not to be located on the landscape generated by the ongoing conflict in some manner or other.

Omidian emphasizes how the militarization of civil services and the effort to win "hearts and minds" creates instability and insecurity among local communities. Her account can be read in juxtaposition to the descriptions of the U.S. Army's Human Terrain Teams, whose members go out in military uniform and are often embedded with military units. Omidian, in contrast, indicates that the presence of armed guards would compromise the security of her staff; she pursues an "under the radar" lifestyle, which is afforded by her ability to speak broken Kabul and Tehran dialects with a Persian accent that helps mask her American origins. The Human Terrain Teams have famously hired social scientists with a wide range of fieldwork and research backgrounds, many without area expertise. Yet Omidian's account made it hard for us to imagine any social scientist without extensive field experience being able to connect with local people and build relationships of trust in the way that Omidian describes. Despite the military's effort to appropriate social science in the way it has "physics," or "engineering," Omidian's account demonstrates that the kind of rich, local knowledge that anthropologists build over many years of field experience is what makes anthropology valuable. Anthropologists are not fungible, and the military and intelligence communities may not be able to transport "anthropology" across contexts as easily as one might engineering or operations research knowledge.

Many of the themes that Omidian discusses in this essay were less detailed in the first draft that she sent us. In our first response to Omidian's essay, we asked her to describe the kind of work that she performed with her NGO employer and how that work was similar to or different from other forms of "humanitarian" work being pursued in Afghanistan at that time. We also requested that she expand her discussion of security, and to discuss its relationship to her own safety and the safety of others around her. In particular, given periodic media reports about private security contractors providing "security" for American, European, and other international staff working in Afghanistan, we wondered how different NGOs approach the challenge of keeping their staff safe, and how this relates to Omidian's concept of "security." We also asked her to elaborate upon her embeddedness within the Afghan community: her use of local taxis, residence in neighborhoods where Americans do not usually reside, her slight Persian accent. We wondered at what point Omidian realized that her colleagues, neighbors, and friends were themselves less safe—and less secure—because of her association with them. Omidian addressed some of these themes in this essay, but she also provided the following addendum to our commentary, in which she elaborates upon some of the questions and ideas that we presented in response to her original narrative.

Omidian Response

Knowing that I could leave when my Afghan colleagues could not increased my sense of responsibility to them. No matter how deeply I was accepted into my friends' lives or into the communities where I worked, I remained an outsider. That meant I had to respect and honor my colleagues and their lives. There are many things about Afghan society that I will never write about, because that would reveal too much personal information and disappoint someone I respect. But, to come back to the issue at hand, it was important that I did not endanger them to a point where they would suffer after I left. During return trips it was clear that they were not harmed by interactions with me, and the experiences they gained translated into better jobs and increased salaries. I continue to worry about their safety and their well-being. By maintaining neutrality, as much as possible, staff were able to continue visiting their home villages, some in areas that were unsafe for visits by outsiders, Afghan or other.

Ultimately, I was never neutral about the Taliban. Their model of governance is counter to the ideals of how Afghans view their world. But I always had the obligation to tell the stories of others. I was not prowar, though I did write what Afghan friends said—those who wanted NATO and U.S. military help. I was also never proinsurgency, though I met some insurgents over the years and knew that in every Afghan family one would find a mix of characters from all political perspectives. What I would have liked to see would have been a strong human rights approach to reconstruction, reconciliation, and justice. Instead of bombs, I would have preferred a police force that was backed by a transparent judicial system. Those did not happen. In the end, I could only try to protect those who were interviewed and surveyed, and those with whom I lived. I did what could be done to support the villagers who invited my colleagues and me into their homes and lives.

For a country like Afghanistan that had no infrastructure, massive chronic malnutrition, and a series of wars that included both invasions and civil strife, a social scientist dropped into this mess, even with language training, would miss critically important cultural markers. I often made mistakes or misread cues. A member of a Human Terrain Team would have a difficult time understanding the subtleties of a situation in any village or urban area. In a discussion with locals, it can be hard to know to whom one is referring since Afghans rarely have last names. Most people have one formal name (used for their national ID) and a nickname that is used by family and friends. Village women will rarely have their name used in public. For example, one donor agency worked for several years with an Afghan NGO never realizing that most of the managers were part of a large extended family, because one could not tell by their names.

I cannot condone the "hearts and minds" projects of the PRTs; war is war and it leaves in its wake countless lost lives and livelihoods. For military actors to pretend to be anything other than a part of that war machine while trying to build schools or bridges or wells contradicts the whole purpose of aid work and development, which should always be a partnership between those who request help and those who offer aid. As an anthropologist I know that even when collaborating closely with a community we can get it wrong. Desperation from hunger or displacement sets up a situation where people feel hopeless because they cannot take care of themselves or their families. Dependency is never comfortable or healthy, nor is it sustainable. The best way to help is to step back a bit and to allow people to help themselves, working in ways that fit their culture and society. As head of AFSC, we enjoyed the process of collaboration. And the success of this method is illustrated by the fact that schools we built continue to thrive long after we have gone.

References

Omidian, Patricia

2009 Living and Working in a War Zone: An Applied Anthropologist in Afghanistan. *Practicing Anthropology* 31(2):4–11.

2011 When Bamboo Bloom: An Anthropologist in Taliban's Afghanistan. Long Grove, IL: Waveland Press.

12

On the Ethics of Graduated Disclosure in Contexts of War

Flagg Miller

Flagg Miller is an associate professor of religious studies at the University of California, Davis. He received his Ph.D. at the University of Michigan in 2001. Miller's research has focused on the roles of language ideology and poetry in contemporary Muslim reform in the Middle East and especially Yemen. Well represented by his ethnography, The Moral Resonance of Arab Media: Audiocassette Poetry and Culture in Yemen *(Miller 2007), his work on religion is widely published and highly interdisciplinary, drawing from linguistic and cultural anthropology, history, media theory, poetics, philosophy, and cultural studies. He has lived and studied in the Middle East and North Africa for more than four years, including Tunisia, Syria, and Yemen.*

Miller is currently working on a book project that focuses on an audiocassette collection formerly owned by Osama Bin Laden, the same project provoking his discussion of graduated disclosure for his autoethnographic essay in this volume. Currently held at Yale University, the audiocassette collection represents the most important archive for understanding Bin Laden's intellectual formation. His project explores the contents of the collection and its implications for new understandings of Bin Laden's militant movement, but also situates these insights in relation to a broader consideration of the role of Arabic language studies for contemporary Muslim reformers.

After the fall of the Taliban in December of 2001, the Cable News Network (CNN) acquired the audiotape collection of Bin Laden from his personal compound in Kandahar, where he lived from 1997 to 2001. The collection contains more than 1,500 recordings of more than 200 leading Islamist preachers from around the world. In the summer of 2007, Miller was invited by Yale to annotate the collection, and has been the sole researcher on the collection to date. An article on the ways speakers in the collection differ over their understanding of the term "al-qa'ida" ("the base") has appeared in the Journal of Language and Communication *in 2008 (Miller 2008). Though Albro and Miller participated in an American Anthropological Association (AAA) panel some years ago, Miller's work came across the radar of the volume editors after Albro heard a National Public Radio (NPR) story on Miller's work with the Bin Laden tapes. At the time, Miller was in the middle of a year in residence at the Wilson Center, and Albro quickly got in touch. This essay was the first case we solicited, and its high-quality and thought-provoking discussion of how Miller has handled his research—with its clear implications for the intelligence community, the changing contexts of research in the Middle East in the post-9/11 era, and the close relationship of ethical to research practice—helped to change how we viewed these essays. His case came to serve as a model for others we solicited, epitomizing in our view the virtues of what we now call our "autoethnographic" approach.*

Miller's essay, along with Rubinstein's, represent the work of scholars who have more traditional academic affiliations but nonetheless are engaging in ethnographic research on subjects of interest to communities in the securityscape. Comparing their research challenges with those experienced by Abramson, Turnley, Holmes-Eber, and McNamara in this volume, all of whom engage in research with different affiliations to the security sector, is an important way these essays engage with each other.

To varying degrees, anthropologists who work with Muslim communities have long faced challenges in translating the potential benefits of their discipline for Muslims. In the wake of United States–led sanctions and bombings against Iraq in the 1990s, followed by George W. Bush's declaration of a "War on Terror" following the attacks of 9/11, American anthropologists have faced heightened suspicions about the objectives of their research. If war and conflict have always been central to the production of knowledge, anthropologists find themselves newly implicated in global orders. This case examines one aspect of knowledge production that increasingly complicates anthropologists' integrity in Muslim communities: the recourse, directly or indirectly, to declassified information and other documents that are acquired by United States–led global security networks—including American military forces, private contractors, intelligence consulting firms, multinational companies involved in data management, and journalists—and that are increasingly being made available to the public.

The staggering scale and particularity of such material was evident enough in 2006 when roughly 48,000 boxes of Iraqi documents, acquired by American military forces after the overthrow of Saddam Hussein, were released publicly on the Internet with Congressional approval. Described by chairman of the House Intelligence Committee Pete Hoekstra as an effort "to unleash the power of the Internet, unleash the power of the blogosphere, to get through these documents and give us a better understanding of what was going on in Iraq before the war," the project instantly ratified such an unorthodox range of intelligence analysts that the materials were taken offline eight months later. Although this initiative fizzled, other archival projects of greater complexity, financial backing, and public influence are under way, giving leverage to an array of intelligence analysts whose qualifications have yet to be systematically studied. They include projects by private and nonprofit research firms such the RAND Corporation, Search for International Terrorist Entities (SITE), and the Institute Investigative Project on Terrorism that produce reports, records, databases, and policy recommendations for clients as well as the public at large. They include projects by companies such as the Fortune 500 Science Applications International Corporation (SAIC) and IntelCenter that routinely supply government agencies with intelligence data. They include government-funded initiatives such as the Conflict Research Records project at the National Defense University that host and provide access to declassified artifacts that have been transferred to American ownership in countries where U.S. military forces operate. They also include archives assembled by nonprofit research centers and professional bloggers such as the Middle East Media Research Institute, the Northeast Intelligence Network, and Jihadwatch, all of which aim to influence public opinion and policy through the translation, analysis, and publication of documents that bear centrally on intelligence and security issues.

Anthropologists have a responsibility to engage openly in discussions about the nature and credibility of such perspectives, especially as the boundaries of government-managed intelligence initiatives are being rendered more obscure. My own participation in knowledge production of the sort traditionally considered intelligence work began when an anthropologist colleague solicited my assistance in studying a collection of al-Qa'ida documents from Kandahar, Afghanistan, that included 60 videotapes, 2 compact disks, and more than 1,500 audiotapes, the latter of which had been formerly deposited in Osama Bin Laden's personal compound in the center of the city. Bin Laden had lived in Kandahar from 1997 to 2001. And in the months following the Taliban's evacuation from the city in December of 2001, employees with the U.S.-owned CNN had acquired the collection while conducting investigative journalism in the city. Featuring more than 200 speakers from across the Islamic world, including 22 unpublished recordings of Bin Laden himself as well as many other amateur recordings of conversations among top al-Qa'ida leaders, the collection offered an extraordinary record of the kinds of debates and leadership that informed al-Qa'ida's most coherent organizational momentum in the years leading to the attacks of 9/11. Of course, little was known about the content of the tapes at the time that we received two dusty boxes shipped to us from CNN's main regional office in Islamabad, Pakistan, in 2003. I was informed that the Central Intelligence Agency (CIA) and Federal Bureau of Investigation (FBI) had been informed of the collection while it was being held by CNN, and had declined stewardship.

While this puzzled me, I was told that the intelligence agencies had found the tapes to be of historical value only (and thus, presumably, not useful for investigating emerging security threats), an assertion that has been confirmed to date by the fact that I have found no tapes recorded after 2000. As an anthropologist only too aware of the ways such an archive might be selectively mined to confirm preestablished stereotypes, I felt that it was my responsibility to help make the tapes a resource for research collaboration across the widest possible fields of enquiry. First, a catalog was needed to summarize the contents of the tapes. Second, I needed to do what I could to contextualize them. Years of living in the Arab world and speaking Arabic, as well as being nearly finished with a book on audiocassette culture, tribalism, and Islam in Yemen, would certainly help. I would additionally need to conduct interviews and further fieldwork with people familiar with the tapes, preferably those with experience in the Afghan Arab movement, especially its incarnation in Kandahar over the years when the cassette collection was assembled.

I looked forward to bringing my anthropological training to public debates about al-Qa'ida, Bin Laden, and Muslim militants that so often veered into groundless speculation and outright misinformation. During fieldwork in Yemen in the 1990s, I had interviewed militants and Afghan Arab returnees, witnessed a militant attack on villagers with whom I had been working, and written about the ways transnational militant movements struggled to tailor their objectives to local cultural contexts. As I took tapes from the two cardboard boxes that had arrived at Williams College, I was daunted at the prospect of making sense of the tapes. At the same time, I wondered about the provenance of the materials that I was working on, well aware of the tendentious nature of document acquisition in contexts of war, state transformation, and population displacement.

CNN had acquired the tapes as the Taliban, Afghanistan's former state authority, was being driven from its final strongholds in the country's peripheries. Although a former Afghan governor of Kandahar had filled in the power vacuum along with regional tribal leaders, and had given license to CNN to operate in the area, a provisional national government had yet to be established. More broadly, the United States' invasion of Afghanistan on October 7, 2001, was announced by the Executive Branch and authorized by Congress, but had not been subject to approval by the institutions and procedures of international law. Although the United Nations (UN) Security Council had passed several resolutions acknowledging the seriousness of the 9/11 attacks and the right of nations to defend themselves, it made no recourse to sanctioning the use of force under Chapter VII of the UN Charter (al-Na'im 2002:168). Such unilateral military action was not the first time the United States had ignored judgments of the International Court of Justice in the interests of invading countries and capturing its leaders in pursuit of its own claims to justice (e.g., Panama in the early 1980s). In light of these complicating factors, should I have left the tapes in their boxes and directed my attention to another research project? Given Bin Laden's terrorist record and public demands for 9/11 accountability, I knew that the tapes would not be returned to their former owner, and Williams College's purchase of the collection from CNN assured their long-term status as a credible research archive in the United States. Should I have left the documentation and research to someone else? In the contexts of a global "War on Terror" that is centrally engaged in producing new knowledge and facts, are there safe zones for researchers?

In acknowledging the urgency with which I committed myself to working on the tapes, I find myself implicated in systems of knowledge production that can only be described as nonscholarly, politically motivated, morally ambivalent, and at times illegal. As a result of such implication, I take continuous measures to explain my goals and associations, whether for academic colleagues in my own discipline and others, for my students, or for informants. To preserve my neutrality, as much as possible, I have refused funding from intelligence and security institutions, instead seeking research support from academic and scholarly communities. I welcome these opportunities to preserve a neutral ground for my research, not simply for my own professional objectives but for working collaboratively with others in thinking about complicity in knowledge production whose benefits are unequally distributed.

Devoid of specific case studies, questions of complicity are, of course, extremely abstract. At their broadest level, they involve acknowledging that as a tax-paying citizen, one's labor provides revenues for government expenditures on policies that one may profoundly disagree with. We may be tempted to absolve ourselves of responsibility for such complicity, arguing that we were presented a "forced hand" and cannot choose simply not to pay taxes. However, deferring questions of complicity to matters of choice is hardly more satisfactory, given our status as subjects to culture, ideology, and systems of knowledge production that lie quite beyond our own influence. My own struggle to practice ethical anthropology while remaining alert to hierarchies of knowledge that structure complicity is perhaps best illustrated with regards the issue of "disclosure" that is so central to the ethics of our discipline. First, some fieldwork details are in order.

In seeking to contextualize the audiotapes, I conducted a fieldwork trip to Doha, Qatar, to interview the students of a Muslim jurisprudent named 'Abd al-Rahim al-Tahhan, whose work was well represented in the collection.

By some accounts, the shaikh was a leading thinker for militants interested in combating the West. One prominent al-Qa'ida figure, for example, had recommended to students who were interested in affairs on the Arabian Peninsula and the growing strength of the Afghan Arab movement that they begin "listening to the lectures and recordings of the symbols of the Awakening in the Land of the Two Holy Sanctuaries [i.e., Saudi Arabia] that were published between 1980 and 1995. They contain outstanding material on creed and legal learning and jihadi movement ideology, especially the tapes of Shaikh 'Abd al-Rahim al-Tahhan ..." (al-Suri 2006). By other accounts, however, the shaikh was a celebrated "quietist" who privileged doctrinal and spiritual issues over political organization and action.

One of the challenges I faced in approaching the shaikh's students was deciding how to present my research in ways that could lead to productive dialogue rather than to immediate suspicion and a foreclosure of exploratory questions by the students as well as myself. I knew that I couldn't simply begin by citing his importance to notorious Muslim militants or by identifying the significance of the shaikh in Osama Bin Laden's former cassette collection. Not only would such an approach likely offend the students, it would also privilege the relevance of extremely marginalized militant voices in ways that could only distort a fuller consideration of the significance of the shaikh's work and life for wider groups of people. The purpose of fieldwork is surely to facilitate such considerations, not foreclose them. While I welcomed the possibility of broaching the Bin Laden connection with the students, and ideally discussing how the shaikh's work might have ended up in the collection, I needed to begin with a less alarmist set of introductions to my broader research goals, my professional qualifications, and my own worldview and background. I needed, in other words, a graduated strategy for "disclosure."

The AAA's Code of Ethics states that "researchers must be open about the purpose(s), potential impacts, and source(s) of support for research projects with funders, colleagues, and persons studied or providing information, and with relevant parties affected by the research." Such a statement provided me with important general guidance, and I was ready to discuss matters of potential impact and sources of support with all specified parties. I was less certain, however, about the ethics of my strategy of disclosing the "purpose(s)...for research projects with...persons studied or providing information." I couldn't deny, for example, that the American Council of Learned Societies (ACLS), which was funding my fieldwork, had likely sponsored my research because of its "purpose" to help people better understanding terrorism and support efforts to achieve greater security for individuals affected by it, foremost among them American citizens. Wasn't this one of the most important objectives of my research project, both for myself and for my funders? How could I fail to acknowledge this in my opening presentation to potential informants?

I decided that my project needed framing. Although I had received funding from the ACLS for a project titled "The Osama Bin Laden Audiotape Library: Echoes of Legality," this title poorly conveyed the specific reasons that I had decided to study the Qatar-based jurisprudent's works and interview his students. I was specifically interested in the shaikh's lectures on asceticism or self-abnegation (*al-zuhd*), a topic that, according to Internet-based newspapers I had read, seemed to distinguish his work from other jurisprudents. In the many cassettes of his that I had heard, I found his discussions of the topic fascinating primarily because although they delved into themes of worldly renunciation and redemptive suffering that other scholars of religious militancy had found central to militant discourse, he discussed them in ways that greatly cautioned against militancy and outward political action, and instead privileged an inward focus on disciplining the self in ways that could just as easily appeal to pacifists. The shaikh's subtle distinctions in discussions of asceticism led to just the kind of complexities that an anthropologist would find productive for revisiting stereotypes of dogmatic militant ideologues. For this reason, I drafted a new title for my fieldwork project in Doha: "Asceticism (*al-zuhd*) in Muslim Reform through the Works of Shaikh 'Abd al-Rahim al-Tahhan." Furthermore, to solicit support for the ethics of my decision, I submitted an application to the Institutional Review Board (IRB) at my university, even though the ACLS had not required me to do so. The IRB could help me decide whether or not my project preserved the rights and protection of human subjects who might be involved in my study.

A month later, the IRB gave me clearance for my project. I immediately contacted students of the shaikh by email to set up appointments during my stay in Doha, attaching an Arabic summary of my research project with my email. Several students agreed to meet with me, although they wanted all interview questions written out in advance. I readily obliged, and the theme of asceticism in the shaikh's works seemed amenable. Two weeks later, I found myself walking through a park in Doha with two long-time disciples of the shaikh, introducing myself and discussing my research project with them in ways that I hoped would elicit further discussions and a formal tape-recorded interview, following the procedures outlined in my IRB proposal.

I began introducing my research project to the students by talking about my life history and interests. When focusing on the reasons for my visit to Doha and interest in the shaikh's life, I began with a general observation that, since the earliest days of my youth, I had always sought to understand the perspectives of the weak and oppressed, hoping that by doing so I could help improve their lives. I backed up this assertion with evidence of publications I had written on this topic, all of which focused on Muslims, and with discussions of my goals as a teacher. In moving to a discussion of my interest in the shaikh in particular, I ventured to suggest that, from what I had heard of the shaikh's sermons, he was an even more committed defender of the rights of the oppressed, though he worked within a tradition of Islam with which I, raised as a Christian, was not as familiar. Hoping to convey my appreciation of the shaikh's relevance to political activists, I added that he often seemed impassionate about corruption and hypocrisy in particular, including in which the ways the West, including the United States, had exacerbated modern Qataris' sense that the world's moral and spiritual orders were capitulating to material and economic power. When the students asked how I had first learned about the shaikh, I explained that I had first encountered his lectures on audiocassettes that had surfaced in the United States, some of which had come from collections of tapes found in Afghanistan (and others I had accessed from the Internet). The students seemed pleased to hear that the shaikh's lectures were circulating widely, and asked no further questions. Our discussion turned to the particulars of asceticism, the details of which occupied us for several hours until my departure. Although we left on amicable terms, they stated that further discussions needed to be conducted via email or phone only. No responses were returned, however, when I tried those channels in subsequent days. No further contact with the students occurred.

Although my interview was short, I gained insight into the broader political and cultural significance of the shaikh's work for the students. When combined with informal interviews I held with others in Doha about the shaikh's work and influence, I was able to assemble a slightly better ethnographic account of the social and cultural contexts that informed the shaikh's work than I had had before my visit. My research in Doha helped me write about the some of the disjunctions between stereotypes of Muslim violence, militancy, and terrorism and lived practice. I wondered about whether slightly *less* disclosure with the students could have resulted in further meetings, discussions, and mutually beneficial dialogue. From discussions I've had with anthropologist colleagues throughout my career, I've heard the refrain "less is more." In the interests of fitting in and more productive participant observation, an anthropologist should disclose information about themselves and their larger research goals only with tact and diplomacy even as ethical standards toward the protection of human subjects are firmly maintained. I have wondered about such reserve, however, when studying people whose work or lives might even loosely be associated with "terrorism" by Western governments, intelligence networks, and media institutions. In recent years, charges of "ideological support" for terrorists bear a heavy burden in the West, especially when combined with "material support," even in the form of monetary contributions to charities which, although originally considered strictly welfare oriented, are later determined to have channeled revenues to terrorist organizations. If one's work suggests any link between given informants and terrorists or terrorist organizations, even if these links are already known to intelligence agencies, must one "disclose"? If not, just how much, and how quickly, does one "disclose?"

Editorial Commentary

We were fascinated by the extent of thought and consideration that Miller brought to the seemingly straightforward project of translating and studying a set of audiocassettes. His contribution illustrates the complexity of intersections among anthropologists, our research, policy- and decision-making, and national security concerns. Miller explicitly rejects direct funding from government agencies with a stake in preventing terrorism or countering insurgency. But as he demonstrates, it is impossible to pursue research on the salient topics of Islam, identity, and violence without engaging national security concerns, if obliquely.

Some of this is due to the perceived relevance of social science methodologies for national security decision-making. In this regard, Miller's work reminded us of the wholesale embrace of social network analysis among many national security experts studying, chasing, and prosecuting terrorist groups. Even before the 9/11 attacks, and well before the military's Human Terrain Systems and Minerva initiatives exploded as topics of scholarly political debate, many institutions in the national security community were exploring social network analysis as a practical method for tracing interactions among suspected terrorists. The "network" has emerged as the dominant metaphor for making sense of and even predicting the dynamics of the post–Cold War world, and marks a significant shift away from the nation-state paradigm that structured twentieth-century international relations and political science discourse. As a result, many institutions in the securityscape are recruiting social scientists with expertise in social network analysis to provide methods and computational tools for mapping the interactions among persons and groups who may be active in insurgency or terrorism activities (see Bohannon 2009; Keefe 2006).

Into this space, enter Miller's research, which reveals ideological connections between the al-Qa'ida conversations and a Muslim scholar in Yemen. As he points out at the beginning of the essay, social scientists working with Muslim groups or studying Islam have long struggled to explain the benefits of their work for these communities. In the wake of the 9/11 attacks, many anthropologists were frustrated at the stereotypes circulating in public discourse about Islam in general and young Muslim men in particular. Miller perceived an opportunity to challenge some of these stereotypes by studying a collection of al-Qa'ida documents and audio recordings captured in Afghanistan in late 2001 and released to the media. Not only does he have the linguistic and historical knowledge required to catalog and summarize the tapes, but his previous fieldwork on the culture of audiocassette recordings in Yemen uniquely positions him to contextualize and make sense of the exchanges recorded on the cassettes.

Miller recognizes that he has developed a project with tremendous scholarly, political, and even moral importance. As he points out, a number of well-funded private contractors and semiprivate think tanks, many with no expertise at all in Arab language, culture, or religious history, have begun producing enormous amounts of information about Islam, the Middle East, and terrorism. He sees an opportunity for an experienced researcher to challenge a rapidly crystallizing discourse about the relationship between Islam and the West using primary source material on al-Qa'ida. Indeed, in some ways, Miller's project is similar to Schoch-Spana's: to use research in the spirit of cultural critique, to use alternative narratives to challenge dominant discourse and stereotypes about the social and cultural worlds imagined by decision makers.

Almost immediately, however, the project is fraught: for one thing, Miller is troubled by the fact that the tapes were captured in the invasion of Afghanistan, which despite massive political support was never officially sanctioned by the UN. His research can be set against the background of recent public controversies over the provenance and ownership of potentially valuable research archives composed of information removed from countries during wars, as with the arguments over the legitimacy of the Iraqi Perspectives Project (see Eskander 2008). As with Rush's essay, Miller's project, as an anthropological intervention, is informed by the changing geopolitics of what is permissible and possible, associated with international concepts of ownership and of patrimony.

Moreover, he realizes that fully contextualizing the conversations he is studying will require additional fieldwork in Qatar with Shaikh 'Abd al-Rahim al-Tahhan, whose thinking seems to have influenced the positioning of some al-Qa'ida followers vis-à-vis the West. These challenges lead Miller to reflect on his own position as a taxpaying citizen of the United States, as a political actor, and as a scholar seeking to practice "ethical anthropology" in the most politically, legally, and ethically charged field of knowledge production today. Not only is he nervous about how to present himself and his research objectives to his potential participants so as not to offend them, but he recognizes that the very act of interviewing the shaikh and his students could quite easily reify a connection between the shaikh's students and al-Qa'ida for a national security community driven to discover and mitigate possible terrorist activity by connecting the dots.

Reading Miller's thoughts on his decision-making, we were struck by his careful consideration of the AAA's Code of Ethics and the decision to engage his IRB as sources of guidance for a fraught research project.

Most anthropologists complain vociferously about the poor fit between ethnographic research practice and IRB rules and regulations, which are primarily grounded in biomedical research models. Moreover, the AAA's Code is a constant object of political debate and discussion within the Association, as people argue over whether its guidance is worded strongly enough, whether the AAA should become a sanctioning organization, and how the incorporation of stronger language and/or an AAA sanctioning process might affect the field and the Association. In contrast, in Miller's discussion, we see him as less concerned about the political positioning of the Code and more interested in the guidance it might provide to inform a complicated decision-making processes. We had the sense that he found the general guidance about disclosure ethically helpful but methodologically troubling, given the goals of his funding agency and the possible implications of his work for raising the interest of the national security community in the activities of the shaikh he decides to study. Moreover, we were struck that he looked to his IRB for additional guidance and assistance, absent any requirement to do so. We are aware of several anthropologists working in the national security arena who also actively seek IRB assistance as a way of invoking formal institutional and legal protections for their research participants.

In this regard, we wondered how Miller presented the project to his IRB and how its members received this project: were they as aware of, or troubled by, the dynamics that Miller was grappling with? The questions raised by the IRB might indicate the extent to which its members understood the nuances of Miller's project. Moreover, given the complexities of this work, we commented that an IRB would have to be fairly sophisticated to provide guidance that Miller could actually implement. We wondered if they were sympathetic to his concerns. Moreover, it would be interesting to know if his IRB was aware of the ethical codes that govern anthropology in the United States (we are thinking here of the AAA and the Society for Applied Anthropology), and if any of the IRB's guidance was drawn from the ethical code of Miller's core discipline.

In the end, it seems as though the research participants in Doha may have protected themselves, perhaps due to Miller's explanation of his work, but perhaps also because they are aware of the extent of U.S. activities to monitor activities defined in terms of "radicalization" or "terrorism." We were particularly struck by the limitations that the students put on Miller's interactions with them: email or telephone contact only, please; and as the contributor acknowledges, his efforts to interact through those channels were ultimately unsuccessful. We wondered if this signaled that the students were as aware of the fraught context of this research as Miller was, and were exercising their agency to mitigate the consequences of his curiosity for themselves. We also wondered if Miller had ever been contacted by any government agency as his work has progressed: although the CIA seems to have dismissed the tapes as irrelevant to their current intelligence pursuits, Miller's work with these materials demonstrates their value in ways that might heighten interest among military, intelligence, or criminal justice professionals trying to make sense of the fields of meaning that nascent terrorist or radicalization movements draw upon as they form particular ideologies.

Miller Response

A discussion of graduated disclosure was not included in my original application for IRB approval largely because I had not yet formalized my thoughts about the concept. As a result, I was unable to assess the extent to which reviewers were aware of the AAA's Code of Ethics. Looking ahead to future interaction with the IRB, I must admit some hesitation at the prospect of introducing the method in my application. As paraphrased by editors of this volume, graduated disclosure opens inquiry into "the ways disclosure is in significant degree a product of the negotiation of the circumstances of research rather than a clearly defined—and separate—ethical responsibility prior to research." Given the IRB's investment in formalizing the parameters of human subject protection in advance of conducting research, I wonder whether the concept of graduated disclosure would be interpreted to license research conducted under false pretenses. I also wonder about the extent to which the concept would be seen as antithetical to an independent ethical review board's commitment to keeping regulation, monitoring, and compliance within its own institutional purview. Would the possibility of contextually negotiated ethical obligations introduce doubts about my "good faith" and my loyalty to the standards of a scientific community?

From IRB responses to my application, I sense that methods approximating "graduated disclosure" raise red flags among reviewers who are trained to remain vigilant in monitoring possible lapses in procedures for selecting, recruiting, and protecting human subjects. Before submitting my IRB application, I had sent an email to the Qatar Foundation, a state institution supervising education, community development, and international scientific collaboration, to inquire whether any contacts might be established with Shaikh al-Tahhan or any of his students. After being sent the names, email addresses, and telephone numbers of individuals, I sent one of them an email in which I attached an Arabic-language description of my research and again asked about the possibility of establishing "contact" (*ittisal*) with any of al-Tahhan's students. For the sake of discretion, my email did not imply that the recipient might be included among these "students," leaving open the possibility for a helpful response without self-identification as a potential research subject. Although I had not yet received a reply from the recipient (this came later and only indirectly from the Qatar Foundation, which informed me that the students were interested in hearing more about my research and that I should call them once I arrived in the country), I did mention the email and my hopes for subsequent telephone follow-up in my application. I received the following response from the IRB: "The investigator states that he has begun recruitment through email, although the study has not been reviewed or approved by the IRB. This contact with potential study volunteers should not occur until the IRB approval is obtained. The investigator should provide a statement to the IRB explaining what recruitment activities he has initiated prior to approval." After English and Arabic texts documenting my email exchanges were provided, the IRB concluded that I had not violated procedures for subject recruitment.

The IRB's only other response focused on a section of my Description of Study in which I explained my procedures for protecting subject privacy and confidentiality. Although I had been meticulous, I was asked to include the phrase "there is the possibility, though unlikely, of a breach of confidentiality" just to be sure that all bases were covered. I assume this statement addressed potential incidents involving extraordinary legal or illegal data exposure, whether through human error or unexpected third-party intervention (e.g., computer theft, a court subpoena, and so forth). In sum, the IRB's most significant concern about my application focused on whether my disclosure of research goals had been overly hasty and in violation of their institutional standards. The graduation of disclosure, it seems, struck reviewers as an ambiguous exercise that was best not left to the discretion of researchers themselves.

The central epistemological question that arises in the notion of graduated disclosure seems to be: when does "the study" begin? It is a venerable and challenging question for anthropologists. For the IRB reviewers, my mention of "contact" (*ittisal*) had precipitated suspicions that I might have already violated procedures for protecting human subjects. The concept of graduated disclosure, however, is premised on histories of contact that far precede the "first encounter" between an abstract researcher and the subject. As discussed in my case study, my identity and goals as an American researcher were heavily mediated before I had even begun my research project on Shaikh al-Tahhan. Implicated in American-led War on Terror discourse that had complex institutional histories in Qatar, I had to begin research inquiries both by acknowledging my implication in these discourses—I was, after all, an American university professor seeking to learn about al-Tahhan's ascetic virtues in a world of clashing ideologies and political projects—and also by signaling my estrangement from the usual procedures of knowledge production. My initial emails made no mention of the universal legal rights of human subjects or the protections afforded by my selection, recruitment, and data-management procedures. I didn't even mention the word "interview" (*muqabala*), aware that this possibility might elicit anxieties about accountability and a prematurely negative response. These details, I sensed, were best postponed until some measure of trust could be established.

Postponing some of the heavier discourse about legal rights and obligations seemed to me appropriate protocol when introducing oneself in the Arab world. The question again arose, however, about when exactly "the study," as I had conceived it through assistance from an ethical review board, would begin. At what point would I decide that the exigencies of an ethical social science would trump those of cultural decorum? When would I present my carefully drafted Bill of Rights and Consent Form and document informants' signatures? In my application, I had explained that these procedures would take place just before setting up a formal "interview." With the goal of preserving the confidentiality of Shaikh al-Tahhan and his students, I had stated that "I will meet with them in a private location of their choosing and will record their responses to my interview questions." When I ultimately met with the students in Doha, my documents and tape recorder with me in the unlikely event of progressing to a formal interview, I was led not to a "private location" but rather to a very public café in the gardens of the city's busiest shopping mall. Reflecting back on this meeting, I wonder: in a part of the world where boundaries between private and public can be highly contextual and vary depending on who enters the room, could the ideal private setting ever have been realized? At a more general level, might not a tendency toward "compromised" interview conditions justify repeated postponement of awkward discussions about legal rights, obligations and recording procedures? After all, as any ethnographer knows, some of the most valuable insights are gathered before the onset of a formal interview.

My own ethical commitments, formulated in collaboration with the IRB, led me to be wary of excessive postponement, however expedient it might have been. Some measure of postponement, however, seems in retrospect to have been not simply culturally appropriate but ethically responsible. The protection of human subjects in this case arguably required deferring my protocols for sound scientific research in the interests of granting informants the space, time, and flexibility to establish more culturally attuned parameters for enhancing their security. Had I initially approached al-Tahhan's students with a research proposal laden with discourse on legal rights and obligations, they would have been less likely to meet with me given implications that a more advanced level of collaboration was expected. It is to be noted that my email to them, and their own responses to me, were mediated by the Qatar Foundation, a major state institution that closely monitors the activities and commitments of Qataris. I am quite confident that my research project description signaled well enough that I was trying to grapple with the controversial legacy of the shaikh. By keeping initial formalities to a minimum, I allowed them greater latitude for diplomacy: they could respond in an accommodating way, agreeing simply to hear more about my research project, but could avoid signaling collaboration with foreign researchers in broadcasting the views of a figure whose publications, recordings, and public life have been severely censored. Through this culturally attuned approach, they were able to negotiate a meeting with me, representing their shaikh to an American researcher in the best possible light, while also securing a legitimate exemption from further obligations. In my meeting, I found the students to be extremely cordial and encouraging of my efforts to understand their shaikh's work. In many ways, I sensed that our encounter was nothing new; they had become well versed in publicly managing their shaikh's legacy with eloquence, sincerity, and good humor. For my part, I am now obligated to write, speak, and theorize an encounter with students who valued al-Tahhan's work for promoting virtues of nonviolence and social justice, whatever may be said of his associations with Bin Ladin's former audiocassette collection.

My discussions with other specialists and professionals about "graduated disclosure," while not phrased exactly in this way, have been various. Government intelligence and security agencies have indeed contacted me. The FBI, for example, asked me to collaborate in a diachronic study of statements by Osama Bin Laden and Ayman al-Zawahiri. In explaining why I had to decline such work, I referred to the AAA's Code of Ethics and elaborated on the importance of full disclosure when building trust among informants in the Arab world. The FBI official whom I spoke with fully appreciated how my efforts in this respect would be compromised by acknowledging collaboration with his own organization. Conferences on intelligence matters involving a range of government and nongovernment participants have been mixed; the most successful of them have been managed by scholars with areal expertise who can help open debates to a wider range of critical and cultural perspectives and resist the drive toward consensus on the merits of Western policy objectives.

My conversations with other anthropologists about graduated disclosure mostly arose when initially inquiring whether I should go through the effort to submit a voluntary application for IRB clearance. Although responses were somewhat predictably bureaucratic, the rationales defending the value of seeking IRB approval were interesting and fall into three types. The first type was the largely self-interested "just to be safe" variety: getting IRB approval is one of the many precautions one should take to prevent one's research from being discredited or its quality compromised. In this response, the safety and protection of informants was implicit while not foregrounded. The second rationale was of the "pretend to be a good citizen" variety: getting IRB approval is tedious and painful, but once you have it you can do whatever you see fit in the field. Rather than a cynical gesture to anarchy (indeed the person who voiced this rationale was herself profoundly interested in questions of citizenship!), I found this rationale to imply that anthropologists have a higher and more refined set of ethical guidelines when conducting fieldwork that are not addressed in the IRB process. Exactly what these guidelines are was left undiscussed. The final rationale was of the "here's how to make the application easier" variety, and focused helpfully on how to justify securing oral rather than written consent. This response was from an anthropologist who taught seminars on applying for IRB approval. Ultimately, it seems to me that deeper and more encompassing discussions are needed about the ethics of culturally situated procedures for building trust.

References

al-Na'im, Abdallah

2002 Upholding International Legality against Islamic and American Jihad. *In* Worlds in Collision: Terror and the Future of the Global Order, K. Booth and T. Dunne, eds. Pp. 162–171. New York: Palgrave Macmillan.

al-Suri, Abu Mus'ab

2006 Da'walla al-Muqawamaal_islamiyya al-Alamiyya. Available at http://www.megaupload.com/?d=D1Q8JDR1. Accessed August 2009.

Bohannon, John

2009 Counterterrorism's New Tool: Metanetwork Analysis. *Science* 25:409–411.

Eskander, Saad

2008 Minerva Research Initiative: Searching for the Truth or Denying the Iṛaqis the Rights to Know the Truth? SSRC Forum on the Minerva Controversy. Available at: http://essays.ssrc.org/minerva/2008/10/29/eskander/. Accessed August 16, 2011.

Keefe, Patrick Raddon

2006 Can Network Theory Thwart Terrorists? New York Times, March 12. Available at http://www.nytimes.com/2006/03/12/magazine/312wwln_essay.html?scp=1&sq=Can+Network+Theory+Thwart+Terrorists&st=nyt. Accessed June 1, 2010.

Miller, Flagg

2007 The Moral Resonance of Arab Media: Audiocassette Poetry and Culture in Yemen. Cambridge, MA: Harvard University Press.

2008 Al-Qa'ida as a 'Pragmatic Base': Contributions of Area Studies to Sociolinguistics. *Language and Communication* 28(4):386–408.

13

Ethical Considerations from the Study of Peacekeeping

Robert A. Rubinstein

Robert Rubinstein, a senior figure in anthropology, has developed a reputation for his equanimity and broadmindedness as it bears on the discipline's debates about and engagements with the national security sector. Such a disposition mirrors the work environments and research subjects to which he has dedicated himself. Rubinstein is a Professor of Anthropology and International Relations at Syracuse University's Maxwell School of Citizenship and Public Affairs. Situated in an interdisciplinary academic setting that values and probes the interconnections among theory, policy, and practice, Rubinstein is skilled at and invested in listening to people who come from diverse perspectives. His work as a political anthropologist has focused on cross-cultural dimensions of conflict and dispute resolution, including negotiation, mediation, and consensus building. Since 1985, Rubinstein has conducted empirical research and policy studies on peacekeeping, examining how the success of peace operations hinges upon cultural considerations, including organizational biases.

Rubinstein is enmeshed in the complex relationship between anthropology and the military on a number of fronts. Certainly, military institutions and personnel are key players in his ethnographic inquiries, and he is keenly interested in understanding how these actors work. And, as his essay suggests, he believes that casting an anthropological lens on the armed forces obliges the ethnographer to put aside any preheld essentialist or totalizing assumptions. Rubinstein is a trusted mentor to young anthropologists working in the military, an advocate for anthropologists pursuing nontraditional careers in national security, and a "matchmaker" among anthropologists working at the military-anthropology frontier. His ties to the editors and contributors to this volume are many and varied. Finally, Rubinstein has emerged as an interlocutor not known to be dogmatic in public anthropological debates about security sector engagements, showing a preference instead for continued dialogue.

Rubinstein received his Ph.D. in anthropology from the State University of New York at Binghamton in 1997, and a master's degree in public health from the University of Illinois at Chicago in 1983. His field research has included work in Egypt, Belize, Mexico, and the United States, and it has entailed pursuits as both a political and a medical anthropologist. Rubinstein has addressed issues of conflict and health as well as disparities in access to health care. He has collaborated with a variety of agencies and institutes on the policy implications of his work, including the United Nations (UN) Department of Peacekeeping Operations, the U.S. Army Peacekeeping Institute, the Georgia Department of Physical Health, and the Onondaga County Health Department. His most recent books are Peacekeeping under Fire: Culture and Intervention *(Rubinstein 2008) and* Building Peace: Practical Reflections from the Field *(Zelizer and Rubinstein 2009).*

In this essay, Rubinstein offers four vignettes illustrating the kinds of research dilemmas he encountered during his first fieldwork experience among UN peacekeeping forces. In doing so, he asks us to consider if fieldwork among military, intelligence, or other institutions in the securityscape presents exceptional ethical challenges, or if we attach special meaning to these sites because they represent particularly concentrated expressions of state power.

When I decided to begin my ethnographic research on peacekeeping in the mid-1980s, I was associated with the Department of Anthropology at Northwestern University. I had been a postdoctoral fellow and interim director of the Northwestern Program on Ethnography and Public Policy. So, a project focused on the international security community seemed a natural extension of that work and my interest in the anthropology of peace and conflict. I started out by attending meetings held under the auspices of the International Peace Academy, a nongovernmental organization that trained military officers and diplomats in peacekeeping. As I've described (Rubinstein 2008), this made it possible for me to conduct ethnographic research among the members of the United Nations Truce Supervision Organization (UNTSO). When I began studying UN peacekeeping in the mid-1980s, it was still relatively rare for anthropologists to conduct ethnography among multilateral institutions, and even rarer for them to work with organizations that have a large military presence. Before I began my work on peacekeeping, I had done ethnographic research in a number of other settings. Those research projects include studying formal institutions like schools in Belize, state public health agencies in Georgia, and medical institutions in Chicago. Each of these settings had elements of what Laura Nader (1972) described as "studying up," that is, a focus on institutions and peoples who occupy positions of power within society. None of these projects, however, was as fully an example of studying up as my research on peacekeeping. In common with other anthropologists at the time, it was unclear to me what unique challenges fieldwork among institutions that could be considered "up" would pose.

As I began to plan for my peacekeeping research, I discussed it with colleagues in the three main institutional settings to which my professional network extended: Northwestern University, the University of Chicago, and the University of California, Berkeley. My colleagues in all of these places were supportive of my work, though they raised a number of issues to think about as I went forward. It seemed likely, for instance, that gaining access to conduct fieldwork would be especially difficult, since in studying up the venues for field research would involve entry into institutional spaces that are tightly controlled. In settings like peacekeeping missions, but also in other multilateral institutions or in government or in business, one's informants would be dealing with information considered classified or proprietary, and this might interfere with an ethnographer's ability to learn about and report on aspects of life important for filling out the ethnographic picture. That is, would the ethnographic enterprise be frustrated by the ways in which these institutions controlled access to areas of social life of interest to the ethnographer? Then there were questions about the day-to-day conduct of research in situations where ethnographers were studying up. Would, for example, interpersonal relationships with informants be different than those ethnographers had among the communities where they usually work? How would the ethnographer achieve a role and status within organizations where these were structured and controlled?

No one suggested that these questions would translate into challenges that could not be met, though we were all interested in seeing where the project would lead. Perhaps because peacekeeping was associated with the UN, the heavy involvement of militaries in the institution was not a topic of particular comment. This changed when in the 1990s I gave a paper at an American Anthropological Association (AAA) meeting in which I discussed the military officers who were associated with the UNTSO group I was studying. In that paper, I confessed to having my previous stereotypes about the military challenged, and noted that some of the military officers who were my informants had become good friends. Some of my colleagues, like Joan Ablon and Margaret Clark, expressed the view that this was a natural outcome of fieldwork, while others, like Marvin Harris, found my new views on these military officers challenging. A few colleagues, who were themselves studying or considering studying military institutions, expressed a fear that doing so would harm their academic careers. I do not know how my career would have been affected by concerns about anthropologists working on military topics, since at the time I did not hold a regular university appointment. I describe more fully my personal and professional reactions to this work elsewhere (Rubinstein 2011).

In what follows, I describe how my research was affected by considerations like those just outlined. I describe four vignettes that posed fieldwork dilemmas. Before describing these vignettes, it is useful to characterize one of the main "takeaway lessons" I derive from this experience: All of the concerns and dilemmas that I encountered in studying up—from the degree of difficulty gaining access to the research site, to the dilemmas surrounding exposure to proprietary knowledge, to questions of what to do when in the field I learned of something that would endanger the life or career of my informants—were things I encountered in more traditional anthropological research, though with obvious contextual differences.

Vignettes: Dilemmas in the Field

Gaining Access

To conduct this research, I had to get permission from several different sources, including the Institutional Review Board (IRB) from Northwestern University, with which I was then associated. As I've described elsewhere (Rubinstein 2008), the process of gaining access to study UNTSO required the approval of several levels of bureaucracy. I'd met the general then serving as Force Commander for UNTSO in a meeting in which I was participating. I explained my interest in studying peacekeeping and in using UNTSO, and especially Observer Group Egypt (OGE), as the site for that research.

After some months, by which time I was living in Egypt, the general called me to tell me that I had permission from the Secretariat to conduct my research. Armed with this permission from UN Headquarters, I found the administration at OGE was reserved yet receptive to my conducting my research among them. As it turned out, I also had to get permission from the national authorities to whom each of the contingents reported.

I began my research when the Soviet Union still existed. Tensions between the United States and the Soviet Union were not unusually high, but there seemed to be a mutual suspicion between the officers serving in each contingent. I learned that the Soviet Embassy would not permit its military officers to speak with me for my research unless they too approved my research plan. I therefore submitted my proposal and interview guide to the Soviet Embassy, and was interviewed myself by the Embassy's political officer. He explained to me that the Embassy was especially concerned that my presence would be a problem for their security. And they were concerned that I might become privy to information that I should not have. They asked for assurances about my work to convince them that this was a minimal risk. A few weeks later I received word that I had received their permission to conduct research among the Soviet members of the Observer Group.

Seemingly, the extended process that was required for me to gain access to UNTSO as a field site confirms fears that when studying up access would be a particular difficulty. On reflection it is clear that this difference in the degree of difficulty is more apparent than real, at least in my own experience. Similarly, my early studies in Belize (Rubinstein 1977, 1979) required the negotiation of access with a wide array of institutions, formal and informal, and the establishing of personal relationships before my work could go forward. These included gaining permission from the appropriate government ministries, from the local government, and from the schools in which I was to conduct research. In addition to these formal permissions, individual "gatekeepers"—people who had formal roles or were informally influential—had to be persuaded to permit me access. Access for my research in Belize took several months. This is an experience not uncommon among anthropologists pursuing "more traditional" ethnographic projects. Some of them have found that difficulties and delays in gaining access to their intended field sites have been insurmountable (Rubinstein 2008:59, 161).

Navigating Social Divisions in the Field

The colonel in charge of OGE informed me that I was welcome to conduct whatever research I wanted within certain logistical restrictions that would be placed on my work. I could have relatively free access to most areas of the Headquarters building, except for offices where security-sensitive materials were kept. I could even enter those areas when invited by the office occupants. In addition, although I was welcome to go to the observation posts (OPs) in the Sinai that were manned by the OGE observers, if they asked me to join them, I could not to travel in their vehicles to get to those posts. The colonel explained that the Secretariat did not want me to travel to the OPs in UN vehicles because they thought my doing so might provide a pretext for a diplomatic protest, and they didn't want to take on that risk.

After several months of conducting research in and around the headquarters of the Observer Group in Cairo, I began to be invited by officers to OPs they were to occupy for a week. I drove myself to these OPs and stayed with the officers there. Their responsibilities involved making regular patrols, during which one officer would remain at the OP's staffing communications. Once I was at the OP, some officers asked me to make their patrols with them. Recalling the concerns expressed about my traveling in UN vehicles to get to the OPs, I was reluctant to do that. Yet, patrolling was an important activity for the group that I was studying, and I knew that I could not fully understand them if I did not participate in those experiences. So, with the insistence of my officer informants, I made several patrols with officers from different national contingents. On some of those patrols we encountered minor problems, and I contributed to their resolution when asked to do so by my host.

Should I have acceded to the urgings of my informants that I join them on their patrols and to participate in their official duties? How ought a fieldworker balance the competing imperatives of institutions and informants who control access to the research site, and those created by other informants? Is there a single proper path in such situations?

These dilemmas are surely an aspect of studying up, and of working among military communities. But, they are not unique to these settings. For instance, as Daubenmier reports in her discussion of the fieldworkers' experiences during the Fox Project, many communities within which anthropologists conduct "traditional ethnography" contain divisions within them which the ethnographer must navigate, sometimes including differences in views expressed among those in formal authority and others (Daubenmier 2008).

Dangerous Practice

Spending the week together in the desert provides lots of time during which the observers were not actually conducting duties required of them. It is not unusual for military personnel to have long periods of time away from their duties. The observers filled this time by watching movies, cooking, reading novels, or listening to music. And they spent a considerable amount of time speaking to each other about their lives in general. When I was at the OPs, I participated in these "downtime" activities too.

One OP I visited was staffed for the week by a Soviet lieutenant colonel and a U.S. major. Their time at the OP was much like that I'd experienced elsewhere, with one exception. It turned out that as part of his professional military education, and in pursuit of a promotion, the U.S. officer was studying Soviet tactics by a kind of correspondence course. While I was at the OP, one evening after dinner, the Soviet colonel sat down and tutored the U.S. major about Soviet tactics, correcting information that was in the course. I was witnessing a two-way exchange of information, some of which was considered secret by the respective national services.

From one perspective, this was a remarkable development, a testament to the pacific work of the UN. The potential of building bridges among potential adversaries was certainly a subtext of peacekeeping. Yet, what I was witnessing would be deeply disturbing to the authorities who made my research possible. Was there a moral or ethical responsibility to intervene in this practice?

During fieldwork among military communities, and in other settings when studying up, the ethnographer may encounter practices the reporting of which would place their informant in some sort of personal danger, physical or otherwise. These may be of the kind I describe here, or they may be matters of life and death. The ethnographer must then decide what, if anything, to do about his or her knowledge of such activities.

Because I found these instances intriguing and informative, I saw them as opportunities for better understanding the social world I was observing and experiencing. As an operating principle, I would discuss my observations with those whom they concerned. Thus, I commented to the Soviet and American officers that I found the mutual tutoring in the "enemy's tactics" to be both interesting and problematic, and I elicited their own views on the practice. Both officers told me that they thought that such an exchange was one of the real benefits of multilateral peacekeeping; it built bridges between those who would otherwise be adversaries. Yet, they asked me not to tell what I had seen, since it potentially put them at risk with their own militaries. I respected this request, and did not speak or publish about this observation until and unless I was sure that in so doing the observation could not be traced back to specific individuals.

Again, however, encountering such a dilemma is not unique to studying up. Indeed, dilemmas such as these have been reported in the "traditional ethnographic" literature. Polsky (1967), for example, encountered these dilemmas when studying people he calls "hustlers, beats and others," groups who are decidedly *not* "up," in Nader's sense, who engage in illegal activities dangerous to themselves or others. Likewise, Humphrey confronts similar dilemmas in his study of "impersonal sex in public places" (Humphrey 1975).

Sacred Knowledge

One afternoon back at Headquarters, one of the civilian field staff who worked with Observer Group's communications invited me to his office. He was clearly agitated. He began to explain that he was exasperated by the behavior of some of the officers. He began to describe how they did not seem to understand how to use the coded communications. Apparently, these officers were broadcasting code keys, which were supposed to be closely held. To help me understand the point he was making, in the natural course of conversation, he showed me the codes and explained their functioning. Although this was information to which I was surely not supposed to be privy, this communications staff member "opened the books" to me. Although this validated in some way that I had achieved a deep rapport and place in the community, it also violated the trust upon which my activities were premised. What kind of action, if any, should I have taken?

Ethnographers who are studying up are bound to find themselves privy to information that they should not know. Yet, this, too, is a phenomenon not uncommon for ethnographers in more "traditional ethnographic" settings. In fieldwork, ethnographers develop deeply personal relationships with other people. Sometimes the intimacy of fieldwork leads informants to reveal to the ethnographer what they might not tell to other outsiders. The ethnographer must then decide how to respond to these revelations. Again, these dilemmas are not unique to those studying up. Turnbull, in his ethnography *The Forest People,* describes the dilemmas that arise for him when he is given access to sacred knowledge by his informants (Turnbull 1968).

Conclusion

In considering the challenges of studying up, Gusterson (1997:116) suggested that anthropologists may well have "to abandon, or at least subordinate, the research technique [participant-observation] that has defined anthropology as a discipline." Yet, rather than being a different kind of practice requiring distinct methodological and ethical principles, studying up has deep resonances with anthropology's extant research practices. Because of these resonances, it is in my opinion important to understand the dilemmas encountered in studying up in the context of the full range of anthropological research, rather than treating them as a special case.

Editorial Commentary

Rubinstein relates some of the practical, social, and ethical dilemmas he faced when conducting ethnographic research among UN peacekeepers (the UNTSO) stationed along the Egyptian-Israeli border. He describes his research as a variant of Laura Nader's "studying up" (1972), with a focus on the "institutions and peoples who occupy positions of power within society." With their bureaucracies, legal frameworks, gatekeepers, public representatives, and hard-to-access information hierarchies, such organizations can thwart the fieldworker's typical mode of inquiry. This is especially the case, we are told, where the traditional expectations of participation-observation are suspended and the power relationships of researcher and subject are potentially reversed.

As such, Rubinstein wonders to what extent ethnography might be possible, and whether traditional research strategies and concerns aren't fundamentally upset in such contexts. Rubinstein's main concern is access: what this looks like, how it is negotiated, and whether it might be a different affair in the mode of "studying up." He describes negotiating access in terms of his extended formal and informal interaction and intercession both with institutions and people prior to and during "fieldwork" proper: the university IRB, UN Headquarters, OGE administration, the Soviet Embassy, UNTSO Force Commander, OGE leader, and OGE officers from different national contingents, and so on. Perhaps surprisingly, he concludes that for his UNTSO research, the problem of negotiating access had "deep resonances" with widely recognized ethnographic practice. So, too, did other dilemmas he encountered in the field, such as being exposed to knowledge reserved only for select insiders and having to weigh conflicting loyalties to informants across the social hierarchy.

We appreciate that what Rubinstein is doing for "studying up" at least in part—to paraphrase Bourdieu—is to make the exotic mundane and the mundane exotic. Whereas the signature disciplinary method of at least sociocultural anthropology—ethnography—has been regularly debated and updated for our times (e.g., the erosion of "place," multisited, as a polymorphous engagement), Rubinstein reminds us that this method can still be effectively employed with nontraditional subjects like the military personnel populating multilateral humanitarian efforts. "Studying up," goes the suggestion, is not atypical but in fact more like "traditional ethnography" than it is different: we are so focused on studying up as a special case that perhaps we forget that the challenges these projects present are part of "normal" field practice, wherever we are.

Moreover, we suggest that whether intentional or not, a distinction between studying up and traditional ethnography is, in other ways, undermined throughout the essay even as Rubinstein regularly invokes it. The vignette about the Soviet officer sharing information about Soviet military tactics with a U.S. officer is a compelling instance. Rubinstein worries that disclosing these kinds of exchanges could jeopardize not only the personal careers of the men involved, but also the willingness on the part of governments to participate in multinational institutions such as peacekeeping operations and the UN. Rubinstein is quite aware of the complex ethical dilemmas involving access to classified information in this context. Rubinstein also mentions an extensive IRB process, one that has additional layers to it in ways that heighten the evident differences between the people and institutions with which he is engaged and what we might imagine as Malinowskian-style traditional ethnography. His careful due diligence is in a sense in tension with his own description of what he is doing as typical ethnography. The questions: what, then, is particular—if anything—to studying up? And what is the extent of flexibility of ethnography as a method?

This unspoken tension between Rubinstein's characterization of ethnography among "up" institutions and individuals as both the same and as different from "traditional" subjects is revealed again when he talks about information to which he is not privy as "sacred knowledge." This is an interesting and important moment. One of the themes that runs through the cases in this volume is people's differing relationships to information and to sources of knowledge production as specifically marked for security contexts. Rubinstein casts this as like when ethnographers encounter the "sacred": in his case, the "secret"—clandestine, classified—is compared to the "sacred." This moment reminds us of the routine fact of secrecy in fieldwork at the same time that it equates one highly politically charged notion of secrecy (at least for anthropology) with "garden variety" ethnographic forms of secrecy. In Rubinstein's case, this is all part of gaining access and rapport among this community of peacekeepers.

Another line of questioning that emerged from our review of Rubinstein's essay was if and how Rubinstein communicated fieldwork dilemmas to his research subjects. In one instance, Rubinstein is asked not to ride in the car of an OGE observer to an OP in the Sinai, because this might provide a pretext for diplomatic protests. Nonetheless, once he is at the OP, the officers participating in his study invite him ride on their patrols. Rubinstein recognizes that patrolling is a core peacekeeping activity and that the completeness of his research depends on observing it. Attitudes toward his presence and where it is and is not appropriate, however, differ: whereas the colonel in charge of peacekeeping operations has asked that Rubinstein not ride in official UN vehicles, the officers encourage his participation. By accepting the invitation, Rubinstein is potentially risking further access to the field site, yet he is also being offered access to understand a fundamental practice of peacekeeping. Moreover, by accepting the invitation to ride with the patrols, he could potentially get the officers he is observing into trouble with their colonel.

In the end, Rubinstein does ride with the patrols. In reading this and the other accounts, we wondered about the extent to which Rubinstein relied upon his informants in weighing his decision to act one way or another. Did he, for example, share his predicament with the officers inviting him to ride with them in official UN vehicles? Did he communicate with these individuals about how (and if) he could include these experiences in his fieldwork accounts? Or, does he only feel able to discuss these encounters 25 years later, at a time that may make it possible for him to describe these issues without worrying about the impact of disclosure on the participants and the institutions involved?

Rubinstein's perspective and observations are most welcome given that his research began 25 years ago, at a time when (as he notes) ethnographic work among multilateral institutions was uncommon and that among military institutions was even more so. We wondered about the initial reactions of Rubinstein's colleagues to his choice of research subjects. Did anthropological peers also see his project as one of "studying up"? What expectations, if any, did colleagues have about the directions his analysis of peacekeeping should go? What position, if any, did they take on the social relationships that he might strike up with military informants?

Rubinstein Response

During the time that I was conducting the study of UNTSO, I moved to Egypt and became part of a research team that had for 20 years been studying and working to prevent blinding eye disease in the Nile Delta. As a consequence, just as I was learning about the new ethnographic area of peacekeeping, I was also learning about the anthropology of the Middle East. One of the things that struck me as I tacked between these two areas of research was that many in the anthropological community would freely talk about people and organizations of the national security state in ways that they would never speak about other peoples or their institutions. I observed (Rubinstein 2003), for instance, that our anthropological community would sharply condemn sweeping statements about "The Arabs" as essentializing and totalizing, appropriately noting that among these peoples and communities there was considerable variation; however, our anthropological community rarely challenged those who routinely spoke of "The Military" as though no such variation exists. Yet, militaries are as varied and complex as other human communities.

Similarly, I saw that for questions of access and method there was a similar separate treatment for those studying up. Both in my own case and later in cases of my students, I found that when proposing a project that "studied up," grant reviewers would comment in disbelief that access could be gained to the institution to be studied, especially when the researcher was a younger scholar or the institutions were part of Western society. And, they would lower their ranking of the proposal on that basis. Yet, I have seen colleagues of all ages receive no such skeptical treatment when they proposed to study in non-Western settings. I puzzled as to why this might be.

Perhaps because we think we know more about our own societies, it seems to me that collectively anthropology often exhibits a kind of exceptionalism when we look at ourselves, especially when the selves we are looking at are elites, or, in Nader's term, "up." I believe that anthropology is still ambivalent about turning its focus on our own societies and institutions and selves. Yet, one of anthropology's most important contributions is the idea that all peoples are fundamentally deserving of the same respect and engagement.

In their comments on my case, the volume editors seem to reproduce the exceptionalisms I noted. To me, the challenge of having to decide what to say and when to say it that is posed by observing (and talking to) two military officers transgressing institutional expectations is no different than the challenge posed by observing (and talking to) the Belizean $2 taxi driver who took me across the Mexican border while smuggling contraband in the hollowed-out fenders of his car. Yes, one is Western and elite and the other less powerful (in an institutional sense) and non-Western. Yet, in both cases, as participants in my research, I believe that I had the same duties to both peoples: to be sure that they were aware of my research, to promise to them only the anonymity I could ensure, and to do my best to do no harm to them. In both cases, there is the coordinate challenge of balancing the researcher's duty to the individuals involved while keeping in mind the broader institutional contexts and responsibilities.

I see this exceptionalism too in the volume editors' distinction between "politically charged secrecy" of studying up and the "garden variety" secrecy of fieldwork. (Though I confess that I do not know exactly what they mean by the "garden variety" secrecy of fieldwork.) In both instances, it seems to me, the anthropologist confronts societies with their own conceptions of power, of what should and should not be revealed to outsiders (including researchers), and what the consequences of such revelation might be.

I greatly appreciate the coproduction of this volume since it gives room for a conversation about these and other topics to begin to take shape. Although I agree with the volume editors' that the actual circumstances of the situations of anthropological research in the "securityscape" are different from those outside of it, to me it seems that the moral and ethical challenges posed by fieldwork within the securityscape are the same in structure and logic as those that confront us when we research other areas.

References

Daubenmier, Judith Marie

2008 The Meskwaki and Anthropologists: Action Anthropology Reconsidered. Lincoln, NE: University of Nebraska Press.

Gusterson, Hugh

1997 Studying Up Revisited. *Political and Legal Anthropology Review* 20(1):114–19.

Humphrey, Laud
1975 Tearoom Trade: Impersonal Sex in Public Places. New Brunswick, NJ: Transaction Books.
Nader, Laura
1972 Up the Anthropologist! Perspectives Gained from Studying Up. *In* Reinventing Anthropology, D. Hymes, ed. pp. 284–311. New York: Pantheon Press.
Polsky, Ned
1967 Hustlers, Beats and Others. Chicago, IL: Aldine.
Rubinstein, Robert
1977 Cognitive Development and the Acquisition of Semantic Knowledge in Northern Belize. Ph.D. dissertation, Department of Anthropology, State University of New York at Binghamton.
1979 The Cognitive Consequences of Bilingual Education in Northern Belize. *American Ethnologist* 6(3):583–609.
2003 Politics and Peacekeepers: Experience and Political Representation among United States Military Officers. *In* Anthropology and the United States Military: Coming of Age in the Twenty-first Century, P. R. Frese and M. C. Harrell, eds. pp. 15–27. New York: Palgrave Macmillian.
2008 Peacekeeping under Fire: Culture and Intervention. Boulder, CO: Paradigm.
2011 Ethics, Engagement, and Experience: Anthropological Excursions in Culture and the National Security State. *In* Dangerous Liaisons: Anthropologists and the National Security State, L. McNamara and R. A. Rubinstein, eds. pp. 145–65. Santa Fe: SAR Press.
Turnbull, Colin
1968 The Forest People. New York: Simon and Schuster.
Zelizer, Craig, and Robert Rubinstein
2009 Building Peace: Practical Reflections from the Field. Sterling, VA: Kumarian Press.

14

Hazardous Field Operations: Romanian-American Joint Humanitarian Training

Peter Van Arsdale

Peter W. Van Arsdale (Ph.D., University of Colorado) is a senior lecturer at the Josef Korbel School of International Studies at the University of Denver and a senior researcher with eCrossCulture Corporation. He has conducted fieldwork in many locations, including the United States, Romania, Bosnia, Indonesia, Sudan, Ethiopia, Guyana, Peru, El Salvador, New Guinea/Papua, Timor-Leste, Israel, and Palestine. He also has long experience in wide-ranging development and humanitarian work and program evaluation, particularly in postconflict societies, including work on questions pertaining to immigration and refugees, mental health, human rights, and military-civilian collaborations.

Van Arsdale was a cofounder and director (2007–2008) of Josef Korbel's Program in Humanitarian Assistance, and recently helped to initiate a program in Timor-Leste with Nobel Peace Laureate José Ramos-Horta. He recently served as chair of the Human Rights and Social Justice Committee of the Society for Applied Anthropology and has served as a member of the Committee for Human Rights of the American Anthropological Association (AAA). Among his many publications are Forced to Flee: Human Rights and Human Wrongs in Refugee Homelands *(Van Arsdale 2006) and* Humanitarians in Hostile Territory: Expeditionary Diplomacy and Aid outside the Green Zone *(Van Arsdale and Smith 2010).*

Van Arsdale worked with Albro for several years on the AAA's Committee for Human Rights (CfHR), a period that overlapped with the work of the Commission on the Engagement of Anthropology with the U.S. Security and Intelligence Communities (CEAUSSIC). At this time in CfHR a recurrent discussion—indeed, controversy—was about what an anthropology of human rights should be in practice. Should CfHR be: a front-line advocacy-type organization, or a group dedicated to exploring the productive intersections of anthropology with human rights as a particular form of engagement with the world? In many ways, this is a parallel universe of concern about "practice," with implications for our discussion of work in the securityscape.

In anthropological arguments about human rights, the long-standing ethical responsibility on the part of ethnographers for the well-being of human subjects of research is brought together with a concern for the historical victims of human rights violations in the form of a research and advocacy practitioner stance. Van Arsdale's long-standing commitment to human rights work informs his private and university-sponsored work training students for mixed military-civilian humanitarian cooperation. His essay in this collection, however, is less about advocacy in a political mode and more about building human rights into the practices of institutions and programs. In this sense, his discussion can be compared with Goolsby's on ethics.

Van Arsdale's essay can also be usefully compared with Rubinstein's, as both direct attention to different facts about civil-military collaborations. His discussion can further be compared with Omidian's, as both engage with the relationship of an applied practice to nongovernmental organization (NGO) work in conflict or post-conflict settings. Collectively, these essays raise what we think are useful questions about the kinds of national, institutional, and legal regimes of which their work is a part, as these, too, fill out the extent of the securityscape.

Military bases and camps serve as the central platforms or "fixed sites" for certain types of training activities and military operations, at home and abroad. When working at the civilian-military interface, where humanitarian outreach is considered to be located, such sites can be used to engage multidisciplinary teams of trainers and trainees. This case study features a fixed site my colleagues and I used in the Transylvanian mountains of Romania in 2004. Fifteen University of Denver graduate students (i.e., civilian personnel) worked in concert with 30 Romanian Land Forces Academy cadets (i.e., military personnel) in the conduct of a joint humanitarian training exercise intended to benefit the skill development of both parties. They were jointly supervised by a group of Americans and Romanians, again representing both civilian and military expertise.[1]

All effective training operations, like all actual field operations, are built upon webs of relationships. They are carried out by teams, variously configured. Ours paralleled what are known as "country teams." In the use of fixed sites to support humanitarian assistance and stabilization operations, as would be encountered in such places as Bosnia and Timor-Leste (where I also have worked), one objective is to humanely engage teams to establish relief camps while clarifying roles and responsibilities so as to mitigate immediate risks to both potential beneficiaries and camp personnel. Considerations of entrée/encampment must complement subsequent onsite work, and in turn be complemented by considerations of exit/departure. Increasingly, threats of external force by NSAs (nonstate actors) must be taken into account. Of obvious importance to beneficiaries, personnel must be familiar with—and practiced in—the humanitarian skills necessary to help an at-risk citizenry while they are encamped.

Stimulated by the insights and field leadership of Derrin Smith, himself a Ph.D. graduate of the Josef Korbel School (and my former advisee), who also is a former U.S. Marine and diplomat, we conceived a set of innovative civilian-military training exercises. These were pretested in Colorado and enacted in a special kind of field school in Romania. One key element was development of a fully functioning relief camp, of the type that would be used in mounting a refugee or internally displaced person (IDP) operation in a conflict or post-conflict environment. Its operations were intended to exemplify core principles of humanitarian assistance at the civilian-military interface: the importance of recognizing the value of armed forces work in post-conflict and noncombat field operations; the significance of field-ready and site-specific training for humanitarian intervention; and the value of stabilization and reconstruction operations in hazardous environments, particularly as partnerships are developed that genuinely integrate the ideas and expertise of soldiers, outside civilians, and the indigenous populace.

As our colleagues with Romania's 10th Land Forces Division told us in 2004, the foundation of a solid, diversified, well-trained, humane military organization long had been bubbling in the post-Ceauşescu era.[2] That some of this could be put into practice through a field training program, aided by U.S. colleagues, would offer an additional boost to those Romanians seeking greater recognition in the European-American sphere. That it likely would be viewed favorably by North Atlantic Treaty Organization (NATO) representatives was another plus. Although certainly intended to help others, recent operations in places like Somalia and Bosnia had been conducted strategically so that Romania's place in the Western panoply of transnational actors could be strengthened. During the past decade, reform has occurred at the strategic command level with the organization of the armed forces into battalions, brigades, and army corps. An interoperability process also was launched with the armed forces of the NATO member states. By 1997, the Romanian units designated for peacekeeping missions had become operational. Specific humanitarian missions to conflict zones were initiated.

The timing of our civilian-military training program *cum* field school in 2004 therefore was ideal from the perspective of the Romanian military.

Public relations opportunities abounded, with both positive and negative ramifications. The Romanian Ministry of National Defense recruited senior Air Force and Land Forces trainers and advanced cadets, and funded 85 percent of the operation (including all equipment costs). The University of Denver funded the remaining 15 percent. This was a first-of-its-kind effort.

The following two vignettes indicate how the field school *cum* camp that we established in Romania engaged its participants.

> The machine gun fire rattled our brains. The gunner was only a few feet away, and the sound was deafening. Our convoy ground to a halt. The walls of the narrow mountain valley seemed suddenly to close. The drivers jumped out and ran into the forest. A burly, ominous-looking man with a bandanna wrapped around his forehead and ammunition belts draped over his shoulders ran into the road and waved his AK-47 in our direction. "I am Dracul. We are taking over!"
>
> "Get out of those trucks, now!" Dracul shouted. He waved his gun in the direction of our students, riding in the cargo bays, and then added: "You'll be sorry if you do not move." Other militiamen and women, following their leader's command, converged around the rear doors of the three convoy vehicles and herded the students off. Some stumbled, since they'd been forced to put on black hoods a moment earlier and couldn't get their bearings.
>
> The militia lined the students up near a small stream. "Put your hands behind your heads, spread your legs, and shut up," one yelled. "Keep those hoods on," another screamed. Female militia then began patting down the female students; male militia began patting down the male students. "All clear," one woman stated in a matter-of-fact fashion.
>
> "You do not have authority to enter our territory," Dracul said. "Did you think you could bring these trucks in without our permission? Did you think you could help those refugees without going through us?" He poked his gun at one of our students, a young man who had been in the military himself, and said: "Did you?" "No, sir," our student replied.
>
> "Then get out of the way. We are in charge here. I only have two friends—my knife and my gun."
>
> With that, Dracul and his 10 colleagues jumped into the trucks, turned them around, and drove them back down the valley. Our students, seemingly dazed, also turned around and began the journey back on foot, trudging the five kilometers to where they had begun their relief operation hours earlier.

This was a simulation. It included all the "bells and whistles." Dracul and his militia colleagues in fact were Romanian cadets in training, members of the Romanian Land Forces Academy (similar to the U.S. Army's West Point). They were enacting a simulation that our staff, in concert with Romanian officers, had concocted days in advance. The 15 students who were "captured" had no idea that this would happen, but had been well versed in country team operations, had been working alongside Romanian soldiers, and had been preparing for unusual and realistic scenarios. As the summer of 2004 went on, they encountered a number of other difficult situations in the Transylvania Mountains, as a second vignette illustrates.

> Our convoy of trucks and military equipment lumbered through a small valley and up a rough dirt road. Although part of a military reservation, it was littered with rocks and potholes. The Transylvanian forest enclosed us on all sides. As our first vehicle crested a steep rise, it suddenly came to a halt. There was smoke and fire dead ahead; it appeared that a jeep and small truck (travelling on a separate, crossing road) had collided just prior to our arrival. Two people lay in the road, seemingly covered with blood and severely injured.
>
> Having trained with the Mile High Chapter of the American Red Cross to assist the injured in such emergencies, five of our students sprang from their truck and rushed forward. The other 10 remained behind along with their Romanian military colleagues, awaiting further instructions.
>
> The first five were in for a surprise. Masked militiamen and women charged from behind a nearby grove of trees and surrounded them. Dracul appeared, ordering the students to the ground, face-first. "You let this little accident we staged distract you! Tell the others to stay away; we're armed and won't hold back if they attempt to trick us." Radio communications were engaged and the others retreated to safety, back into the small valley.
>
> "There's an abandoned farmhouse nearby. We're taking one of the women there as a hostage," Dracul shouted. "The other four can go. We'll relay you our demands shortly." One of the female students was bound, hooded, and led away by two armed militia women.
>
> For half an hour, there was silence. No militia could be seen, no sounds could be heard. Then a single masked man appeared. "Dracul is ready to negotiate. You can have the woman if we can have one of your trucks. Meet him in the farmhouse, half a kilometer to the west." The remaining students walked cautiously there, accompanied by their Romanian colleagues. They found the student sitting on a stool in the corner of the

> living room, still bound and hooded. A gun was pointed at her head. The room itself was filthy.
>
> "Do we have a deal?" Dracul asked. "One truck for one woman, a more-than-fair bargain." The students huddled, discussed the offer, and told him he had a deal. The woman was released; the simulation ended. All totaled, about an hour had elapsed.

This overall exercise represents an extreme field school outlier. Built in part on service learning principles, the country team operations model incorporates training exercises, scenarios or simulations, and onsite study and guest lectures. It is maximally experiential.

On the U.S. side, preparations for a summer of training operations in Romania began with a five-credit, campus-based, graduate-level class titled "Country Team Operations: Theory and Training." Smith and I offered this during the spring quarter of 2004. "Best practices" associated with materiel deployment, refugee camp operations, recovery operations, and field communications (including report writing) were featured. Basic Red Cross training was included. Case-based examples of emergency operations worldwide (including some associated with natural disasters) rounded out the classroom lectures.

The class ended with a kind of pretest, a set of field exercises. These took place over three days near the small mountain town of Creede, Colorado, located near the headwaters of the Rio Grande. In addition to Smith and myself, our professional field staff consisted of three non–university-based professionals. Two had extensive military experience.

These skills again were used when the students arrived in Romania several weeks later. During the first phase of our trip, a kind of "grand tour," we were primarily aided by officers of the Romanian Air Force and were billeted at the equivalent of that nation's Air Force Academy. Several guest lectures were presented. During the second phase of our trip, a targeted "onsite training," we were aided by officers and advanced cadets of the Romanian Land Forces Academy. We were based at one of their training camps and shuttled 30 miles west to one of their primary field camps.

The process of entrée to the Transylvanian field camp site was designed in such a way that students were divided into two teams, each charged with mapping out a route, arranging a convoy of military vehicles, loading and transporting supplies, and coordinating radio communications. One team took the "high route," through hills and low mountains. The other took the "low route," through a system of valleys. It was on a follow-up relief operation through the "low route," after both teams had joined, that they were "captured" by Dracul and his band of militia (as summarized in the first vignette).

Within the military field camp's perimeters, a complete relief camp was built, literally from the ground up and centered around large military tents, in a gently rolling field about a mile from the academy field headquarters. Outhouses were constructed and latrines installed. A small communications command post was established on an adjacent hilltop. A helicopter landing pad was set up. A generator-run electrical system was installed. In short, we established a camp that would serve as the center of field operations and as a base to assist "refugees" and "IDPs," whose arrivals were anticipated.

During the next few days, and following scenarios that had been scripted by members of our team in conjunction with the Romanian officers and cadets, a number of difficult situations unfolded. At the ready and working 24/7, our students were variously confronted by "irate peasants" from a "neighboring village," who claimed that our camp's new operations were upsetting the local political situation; the same group, who came again on a subsequent day and now claimed that we had inadvertently but thoughtlessly constructed our camp over several community gravesites; "IDPs" who required nighttime medical assistance based on a protocol and triage system we previously had practiced (with Red Cross assistance) in Denver; "guerrillas" who attacked our camp at midnight; "refugees" who needed to be evacuated; and the "hostage situation" reported earlier (in the second vignette).

These exercises illustrate both the realism that our mock operations engendered and the financial costs that our program incurred. The "refugees" were evacuated on Romanian military helicopters. We had access to these for two days, including training in flight operations, the loading of supplies, care of the wounded, and radio communications. The woman's capture was preceded by a battle that included the use of training explosives, dummy mortars and gunfire, and the mock automobile/truck accident already noted. We had six trucks, two ambulances, and 10 senior Romanian military officers at our disposal throughout this set of field exercises. We had eight helicopter crewmen at our disposal for two days, including one of the country's senior flight instructors.

The initiative allowed master's degree candidates from a wide range of concentrations, all within the University of Denver's Josef Korbel School of International Studies, to work together. It also allowed a scaled-down version of the field project to be reinstituted at the school in 2008; it continues today under my direction. M.A. candidates focusing their studies on homeland security, human rights, international development, and international administration predominate. It affords students whose political views are more conservative to work alongside those whose views are more liberal. It affords students who have had military experience themselves to work alongside those with no such experience; indeed, some in the latter group had been vocally outspoken against the military prior to joining our program. Of equal importance, it affords students the opportunity to merge theory, ethical interpretation, and practice—our definition of praxis—and to hone skills essential to careers involving onsite work in refugee camps, civil-military relief operations, or disaster assistance activities.

Through country team training operations in Romania in 2004—including the preparatory work in Colorado—students learned disaster relief planning (including refugee camp development and maintenance), mass casualty aid (nonmedical), emergency first aid, triage needs assessment (nonmedical), techniques for maintaining site security and the fixing of perimeters, the process of threat assessment, the process of personnel deployment and task assignment, map interpretation and intelligence, and radio communication. These are field skills of direct use to those who move on to careers in practicing anthropology, overseas development, NGO outreach, and other fields. A student practicing on- and off-loading of supplies with a helicopter in Romania is authentically preparing for assignment to the most challenging of field situations.

This program also enabled our students to improve their writing skills, specifically in ways that are useful onsite and under stress. Students maintained daily logs of specific activities, these tied to the administrative and service components of the program. The writing of briefs, issue papers, "hot washes," and field reports summarizing "best practices" and "lessons learned" were essential.

Therefore, as discussed in detail elsewhere,[3] this type of field exercise must be accompanied by a systematic review of "best practices" and "lessons learned." In Romania, we conceptualized these at three levels:

1. **Basic, establishing "ground truth":** An example of a best practice would be gaining effective entrée and establishing rapport with beneficiaries. A lesson learned was detecting and interpreting deception by "indigenous refugee camp leaders" (cadets) in a cross-culturally tense relief setting.
2. **Intermediate, establishing "field readiness":** An example of a best practice would be development of an emergency action plan (EAP). A lesson learned was identification of camp ingress and egress routes, accompanied by nonencrypted intrateam radio communication protocols.
3. **Advanced, maintaining "site operability":** An example of a best practice would be knowledge of local authority structures. A lesson learned, as "relief workers" (students) negotiated with "leaders of a nearby host village" (cadets), was that relief workers' priorities for refugee well-being did not correspond with those of the refugees'

> hosts. The local village authorities placed upcoming local electioneering needs ahead of refugee infrastructural needs.

Basic, intermediate, and advanced "learning" all are recommended to effectively complete both joint civilian-military humanitarian exercises and actual field operations.

The Romanian initiative incorporated elements of what we refer to as "pragmatic humanitarianism." Tied to an emerging theory of obligation, which I have elaborated elsewhere,[4] this notion of humanitarianism features hands-on training with at-risk populations. It respects rather than castigates humanitarian intervention involving military and peacekeeping personnel. It engages the simple liberal premise that what one person does within one grassroots agency or field site makes a difference. Through what are known as "obligated actions," the materially possible (e.g., a network of service providers) is linked with the morally possible (e.g., institutional accountability and the protection of confidentiality).

The consideration of ethics is paramount. Smith and I have suggested a set of ethical "rules of engagement," this in turn linked to understandings of rights-based development where longer-term, post-relief assistance is required. Students therefore study cases, such as Operation Provide Comfort for the Kurds in the 1990s, where military and civilian partnerships were engendered and where ethical dilemmas were encountered. We employ a neo-Kantian stance, one that emphasizes the need for informed consent as interventions are considered and that sees value in the evolution (but not forced implementation) of liberal democracies.

A "critical realism" also is suggested. The diverse voices of beneficiaries, military personnel, civilian/NGO personnel, and government officials must be weighed equitably as outreach strategies are considered. Some of these might counter conventional U.S. military thought. "Command-and-control" might well be replaced by "command-and-collaborate" as humanitarian field operations commence.

In terms of benefits derived, several of the students from 2004 subsequently used their experiences as "springboards" to other university-based overseas opportunities, some of these also in the Balkans (e.g., Bosnia, Croatia, Albania). Several followed up with M.A. theses or major research papers that dealt with topics of humanitarian intervention, international security, disaster relief, and refugee assistance. Career-wise, some went on to work for intergovernmental organizations (IGOs) and NGOs. One currently serves as a specialist with the American Red Cross. Another is a Foreign Service Officer. Still another is an intelligence analyst with the U.S. Navy.

Current courses offered through the University of Denver's masters program in humanitarian assistance build upon what was accomplished in

Romania. Issues in international law and ethics are featured. Classroom discussions revolve around complex humanitarian emergencies and the viability of Human Terrain Teams, Provincial Reconstruction Teams, and—most recently as proposed by Derrin Smith and me—Diplomatic Expeditionary Field Teams.

Editorial Commentary

Van Arsdale describes a training initiative within the University of Denver's School of International Studies to prepare graduate students for civil relief field operations that rely upon a partnership with military forces. Given regular emphasis on Iraq and Afghanistan, it is interesting to see a discussion of training partnerships with a completely different region—in this case, Romania and NATO. The initiative that Van Arsdale's work supports accepts as a given that certain humanitarian interventions—such as the establishment of a refugee camp in a conflict or post-conflict environment—depend upon effective civilian-military interactions. Students are afforded experiential opportunities to test out what that relationship may mean in simulated field settings.

In this case, graduate-level students actively take part in cooperative training exercises with the Romanian military in Romania. For the students, this direct experience with the "skills" of humanitarian assistance is understood to be useful for a variety of humanitarian-type career trajectories, including civil-military relief operations, work in refugee camps, and varieties of direct assistance activities. As a University of Denver field school, this program combines elements of study abroad, service learning, and onsite study, with training and simulation activities. The program also teaches practical skills such as how to write after-action briefs.

Anthropology has had, at best, an awkward relationship to the teaching of "skills." We are reminded of the professional pedagogical silence that largely characterized the teaching of field methods in anthropology, and in some ways, still pertains. The language of "skills" carries overtones of business school–style preprofessional training, as this is increasingly reflected in the proliferation of "skills institutes" on college campuses and elsewhere. It runs in another direction from anthropological practice toward the emerging and interdisciplinary estranged sister field of "cross-cultural communication," for which anthropology is a progenitor field, with the likes of E. T. Hall and others, but over which it rarely exercises any ownership and of which it is often quite critical. The question of "skills," as this is related to expectations for the value, utility, or instrumentality of anthropology, comes up across the essays in this volume in various ways, and indicates the extent to which work in the security sector is informed by the expectation of the application of well-identified forms of expertise to the end of solving a definite problem or creating an applicable product. This is not a new concern along the academic-applied frontier, but it is posed here in new forms.

This set of arrangements also reminds us of the extent to which the anthropological debate about engagement with the security realm has been framed primarily in terms of the ethical quandaries presented by participation in the Human Terrain Teams. Van Arsdale's account points to another kind of setting for engagement with armed forces—the post-conflict environment, that liminal state in which social groups are retreating from the battlefield, withdrawing from the use of force, and putting an end to violence.

We noted that Van Arsdale spends relatively little time reflecting on the theoretical and methodological relationships between anthropology and his work, though we did think it interesting that his program requires the students to maintain journals, much as graduate school anthropologists are instructed to take copious field notes. Even if in his case Van Arsdale is not training anthropologists, this example is relevant to his work and emphasizes the salience of the contexts of security, war, and civil trauma as contexts in which a lot of projects today must be conceived and done. Indeed, anthropologists may find the securityscape permeating the environs of fieldwork in ways that we have not previously encountered.

The arrangements that Van Arsdale describes highlight the extent to which the anthropological debate about engagement with the security realm has been framed primarily in terms of the ethical quandaries presented by participation in the Human Terrain Teams. Van Arsdale's account points to other kinds of intersections that are less popularized in anthropology's discourse about practice, security, and warfare. One of these is the relationship between anthropology and international relations, whose history is perhaps best described as a "ships-passing-in-the-night" relationship. In this sense, Van Arsdale's account is not dissimilar to Robert Rubinstein's: both are affiliated with international relations programs, and both have assumed roles as "trainers" in programs aimed at reducing conflict.

Second, both Van Arsdale and Rubinstein's work point to another setting in which anthropological work intersects with the armed forces: in the post-conflict environment, the "peacekeeping" environment in which one set of groups is retreating from the battlefield as other organizations take on the challenge of "reconstruction" or "stabilization." For example, in her discussion, Holmes-Eber notes that the Marines are doing quite a bit of humanitarian and "nonkinetic" work; Van Arsdale is perhaps also telling a story about how stabilization and reconstruction operations work, and the role of military forces and "security" in that regard.

Given this, two questions occur to us in Van Arsdale's essay. First, he points to a different role for anthropology and anthropologists in the securityscape; as a member of international relations faculty partnering with a foreign military to train humanitarian workers, Van Arsdale's work represents the intersection of applied work, academia, humanitarianism, and war. In doing so, his essay raised questions about whether anthropology's professional organizations have paid sufficient theoretical, ethnographic, and political attention to processes of demilitarization, so that we might be in a more qualified position to examine how our ethical commitments play out in the settings described by Van Arsdale.

Second, as an exercise in "civilian-military training," the University of Denver's program is similar to others across the landscape of higher education, and might also be thought of as an indicator of the prominent role of militaries in humanitarian relief efforts worldwide—a fact not without controversy. In 2007, the U.S. Institute of Peace brokered the writing of "Guidelines for Relations Between U.S. Armed Forces and Non-Governmental Humanitarian Organizations," which laid out specific rules of engagement between military and nonmilitary humanitarian agencies, in response to concern about the military presence in response to humanitarian disasters. This program also raises the specter of the potential militarization of higher education. Such efforts are often incorporated into new graduate-level programs and housed in new "centers of excellence" and institutes on campus, and are becoming a greater part of the landscape of higher education as well as often important sources of revenue for universities.

Van Arsdale's essay indicates the multiple dimensions of the "civilian-military" interface at the heart of the program, and the subtle permeation of security discourse across higher education. Critics might point to the ways lines are being blurred between, for example, the mandate of higher "education" and "training," with the latter about inculcating a different set of military-relevant skills. Likewise, others might note the blurring of study abroad experiences with field schools that appear to work with formal military ventures. We are thinking here of Mojave Viper, a Marine Corps predeployment program at Twentynine Palms, California, that—among other things—offers training in security and stability operations by way of a simulated Iraqi town. The cross between field school and the old Air Force survival training (which leads to the capture and intimidation of airmen as the model for enhanced interrogation) is provocative. Such examples point to tensions between a liberal education, broadly conceived, and the tasks of "social engineering," as such humanitarian work is characterized here.

Describing the program, Van Arsdale promotes a "pragmatic humanitarianism," that is, the notion that what one person does as part of a grassroots agency "makes a difference." Personal convictions about how best to "make a difference" appear to be central to decisions to participate in this program, an issue that has also come up more than once throughout this volume. Such a pragmatic humanitarianism, at least potentially, promotes the idea that one individual in one agency can be effective. This leads to a third question: as part of an "emerging theory of obligation," as Van Arsdale puts it, how might this tie back to anthropology's increasing propensity to talk about the pitfalls and possibilities of "engagement?"

The field training that Van Arsdale describes does not hold ethical debates at an abstract level, but puts students in simulated environments that concretize tough choices and competing priorities. Training programs of this sort raise a range of ethical questions. For example, despite our discipline's normative commitments to peace and human rights, we expect that few anthropology programs have developed sufficient tools to help students plumb the depths of the ethically fraught contexts they may encounter in such military-humanitarian contexts, and the importance of developing training materials and providing experiences that give students some sense of how ethical dilemmas play out in real life.

In our response to Van Arsdale's essay, we asked Van Arsdale to describe the interinstitutional relationships between the University of Denver and the Romanian military to get a better sense of the risks and potential benefits that each perceived in this relationship. We asked about the history of the training program, its relationship to the Korbel School, and the support that the school provides the program. Last, we wondered about the extent to which Van Arsdale and Smith's work has influenced the U.S. military's approach to working with NGOs in demilitarizing zones, as Iraq will soon become.

Van Arsdale Response

As noted in my essay, the 2004 Romanian training program contributed to the development of the Josef Korbel School of International Studies' current Program in Humanitarian Assistance. Graduate-level students like those who participated in the Romanian initiative are afforded the opportunity to earn certificates or concentrations that complement their degrees. Since its founding in 2007, it has been the school's fastest-growing program. Current core and elective courses build upon what was accomplished in Romania. Issues in international law and ethics, complex humanitarian emergencies, health and humanitarianism, and civil war/peace-building are featured in the core courses. Classroom discussions include the viability of Human Terrain Teams, Provincial Reconstruction Teams, and—most recently as proposed by Derrin Smith and me—Diplomatic Expeditionary Field Teams. Our current dean, former U.S. Ambassador to Iraq Christopher Hill, strongly supports us.

To these students, the emergent securityscape is of great concern and great interest. Interviews with those who have completed the program, without exception, have emphasized the value of conducting training exercises in harsh environments that include military simulations and analysis of military operations. Issues "at the military-civilian interface" are featured in three of the core and two of the elective courses. Students strongly express the desire for a curriculum that features a balanced array of classroom, internship/field, and applied research opportunities. It should be noted that approximately 85 percent of these students are women.

In complement to the points made by the editors of this volume, ethical "rules of engagement" are emphasized in this training (Van Arsdale and Smith 2010:33). The understanding of "soft measures" which balance diplomacy/aid/service with ethics/research/advocacy are stressed in classroom discussions and in briefs written by the certificate and concentration candidates. In prefield classroom debates, students are required to analyze the points and processes indicated in Figure 14.1. Role-playing exercises sometimes are engaged. Cases drawn from the development literature, in particular, are used as referents.

The editors of this volume, in their commentary on my essay, are correct in noting that—at one level—I am telling a story about how

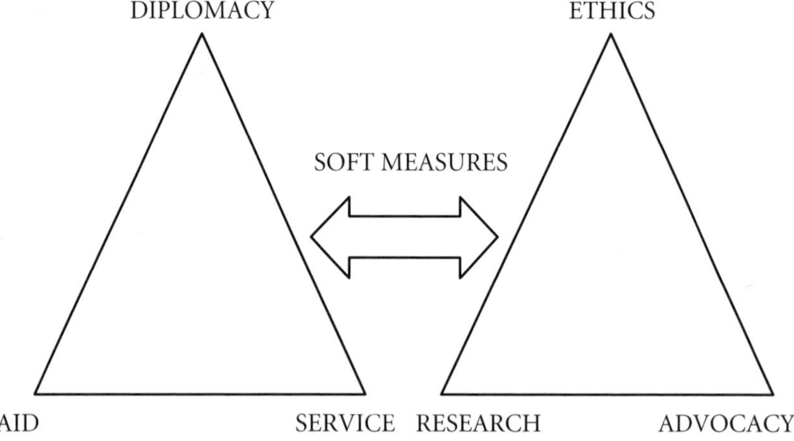

Figure 14.1. Ethical "rules of engagement" require consideration of so-called soft measures. In our interpretation, these consist of the intersection of the six factors shown here. Inevitably, there will be an imbalance "on the ground," but both humanitarian assistance and humanitarian intervention benefit from tactical analyses involving the first set of three and strategic analyses involving the second set of three. Free, prior, and informed consent (FPIC) must be pursued simultaneously. Reprinted from Van Arsdale and Smith (2010).

stabilization and reconstruction operations work, and the role of military forces and "security" in that regard. Students destined for overseas assignments in conflict and post-conflict environments, as well as those destined for offices in places like Geneva, need to know this. At another level, I am suggesting that students want tough opportunities presented to them. They want to engage debates about the roles of the military in stabilization and reconstruction operations. They want to be able to decide for themselves whether they should be engaged with military personnel in the conduct of humanitarian operations. In my experience, whether they come to a university as promilitary, neutral/undecided, or antimilitary, and whether they come as students of anthropology or of other social science disciplines, they most certainly do not want to be told what to believe in this regard. Professional anthropologists can play a better role in facilitating a newer form of open discourse in this regard.

All of the queries included in the editors' commentary are extremely useful. None are meant by them to be rhetorical. But this is not just about students, it is about me as a professional anthropologist—and it is about my colleagues. For me, the second query about the extent my work might be influencing current U.S. military training for stability, security, transition, and reconstruction (SSTR) operations, is of particular interest. Building on what I had learned in Romania, as well as what was then transpiring with CEAUSSIC, in late 2008 I signed a contract to work part-time with the for-profit consulting firm eCrossCulture Corporation. Based in Boulder, Colorado, this firm specializes in a wide variety of projects "at the military-civilian interface," and has been awarded a number of contracts by the Office of Naval Research. From social perspective taking in conflictive cross-cultural settings, to the better employment of Rapid Assessment Program (RAP) methodologies under duress, to the development of geospatial maps attuned to the ethnoterrain of Africa's newest nation, the Republic of South Sudan, promising work is under way. In most instances, University of Denver graduate students are given an opportunity to work with us. In each project, a number of questions are asked. How might a U.S. soldier use this information or tool to benefit a local population? How might an NGO outreach worker use the same information or tool to benefit the same population? How can they better collaborate under an "ethical umbrella" that does not damage the indigenous population?

Notes

1. Parts of this article are adapted directly from Van Arsdale (2008) and Van Arsdale and Smith (2010).

2. The history of Romanian military operations before 1989 (during the regime of Nicolae Ceauşescu) and after 1989 has been effectively summarized by Călin Hentea (2007).
3. Van Arsdale and Smith (2010) provide a series of humanitarian "best practices" and "lessons learned," drawing primarily upon work in Romania, Iraq, and Afghanistan, for those training for civilian-military operations.
4. This theory of obligation is built upon evaluations of the needs of refugees and the work of those assisting them, both in the United States and abroad (Van Arsdale 2006).

References

Hentea, Călin

2007 Brief Romanian Military History. Lanham, MD: Scarecrow Press.

Van Arsdale, Peter W.

2006 Forced to Flee: Human Rights and Human Wrongs in Refugee Homelands. Lanham, MD: Lexington Books.

2008 Learning Applied Anthropology in Field Schools: Lessons from Bosnia and Romania. *In* Careers in Applied Anthropology in the 21st Century: Perspectives from Academics and Practitioners, Carla Guerrón-Montero, ed. pp. 99–109. NAPA Bulletin No. 29, Arlington, VA: American Anthropological Association.

Van Arsdale, Peter W., and Derrin R. Smith

2010 Humanitarians in Hostile Territory: Expeditionary Diplomacy and Aid Outside the Green Zone. Walnut Creek, CA: Left Coast Press.

15

Retaining Intellectual Integrity: Introducing Anthropology to the National Security Community

Jessica Glicken Turnley

Jessica Glicken Turnley (Ph.D. Cornell University, Anthropology and Southeast Asian Studies, 1983) brings a unique perspective to this volume by virtue of her diverse and peripatetic career inside and outside the national security context. As she discusses here, she first interacted with the world of national security as a graduate student, when she interviewed for a position with the Central Intelligence Agency (CIA). It is not until the end of the Cold War, however, that Turnley's career as a practicing anthropologist shifts from a focus on small business development in the United States to "national security" in a range of forms. Like Mark Dawson, Turnley is an independent consultant whose business is oriented toward military and intelligence work. Unlike Dawson, Turnley has worked with the Department of Defense, the Department of Energy, and several agencies in the U.S. intelligence community, and has also held a research and management position at Sandia National Laboratories, where she and Laura McNamara met and worked together for a brief period in the mid-2000s.

Turnley's narrative intersects with several in this volume: her experience teaching anthropology to military professionals echoes themes in Simons', Holmes-Eber's, and Fujimura's essays, whereas her interactions with computational social scientists evoke many of the same themes that Albro and McNamara raise. The intersections are numerous because Turnley's work portfolio is perhaps the broadest in this volume: her research topics include sociocultural analyses of various aspects of the military, intelligence, and national security communities; contributions to the development of cultural intelligence products; terrorism analyses; support for computational social science projects; and teaching and advising of military professions at the U.S. Special Operations Command (USSOCOM). She was a contributor to a National Research Council panel on computational social science that is described in Robert Albro's essay in this volume; both Albro and McNamara advocated for her participation in the volume, given that her career spans so many of the institutions comprising the securityscape: military operations, intelligence, and policy-making; civilian science and technology and intelligence; and academic research, private contracting, and professional military education. Currently, she is President of the Galisteo Consulting Group, which is located in Albuquerque, New Mexico. She has published under the names "Jessica Glicken" and "Jessica Turnley."

As a student of anthropology, both undergraduate and graduate, I never dreamed I would end up running a small business with work focusing heavily on the national security sector. As with many career and life stories, mine took on a life very different from what I had envisaged as an anthropology student coming of age in the late 1960s and early 1970s.

Running a business and working for the national security sector were almost unimaginable while I was a student for two reasons. The first was the general political climate. I did my undergraduate work at the University of California (UC) Santa Cruz in the early 1970s. My friends and I participated in marches protesting the government's decision to become involved in Vietnam, and there were many late-night discussions in dorm rooms in the redwoods about the appropriate role of the government of a state and the role of the citizen in government. (Many of my friends were majoring in political theory, which gave these discussions a particular edge.) Prominent in all these discussions were the mechanisms by which a citizen could appropriately question a decision of a state. The second reason such a career trajectory was unimaginable was the nature of the discipline. At that time—and, indeed, until relatively recently—there were very, very few anthropologists working in nonacademic environments. It certainly was not considered an appropriate career path at any of the universities I attended (UC Santa Cruz for an undergraduate degree; University of Michigan, Ann Arbor, for an M.A.; and Cornell for an M.A. and my Ph.D., all in anthropology.) There were no classes or conversations on translating the discipline from academe to the applied world: the assumption was that we would all create careers within academe in some way.

Unfortunately (or, perhaps in the long run, fortunately), when I received my Ph.D. in 1983, the last of the baby boomers (of which I was one) were finishing up programs in higher education. Enrollments were dropping, and faculties were being cut. At one point it was claimed that it was easier to get a job in English literature than anthropology—then, as now, our perceived relevance was very low.

To pay the rent, I got a job in the private sector. I went to work in marketing and public relations in the emerging computer and high technology sector in Silicon Valley. This was 1982 and 1983, and few in the workplace understood or cared about computing technology. There was, as I saw it, a niche to be filled translating the technology of bits and bytes into the language of documents, editing, and printing. Although I got my first job in a public relations agency because I could type, I quickly became an account manager. I worked in an agency serving Silicon Valley for a few years, and then moved in-house to a small computer company in Connecticut. I woke up one morning there to scrape the ice off my windshield in the freezing rain, and realized that there were places to live where I did not have to do that. My then-husband and I picked Albuquerque for personal reasons, but also because it appeared then (in 1986) to be on the verge of an economic boom.

We moved, and set up a small marketing and public relations firm in Albuquerque. Through a variety of accidental meetings, I became involved in economic development in central New Mexico. It matched some of my anthropological skills as well as my experience with fast-growing businesses in Silicon Valley.

Economic development requires organizational change on the part of firms and other organizations in the target area, as well as changes in some of the values of the resident populations. I worked with Senator Bingaman (D-NM) as he helped to develop and then implement much of the federal technology transfer legislation of the late 1980s and 1990s. Partially as a result of this, I became particularly interested in the relationship between what was identified as the engine of economic development in central New Mexico—Sandia National Laboratories—and the small businesses that were to benefit from it. There clearly was a cultural disconnect between the two communities, one that generally was ignored as technology transfer programs were put into place and executed. As a result, the programs did not perform as well as many expected. I described this cultural rift in a paper I gave at a session of the Society for Applied Anthropology (SfAA) in Santa Fe (Glicken 1989). The session focused on the interface between theory and application in economic development from an anthropological perspective. It was attended by several key figures from the New Mexico political arena and technology transfer.

My presentation at the SfAA meeting created a profile for me in the political and business community, which was supported by the small businesses that made up the bulk of the private-sector economy of Central New Mexico. (Intel Corporation became a major private sector presence about this time with the construction of a fabrication plant, but its gaze was generally focused on its headquarters on the West Coast.) I also became President of the New Mexico Entrepreneurs' Association, which gave me visibility with the labs as they worked the technology transfer issue with the small business community.

It was in this context that I met the senior manager from Sandia who was working on technology transfer. He was later asked develop a policy center at Sandia, and asked me to help with the planning. After we completed the discussions on organization, I pointed out that Sandia is an engineering laboratory populated with individuals who have self-selected themselves out of disciplines which focus on human interaction, the basis of policy development. He promptly offered me a job, and I entered Sandia through an organization that had a policy focus. This was my entré to the Department of Energy (DOE) world.

Working at Sandia as a social scientist was a difficult path to follow. I was told that I was the first social scientist to be hired into a technical line organization in Sandia's 50-plus-year history. Whether that was actually true or not, I certainly was an oddity. In the early 1990s when I joined Sandia, they were still heavily focused on nuclear weapons, their historic core mission; it was not clear to most staff members what social science had to offer in that domain. Although DOE had adopted economic security as part of its formal mission, an institution like Sandia, which had developed a very strong corporate culture centered on nuclear weapons, takes a very long time to change direction.

In my tenure at Sandia, I had, indeed, project-level opportunities, although programmatic support was difficult to find. The intelligence community and other agencies (including the DOE) had become interested in ensuring that the United States remained economically competitive on a global scale: this had become a national security concern. My economic development experience made me attractive here, particularly when combined with my anthropological background. What became known as "national systems of innovation" play out very differently in different parts of the world due to the ways in which they embody sociocultural values. Other projects sprang from my interest in the social study of science: was DOE (or offices within it) appropriately organized to accomplish their mission? I also worked on technology-based projects that required an understanding of the use of environment for successful development and deployment. And finally, I contributed substantively to certain projects that did require an understanding of the human dimension. These early years at Sandia helped establish my professional pattern, in which about half my work focused on issues of organizational development or change, and about half on substantive programmatic concerns: a balance I have since sought to maintain.

I established credibility by looking as much like other Sandians (that is the term that people at Sandia use to describe themselves) as possible. I made sure that my project contributions exhibited methodological rigor (no, an interview is NOT just a conversation in the hallway!) and demonstrated intellectual pedigrees (through citations, for example) that showed the work to be more than my own casual observations. I developed customers in the same organizations as other Sandians. And finally, I discovered that Cornell (the university from which I got my Ph.D.) had a very highly regarded physics department, and I was able to bask in some reflected glory. (Although this sounds like a throwaway line, it is not. Sandia was a very status-conscious culture, and one of the markers of status was an individual's Ph.D.-granting institution.)

Some of this work required that I get a security clearance. I had wrestled with my conscience to some extent when I took the position at Sandia. I soon realized that nuclear weapons were not going to evaporate any time soon. The position I was offered and the work I saw as available to me would contribute in some small way (I would hope) to the responsible management of those weapons. I was still free to act politically as a citizen in any way I saw fit, including (if I chose to do so) supporting the abolition of those weapons. The same sort of arguments held true for the security clearance. Every political entity has secrets and spies—always has, probably always will. I do not have a problem with the concept of information that not everyone can know everything. Much of my private sector work required that I sign nondisclosure agreements. I did, however, have personal difficulty with some of the requirements for operators ("spies" in the field) as they were presented to me during an employment interview with the CIA when I was a graduate student. So I chose not to go that route. I determined before I got my clearance through Sandia that I could resign it at any time, should I find that the requirements for an analyst had changed to the extent that they crossed my personal ethical lines. To date, that has not happened.

Back to the story. I resigned from Sandia in 1997 and entered into a contractual relationship with them. This allowed me to stay in Albuquerque, and to broaden my portfolio beyond Sandia itself. I did not resign from Sandia because of concerns or issues with the topical nature of the work or because of its location in the national security domain. One of the primary reasons I resigned was that I was becoming very tired of the need to defend the intellectual credibility and depth of my discipline. As Sandia discovered the importance of the human dimension in many of its new missions and programs, many of its staff began trying to quickly improve their knowledge in this area. I received several requests during this period for the "six fundamental articles I can read in anthropology" by individuals seeking to quickly become more expert in the field. Informing them that, unlike physics, there are no "fundamental laws" of human behavior that are laid out in three or four articles was, itself, a revelation to them. We had many discussions in this area. However, there still were those who felt that reading one book on a policy or social topic made them enough of an expert to contribute at the same level as I did. That said, I believe that I had been making progress with that argument for credibility of the discipline. I had been promoted to a technical manager position (itself a recognition of the "technical" nature of my type of work), and had built an externally funded department. Most important, the staff in my department (many of whom had social science educations if not degrees) were getting requests from others in the labs to support their projects. Sandia was beginning to recognize the contribution of social science to the mission, and, equally important, I believe, the need to have qualified social scientists make that contribution.

Just after 9/11, the individual who had facilitated my hire into Sandia was invited to a panel that was one of a series put on by USSOCOM, headquartered in Tampa, Florida. USSOCOM is the military command that is responsible for recruiting, training, and equipping all the military's Special Operations Forces (SOF): the Army's Special Forces, the Navy SEALs, the Marines Corps Special Operations Command (MARSOC), and the Air Force Commandos. In 2004, USSOCOM was designated the lead combatant command with responsibilities to synchronize military efforts in what was then called the "Global War on Terror." It has continued its own efforts to leverage the unique capabilities of SOF, including their ability to interact with and leverage local populations. This panel was an effort by USSOCOM to mix social and physical science, and figure out how to leverage the combined contribution. USSOCOM was interested in having a social scientist involved, and the individual with whom I had been working (now a vice president at Sandia) suggested that I attend.

The panel series was run by USSOCOM's Joint Special Operations University (JSOU). This was a new effort on the part of USSOCOM to establish an educational capability to provide SOF-specific courses and training. There were only a few faculty members at the time (the faculty are known as Senior Fellows), and they were in the process of recruitment. Apparently I exhibited the qualities they were looking for; they approached me after the panel and asked if I would like to join as a nonresident (part-time) Senior Fellow. I accepted. Being a Senior Fellow means that I get paid to do one large research project per year and teach classes. This served my desire to remain based in Albuquerque (although it added to the time I was already spending in airports and hotels). I currently teach a class on organizational structure (relationship-based [networked] and rule-based [bureaucratic] organizations and the implications of such structures for military action), language, and culture, and an "introduction to culture" in a series on irregular warfare. The students vary. Often my students are special operators—an operator is someone with actual operational experience—who are in their first round of training, or who have just completed an operational tour and are doing training in the interim. They work closely with indigenous populations. In other cases, the class is directed to an interagency audience, teaching the students about irregular warfare. Here I get analysts of a wide variety of types, often mixed in with military operators. Yet another series is directed at officers from foreign SOFs.

In any military environment, including JSOU, USSOCOM, or in front of the classes I teach, I make a concerted effort to make it clear that I have no military experience and, in fact, have not even been to the Middle East. I do tell my students and my colleagues that I have read a lot about the types of experiences they have had, watched movies and videos, and talked with people, but I do realize that is all a far cry from "being there."

I have been trying to find a way to go even if I simply sit on a military base. I believe this would help at the very least to give me a sense of atmospherics and to talk to the forces immediately after their contact with indigenous populations. At best, I would be able to move off the base and watch them in that contact. I am not interested in collecting information on indigenous populations, but on understanding how our forces interact with them and how that interaction can be improved. Data/knowledge is always helpful, but how one moves through an encounter whether one has or does not have that local knowledge also is critical. We all know people who can be rude in many languages.... However, the liability issues around sending a civilian contractor to a high-risk zone usually preclude me from getting there.

When I teach, I let my students know that my job is to give them frameworks to help them think about what they are doing when they are in the field. I ask them questions about their experience, and if the intellectual frameworks I present make sense. I challenge them to apply the frameworks we are discussing to their experience. In this way, I get stories from them on how it "works" or doesn't. Every now and then, I do get the "lightbulb" going off: "Oh yeah, now I understand why this played out the way it did...!"

This also works for the interagency audiences. One of the platforms for interaction in the type of national security environment we find ourselves today is a "whole of government" approach. Interactions among American agencies can often provoke serious misunderstandings. Think, for example, of an intelligence analyst talking with a Marine and a U.S. Agency for International Development (USAID) worker in Washington, D.C.: they have very different conceptions of how one moves through a meeting, what constitutes a "productive" interaction, and the like.

One of the most challenging classes I had was with a group of young Navy SEALs. My segment followed a three-hour segment given by someone describing how to run an operation. He spent much of the time talking about an operation he had just run, describing weapons, firefights, and sneaking through difficult terrain—and some small amount of time discussing his engagement with the local population. Then I stood up and said, "Hi, I'm not an operator, I'm an anthropologist, and we're going to talk about culture." Initially, they had a hard time switching gears, seeing how this would fit into their world. I told them, "This is not about understanding the adversary to death. This is about learning how to do your mission better." I try not to oversell what I am doing: it is not a silver bullet. I tell them that I can only give them some tools to think differently, to engage with their operational environment in a more effective way. And yes, I do believe that if we are more effective at achieving stated missions, we can shorten the life of any engagement and so save lives on both sides. And I still reserve the right as a citizen to disagree with the mission, although it would be inappropriate to voice that disagreement in a classroom.

In teaching about culture, I borrow from my colleague Kerry Fosher, and I tell them, "You don't have to like what the local population does, but your job isn't to change what they do culturally." I try to get examples from them of things with which they are uncomfortable when on an operation. We discuss how they manage their discomfort so that they can achieve their mission without being a cultural change agent. One of the examples I had used, particularly for the operators, is pedophilia. I have heard stories that the operators frequently encounter it in the field, seeing old men with "child brides." However, I usually get no reaction from the class: they listen, we move on. One day, a guy in one of my classes said, "How do we deal with homosexuality? We see these guys all over each other, and sometimes they want to get with us." That definitely got a reaction from the class, and from every subsequent group where I bring it up. So we talk about how these values play out with the guys that they're working with—and at what point it interferes with their ability to achieve their mission, to do what they need to do. And we also discuss how they can appropriately disengage when necessary (i.e., decline homosexual contact).

I believe that the most useful thing I can give to my students is a recognition that the rest of the world does not see things the way they do, and that they may have to learn to adopt other perspectives to get done what they need to get done. Computer models and phrasebooks have their place, but the students in my class are in environments where they need to go beyond them. I want the students to recognize that people in other places think and operate differently. People in other cultures have power structures, for example, but they just do not look like ours. And if you need to engage with the "head man" in a village, just how are you going to recognize him? Sometimes it is not the guy who is front and center in every meeting, but the one sitting quietly in the back. And in some places it is not only okay to hire your brother, it is expected—and if you do not, you may be socially ostracized. So how can you make that expectation work for you?

Most of the students have never had an anthropology course, and they are interested in application, not theory. I learned this quickly. At the end of one of the first classes I taught, one of the students (a special operator with several deployments under his belt), raised his hand and said "Ma'am, this is all mildly interesting, but just what do I do with it when I walk into a village?" So I use a lot of concrete examples in my classes to show them how to use it, but I also talk about theory. I think we sell ourselves short if we don't. I give names of theorists so they can read more if they like. (For example, if I talk about "thick description," I will, of course, reference Geertz. If I introduce the notion of sense-making, I point them to organizational scientist Karl Weick.) I want to get them past the notion that we can compose a checklist that you can follow as you walk into a village. I want to emphasize that if we really believe that "the people are the center of gravity" (one of the tenants of irregular warfare), we are going to have to spend time and intellectual effort to understand those with whom we engage. Learning about culture is not easy.

Most of my colleagues at JSOU are retired special operators, and only one or two are academics. Then there's me: I am the only Senior Fellow who is a woman, and one of the very few without operational experience. Despite all this, my JSOU colleagues, as well as military colleagues on other contracts I have worked, have unanimously been very welcoming to me. My JSOU colleagues, at times, forget I am a woman. I asked about dress code for a particular event (the military is very conscious about dress and almost every event announcement/agenda carries a statement about appropriate attire). I received a response that a sports coat without a tie would be appropriate. (The sender—whom I knew pretty well—was mortified when I pointed out that this was good, as I would have to go purchase a tie otherwise.) I see this not as a mark of disrespect but as a mark of acceptance. However, where my difference would matter substantively (my lack of operational experience), I make sure that distinction is recognized so the information and knowledge I convey can be appropriately contextualized.

One of the most important things I do is push back against what I call "social science lite." For example, a class I teach frequently is about networks and other organizational structures. The impetus for developing the class came from my participation in many conversations about networks in the military environment. It became clear quickly that most participants did not really understand what a social network is, the limitations (as well as the strengths) of social network analysis, and the negative and positive implications of that particular type of organization structure on military action. For example, as organizations based on highly personalized relationships, networks cannot be tasked (individuals in the network must be persuaded), and an officer will lose the certainty of command he has in a rule-based organization (a bureaucracy). Sometimes that is acceptable and sometimes it can be dangerous for all concerned. Recognizing what a social network can and cannot do for an organization as it works to discharge its mission is very important before significant changes are made to organizational structure. Of course, such knowledge also can help us leverage the organizational structure we do have in ways that previously may not have been clear.

My goal through my JSOU classes and through the work I do for other organizations in the national security environment is to help my students and the organizations with which I work to understand the social science behind terms like "social networks" or "legitimacy," to understand what they really mean and their implications for action. Otherwise we are dealing with "social science lite": using a term without full awareness of all of its dimensions. If we take action based on that limited knowledge, we could do more harm than good.

The same is true for the whole. "Culture" is another term that has suddenly become popular in the national security environment. Irregular warfare, such as those we are fighting in the Middle East and elsewhere, depends heavily on engagement with a local population. This is a very different approach than the force-on-force model of the Cold War, in which the local social environment was not relevant in an engagement. However, culture is not a concept that was invented when we engaged in our current version of irregular warfare, but a highly complex and richly textured one that has been around for a while. In some cases, simple tools like "culture cards" may be appropriate. But in others, particularly in many of the environments in which SOF engage, a full understanding of the complexities of culture can be critical.

Learning about "kulture"[1] is easy; learning about culture is hard. Engaging what I call a "pet anthropologist" on a project does not enable learning about and engaging with the culture concept. A pet anthropologist is a project member who is recruited when a project lead realizes it is politically necessary to demonstrate that one is engaging with the culture concept. Shortly after the now-famous counterinsurgency manual authored by General Petraeus and his team was released (FM3-24), it became necessary (popular) to include a consideration of culture in efforts to understand or manage counterinsurgency. One of the things

I do is contribute to the design and development of computational social models. Most calls for proposals from national security organizations in the last few years for these types of models have required that the responding team demonstrate their ability to incorporate culture (or, actually, kulture. When I read many of these Request for Proposals [RFPs], it was clear the issuer did not know much about the culture concept either). I have received several calls over the last few years from people whom I did not know asking if I would like to participate on their modeling team. When I probed as to what "participate" meant, it became pretty clear that it was "lend your CV to our proposal." The search was on for a pet anthropologist. It would be easy money, very attractive for the proprietor of a small business. I declined. Not me, babe.

Computational social models are part of the new analytical toolkits the national security community is developing to help it better understand and plan for operations in an irregular warfare environment. A computational social model is a mechanism to present and manipulate social actors and their relationships over time. Some approaches to a sociocultural environment such as social network analysis lend themselves quite well to this type of manipulation. Others, such as Geertz's thick description, do not.

Computational social modeling is a relatively new field, and certainly new to the national security environment. About five or six years ago, I went to what was the first meeting of a new professional society focusing on this field. There were about 125 people there. At one of the plenary sessions, I asked how many present were social scientists, as the target application was social behavior. There were three present, including me. The remainder were computer scientists, mathematicians, physicists, biologists, and the like. The attendees were methods experts, but were not engaging with domain experts. They thus were uncritically transferring many domain characteristics from fields like physics and biology, and not developing a method that accounts for the distinctive characteristics of the sociocultural domain. Although this is changing today, with an increased engagement of social scientists in the modeling process, the field of computational social science still tends to be dominated by the methods developers. It is far from an equal partnership with domain experts.

The field of computational social modeling and simulation as practiced in the national security community often provides excellent examples of the representation of kulture. As I mentioned earlier, I have received frequent requests to function as a pet anthropologist on model-building projects. (I must say here that some of those requests may have been made in good faith, without realizing that the very structure of the project team and the flow of work as they had designed it relegated the anthropologist to a relatively minor role of data provider or as an expert to validate activities after the fact.) Model structures, which should be driven by social theory, are often constructed without engagement with domain experts. Model formulations (descriptions of model structures) show no reference to social science literature.

One project on which I was working was headed by a group of modelers with operations research background. It was a counterinsurgency project. As the end game of counterinsurgency is legitimacy for a particular regime, they were working to incorporate that in the computational model. I went to the literature to develop a deeper understanding of legitimacy so I could help them with the representation. Ultimately I concluded that they were modeling power, not legitimacy, and that it may not be possible to computationally express legitimacy. They may, indeed, have intended to model the actions they did, but they then needed to be sure that they labeled the representation as power, not legitimacy. They were not happy, but did listen, and appropriately incorporated what I had provided them.

I had another engagement with a colleague who was working on a project related to validation of computational social models. I have some serious concerns related to how this concept is applied to computational social models, as I believe they have some characteristics which make them different enough from physical or biological computational models that we cannot simply transfer the method from one field to another. My colleague refused to engage in that discussion, retreating to her statement of work that focused on validation of computational social models. I believe that in situations like this we must push back, even at the risk of alienating sponsors/clients.

I still do some organizational analysis and assessments for Sandia and others, following my interest in the social study of science. I run into similar situations in these areas. Clients frequently do not understand our method and its associated rigor. This takes us back to my earlier aside: an interview is NOT a conversation in a hallway. I had one instance where I had developed a series of focus groups around a particular topic for a client. After we had recruited for the groups but before they were run, she requested that I add discussion topics from a completely different topic area—a different project on which she was working. I declined, saying that we had developed a recruitment strategy based on the original topic so the population would not be appropriate for her second topic, and that the group process would not allow the introduction of orthogonal topics. She accepted my pushback, noting that she had not been aware of these methods concerns.

By the same token, I ensure that the organizational assessments or studies I do reference appropriate literature. This helps me address the "I read one book" phenomenon that I often encounter when nonsocial scientists attempt to assess their organizational environment. These individuals often do not recognize the depth and breadth of theory and argument surrounding a particular concern as a study begins. However, in general, they are receptive to well-researched and documented arguments.

It is important to remember that there are individuals in the sponsor/client world who will engage in debates about method or theoretical approach and who will ensure not only the integrity of a particular project but the advancement of our field as they contribute a different perspective. However, if we do not push back, not only will we not discover who those are, we will compromise the intellectual integrity of what we do.

Editorial Commentary

Turnley's account is interesting because of the wide array of activities in which she is involved. This makes her unique among our contributors: she has moved in many circles, and perhaps of all the contributors, has the most mature "national security" career. Her account is also striking because her varied career path is so different from the academic one- or two-institution path. Her account is also unusual among the essays we received in that she does not assume that her work needs to be defended. She is frank about her desire to have an effect on the national security sphere, and has openly and ambitiously engaged in a diverse array of efforts, developing a great deal of breadth.

Although Turnley notes that the CIA interviewed her for employment soon after she finished graduate school, her intersection with the national security community seems to have been a later development in her career. At the time, the Cold War was drawing to a close and the DOE's national laboratories were seeking ways to create the "peace dividend" that the nation expects through technology transfer. Turnley was working for an Albuquerque, New Mexico, nonprofit focused on regional economic development, through which she meets a senior executive with Sandia National Laboratories. She asserted that social science is missing from Sandia's technology transfer and economic development issues, and he challenged her to make a difference by working for the laboratories.

Unlike many of the volume's contributors, Turnley does not seem overly concerned about her decision to work for a nuclear weapons laboratory. She is frank: nuclear weapons exist. Whether or not she is working for a laboratory is not going to change the fact of their existence. And perhaps in her own way she can contribute to the responsible maintenance of these weapons. This raises the question: did Turnley's economic development work intersect with the weapons programs? This is not just relevant to Turnley's work history, but to the larger question of how these national security institutions perceive and practice what they believe to be their "mission." We assume that prior to the Cold War's end, nuclear weapons were the dominant core of the laboratory's mission, but wondered if the end of the Cold War meant that weapons work became secondary to these new missions. Or was her work somehow located in a separate, distinct organizational sphere? And to what extent does it continue at the laboratory?

We were also struck by the way that Turnley dealt with the issue of getting a security clearance. The decision to accept a security clearance seems to be a significant rite of passage into the national security community. It troubled other contributors: Paula Holmes-Eber, for example, was concerned about the impact of a security clearance on her relationships with her colleagues in North Africa, where she had done a great deal of her fieldwork. In addition, Holmes-Eber's lack of a security clearance becomes a kind of buffer between her work teaching Marines and activities in which she does not want to participate. Turnley, in contrast, pragmatically accepts the clearance as a fact of her decision to accept a position at Sandia, asking only if it is something she can drop at a later date if it puts her in ethical or professional situations that make her uncomfortable.

Along the way, Turnley's career trajectory is strongly linked to major shifts in U.S. national security history and policy: her economic development credentials, for instance, become salient at Sandia as the definition of national security morphs at the end of the Cold War to include global economic competitiveness and as the national laboratories adapt their mission to this new definition. With the shift to counterterrorist and counterinsurgency frameworks after 9/11 and with the military's newfound interest in culture, her expertise as a scholar of culture becomes more valuable and she then has an opportunity—facilitated by the same vice president—to teach at JSOU. In doing so, her path through the national security community instantiates a broad range of institutional relationships and encounters: between the social and the physical sciences, among different elements of the national security community, and between anthropology and the military.

At Sandia, for example, Turnley becomes a representative of the social sciences in an environment where her field is seen as "soft," even though she recognizes that the laboratory's mission is changing to encompass areas of expertise that are unquestionably social in nature. As a social science trailblazer, she pursues projects—and a version of social scientific practice—emphasizing methodological rigor, well-documented intellectual pedigrees, a "customer" base in the same organizations as her Sandia colleagues, a focus on "national systems of innovation," and the acquisition of a security clearance. Yet Turnley suggests that her Ph.D.-trained engineer colleagues do not seem to return the favor, as they are wont to read "one book on a policy or a social topic" and assume that they have done adequate study. The implication is that her colleagues believe that a degree in mathematics, physics, or engineering is sufficient to understand social science topics. Not surprisingly, she eventually tires of asserting the intellectual credibility of anthropology and leaves.

However, Turnley seems to have maintained a successful and productive career in national security outside the institutional framework of the national laboratories. She is offered a position teaching and conducting research for JSOU. Once again, the DoD's professional educational system is the institutional locus for an intersection between anthropology and the military, as Fujimura's, Simons', and Holmes-Eber's essays also reveal. The DoD maintains an extensive hybrid military/professional/academic system distinct from, but modeled on, civilian academic institutions.

Once again, Turnley discovers that anthropologists are a rare breed in this environment, and sets out to demonstrate and refigure her expertise to meet the demands of the people she is teaching: in this case, military special ops personnel. Her experience at JSOU is in some ways similar to her experience at Sandia. She is confronted by a desire for and an interest in gaining access to social science knowledge, along with demands that her expertise be presented and packaged in a way that meets the institutional requirements of the military. Teaching courses on organizations, society, and culture in the context of irregular warfare, she focuses on providing the special operations personnel with "some tools to think differently," allowing them to "engage with the operational environment in a more effective way." At JSOU, Turnley is engaged in a project of translation; she must present anthropology in a way that is pragmatic and efficacious for military personnel. This begs the question of her pedagogy: practically, how does she accomplish this? What does she provide them—articles, books, videos? Does she do exercises with them in class?

This is not a small matter, as Turnley's courses are one channel among many through which anthropological and cultural expertise are being presented to an audience that is unfamiliar with them and which has traditionally valued mathematics and science at the expense of developing an understanding of the social sciences. In several essays—Milliken's, for example, and Holmes-Eber's—we read about anthropologists being asked to translate and document anthropological expertise into a "tool" (Milliken) or a "manual" (Holmes-Eber). Turnley writes about frames and ways of thinking. What, exactly, is an anthropological "frame" that special operators can grasp and use? In a Sahlins-esque (1976) mode, then, an important question becomes: to what extent is anthropology—as disciplinary method and knowledge—reduced to being just a means-ends form of practical reason in this work climate?

We also wondered about how her approach fits into the broader context of anthropological training in the military educational system. Turnley tells us she refers to Fosher's ideas and messages, but we wondered if she also draws on other resources—such as Holmes-Eber's bestselling manual—to develop her message. Throughout her career, Turnley describes pushing back against what she calls "social science lite" and against the role of "pet anthropologist" on project teams dedicated to the computational modeling of social behavior. Her primary ethical concern is making sure that others respect and value the intellectual integrity of anthropology as a discipline, in a context where nonexperts seek to appropriate it in simplistic ways. In doing so, she must constantly position herself against the intellectual values and norms of the institutions where she is working. As exhausting as this must be, we had the sense that she enjoys it tremendously.

Turnley Response

I will start by addressing one of the comments in the editors' closing paragraph—yes, I do enjoy what I do tremendously. I think that is a critical part of what both keeps me going and allows me to engage with a world that is at best a little skeptical and at worst dismissive of what I do. I believe the anthropological perspective is an important one, no matter what we do in life. And when what we do is of the high consequence nature represented in our national security community, the perspective becomes even more important.

I do believe anthropology is a perspective, not something you "do." In that sense, it is an enabler, albeit a critical one. It shapes interactions and conditions responses. It does allow us to see things that otherwise would be, as Fosher said, "hidden in plain sight." And once they become visible, we can leverage them.

When I began this journey into the national security arena, there were no other anthropologists (and very few social scientists of any ilk) that I knew of working in the area. Since then, there has developed a robust group of anthropologists and other social scientists who are making a wide variety of contributions. I draw on their material when and if I can. I read what they write, and use tools that they produce as appropriate. However, I think it is important to remember that the military, the intelligence agencies, and other organizations in the national security community are organizations with dynamics, values, structures, and populations, just like any other organization in any other domain. As anthropologists and social scientists, we have a whole body of theory on which to draw—I think we need to be careful about limiting our resource pool to literature on the military or national security community.

This brings me to another of the editorial team's points. I intersected with the labs at a particular time in our national history. I had been in New Mexico for several years before the "end of the Cold War" stimulated the technology transfer/dual use programs. Those programs arose out of a national interest to capitalize on the intellectual and physical infrastructure invested in the nuclear weapons complex at a time when it was not clear how much of that infrastructure would continue to be focused exclusively on weapons. That said: yes, it was a serendipitous intersection. But recall that I did not set out to get a Ph.D. in anthropology so I could work in Silicon Valley and learn about technology and marketing and applied organizational development, or help the small business community in New Mexico capitalize on the national laboratory in its midst, or start and run a microeconomic development nonprofit to help women start their own businesses (a portion of my biography left out because it wasn't directly relevant). This was not a planned career. Yet all these experiences and many others positioned me so that I was able to take advantage of opportunities when they presented themselves. They also taught me to look for those opportunities.

One last point. Ironically, it is only recently and only in the national security community that I have been able to "sell" myself as an anthropologist. Outside of academe, few understand what anthropology "is" or "does." Historically, I have demonstrated the value of the anthropological approach by solving problems, and only then "labeled" it as anthropology. The people with whom I work—military and otherwise—want solutions, not a discipline. However, I believe that by bringing the depth and breadth of the discipline of anthropology to bear, we can provide all our target communities with the most robust solutions to important problems. Anthropology "lite" or kulture will provide only a gloss, and that will quickly wear off.

Note

1. I use the term ironically to imply a very limited understanding of the depth and breadth of the concept of culture. It has historically been used as a very limited characterization of German civilization, highlighting aspects such as authoritarianism and earnestness (see Collins English Dictionary—Complete and Unabridged © HarperCollins Publishers 2003, available online at http://www.thefreedictionary.com/Kultur).

References

Glicken, Jessica

1989 Technology Transfer in New Mexico: Subcultural Conflicts. Paper presented at Society for Applied Anthropology Annual Meeting, Santa Fe, New Mexico.

Sahlins, Marshall

1976 Culture and Practical Reason. Chicago: University of Chicago Press.

16

How Critical Should Critical Thinking Be? Teaching Soldiers in Wartime

Anna Simons

In the past decade, Anna Simons has emerged as one of the foremost social scientists studying defense, security, and military matters in the United States. Her 1997 ethnography, The Company They Keep: Life Inside the U.S. Army Special Forces, *details the training and socialization of the Army's Special Forces units, which are responsible for some of the most sensitive and dangerous missions the military undertakes (Simons 1997). In her career as a Professor of Defense Analysis at the U.S. Naval Postgraduate School (NPS), Simons has taught, mentored, advised, and interacted with Special Operations Forces (SOF) professionals from the Army, the Navy, and the Air Force, and has both participated in and observed the shifting paradigms of preparedness and training as the United States has moved out of the Cold War and into the post-9/11 era of counterinsurgency, counterterrorism, and nation-building.*

Like Clementine Fujimura, Simons has been teaching in the military's educational system for well over a decade. Simons, however, is a professor at the only graduate institution in the Department of Defense's Professional Military Education system, which makes her student interactions somewhat different than those that Fujimura and Holmes-Eber experience. Like Fujimura and Holmes-Eber, Simons has tacked back and forth between the world of academic anthropology—she taught at the University of California at Los Angeles (UCLA) and has published numerous articles about anthropology, the military, and warfare—and the world of military education and training. Because of her role as a graduate professor and adviser, however, we felt she was particularly well positioned to speak about the institutional dynamics attending the emergence of the "new culturalism" among elite military operators (those with actual operational experience in the field) and decision-makers.

Simons received her Ph.D. in social anthropology from Harvard University and taught at UCLA, where she chaired the graduate program in African Area Studies. In addition to The Company They Keep, *Simons wrote* Networks of Dissolution: Somalia Undone, *which details the tumultuous collapse of the Somali state in the 1990s (Simons 1995). Simons' interdisciplinary publishing ranges from the* Annual Review of Anthropology, *for which she contributed a review of anthropological research on warfare, to political science and security studies journals including* The American Interest, The National Interest, Orbis, Third World Quarterly, *and* Parameters.

Many anthropologists have identified and lamented a range of dangers and threats that are posited to emerge when military decision makers and operators appropriate anthropological theory, methods, and information to support military operations, no matter how development-oriented those operations may seem to be. In her essay, Simons turns anthropology's concerns inside out by reframing the "new culturalism" of the post-9/11 era in the context of the military's politics, practices, and epistemology. In doing so, she challenges anthropologists of all persuasions to reconsider what we think we know about the dynamics, implications, benefits, and dangers of incorporating "culture" into military planning, decision-making, and operations.

One thing that has troubled me considerably since the invasion of Iraq is how much skepticism we who teach officers should convey regarding a war (or set of wars) our students have to fight. What is our role? To what extent should we worry about—or, is there a difference even—between stoking cynicism and encouraging critical thinking? Do we have a responsibility to temper our remarks, knowing that officers will re-deploy to difficult, maybe even impossible war zones? Or, by questioning policy, do we help gird them for the grim worst that might lie ahead?

My field site for this inquiry is my academic department. My students are midcareer, field-grade officers, which means they hold the rank of major and above.[1] Virtually all are operators. These days, most have served numerous tours in Afghanistan and/or Iraq.[2] Or, they have deployed to the Philippines. A number have also spent considerable time in what some call the third front in what used to be known as the "War on Terror": Colombia.

Typically, our students graduate after 18 months and, if they're in the U.S. Army Special Forces, either attend a three-month-long career course and then deploy, or go straight back to units gearing up to return to a war zone. Navy SEALs likewise head back to their units and deploy. In contrast, many of our Air Force officers (pilots, navigators, intelligence officers, and former Weapons School instructors) get swallowed by staffs.

One observation with which I would have concurred prior to 9/11 is that some graduate education can be a dangerous thing, since at least a few of our students graduated with the unhealthy conviction that they now knew plenty because they knew more than their peers who had not been exposed to the 40 or so books they'd bought and (ideally) read on their way to receiving an M.S. in Defense Analysis. No question, simply sitting through our classes before 9/11 enabled students in our curriculum to quote and cite various theories related to counterinsurgency in ways that few others could. But, whereas in the pre-9/11 Special Operations Forces (SOF) world this would have lent them a bit of an edge; today, it grants them incomparable additional advantages since counterinsurgency has become *the* military topic du jour and they, literally, are the masters of irregular warfare knowledge.

To set a bit more of the scene: as is true in most academic settings, much of what our students learn comes prepackaged for them by faculty who, like faculty elsewhere, vie to get our points across and enjoy being talking heads in our own classrooms. I mention this because our version of graduate education differs from "normal" graduate education in at least two regards. First, our students are already professionals; we are not grooming them to become professional academics in our particular discipline(s). Most faculty who teach in "normal" universities can probably agree that there is some body of foundational knowledge and certain disciplinary methods all students *should* learn to be professors in those fields. In contrast, we offer a terminal degree. We are not helping to train the next generation of anthropologists, or political scientists, or even defense analysts. As it is, fields like Security Studies, National Security Affairs, and Defense Analysis also are broadly interdisciplinary. Of the tenure-track faculty in my department, something like six have degrees in political science, three in mathematics, one in history, one in computer science, one in sociology, and one in anthropology. Thus, it is not clear that even if we wanted to we could agree on the content we would like our students to leave with. However, we all are in accord that the 30-something-year-old officers we teach should go back to the force with more analytical methods than they came with. Worth noting is that they seem to want this, too.

The Cult of the Unconventional

I am sure all my colleagues at NPS, the military's only graduate research university, feel the weightiness of teaching men and women who, in their real-world jobs, are used to managing millions of dollars worth of equipment and making life-and-death decisions. But I'd say there are two added challenges in my department. First, there is the specter of the cult of the unconventional. Second is the tricky business of trying to counter not just military, but SOF conditioning. Both are interrelated. Let me tackle the cult of the unconventional first.

In SOF circles, "unconventional" is used to describe certain kinds of military units, a distinct mode of warfare, and a superior manner of thinking. This leads to any number of elisions. Take thinking, for instance. A common presumption is that people who think unconventionally think outside the box. For those who think they think outside the box, this is, not surprisingly, considered the best and smartest of all possible approaches. Not only do many members of unconventional units consider themselves elite—which they are by virtue of having made it through rigorous assessment and selection filters—but further proof comes with their higher-than-average General Technical (GT) (or IQ) test scores. Smart men, smart units. From here it is but a short slide to then thinking *their* method of warfare is itself the smartest kind of warfare there is; just look at who wages it. Indeed, at times, devotees of the unconventional use the word "conventional" as if it were a slur.

Unfortunately, this attitude poses serious problems. First, it essentializes. Once tribalized, members then get sucked into spending far too much time countering, dismissing, and trying to undermine members of other tribes (or, in military parlance, branches and services). Second, this conventional/unconventional dichotomy itself is falsely based; there is no solid history to support it, which means, third, those who read this divide into the past distort a record from which they are prone to learn faulty lessons.

Advocates of the unconventional often cite Liddell Hart's *Strategy* (1954) as one of their ur-texts.[3] However, for anyone who reads it, Hart's emphasis is on the indirect approach in warfare, which does not really line up with current conceptions of the unconventional. Take, for instance, a classic military action, like an ambush. Ambushes are sneaky; they are nothing like frontal assaults. That makes them (technically) indirect. But, are they unconventional? The correct answer has to be no, since they are a tactic that has been used by most if not all armies from the beginning of time. Indeed, *any* kind of commander hailing from any kind of unit should be capable of taking either a direct (overt, frontal) or an indirect (flanking, behind-the-lines, sneaky) approach when trying to overcome the enemy or seize an objective. It's the situation that should dictate which he chooses, though truly great commanders will artfully combine both for maximum effect.

In other words, it makes no sense to treat the direct/indirect distinction as if it's a dichotomy, which is what has essentially happened with unconventional versus conventional. Though in what is perhaps the ultimate irony, Hart's version of "indirect" turns out to be a far better descriptive for what U.S. Army Special Forces, the preeminent unconventional force, is designed to do: work by, with, and through indigenous personnel.[4]

Not only does "by, with, and through" represent *the* consummate indirect approach to waging war, but "by, with, and through" is also the only way the United States will achieve a credible exit from Afghanistan, according to most observers. Yet, this is an exit that will only be achieved by, with, and through the development and strengthening of Afghanistan's *conventional* security forces (e.g., its army and police). Ironies really do abound.

Here is another: scan modern history, and among three of the most successful variants of a "by, with, and through" approach to warfare are T. E. Lawrence's work with the Bedouin in the Arab Revolt (during World War I); Americans' leadership of Filipino guerrilla bands on Luzon in World War II; and Detachment 101's employment of Kachins, Karens, and other Burmese against the Japanese in Burma during World War II.[5] What distinguishes these three examples, or a host of others, is that each was its own work in progress.[6] None came from a template, a doctrine, or a model. But each was also just one component in a much broader war effort, which itself was orchestrated by "conventional" military leaders, none of whom had received either "unconventional" training or training *in* the unconventional. Worth noting, too, is that, together, these cases represent three of the most successful lash-ups ever achieved between Western and non-Western forces, though the even more profound point is that in no case of which I'm aware has any unconventionally organized, trained, or equipped military force, acting on its own, "won" or even orchestrated the winning of a war.[7]

Yet, for a number of years now, a number of SOF advocates, to include many of our students (and some of our faculty), have been saying: remove the Big Army (and Marines) from the controls, relegate conventional units to a supporting backup role, put SOF in charge, let it do its thing, and we could win in Afghanistan, just like we would have prevailed faster in Iraq. At best this is questionable. Among other things, it presumes that those serving on U.S. Army Special Forces teams or in SEAL platoons would have been aware of what they or, rather, the United States was (and presumably still is) trying to accomplish. It also presumes that there are enemies in Afghanistan that *can* be crushed or can eventually be made to surrender, *and* that counterinsurgency techniques work. Not only does each of these presumptions merit a book in its own right, but to treat them *as* presumptions would itself be considered presumptuous by many in SOF circles because doing so would call into question the very notion that SOF's expertise in counterinsurgency and unconventional warfare *should* suffice.

Heresy

Because my own reading and research (to include my ongoing "field-work" in the classroom) has led me to increasingly question whether the United States really does have the capacity, nevermind the national stamina, to prosecute a long, drawn-out war of finesse, I'd have to be an actress, rather than a teacher, to avoid raising doubts when I teach. However, I am also always reluctant to suggest to American officers who need to believe they *can* make a difference that while they might excel at the tactical and operational levels—which means they do extremely well on missions or when it comes to planning missions—the overall strategy (if there is a strategy) that they're working so hard to support may well fail, and may well fail them. Even so, I probably do get too negative at times.

In the annals of military advising, there are plenty of occasions when the United States' overall advisory efforts failed. It is no coincidence that many of the United States' most effective military advisors returned home distraught and embittered. I joke in my class on military advising that being embittered—like having a bounty on one's head—may be the ultimate proof of advisory success. But, it surely is no joke for participants on the ground whenever the U.S. government pulls the plug early on what has been an all-consuming effort. Yet, since the Korean War this has been our government's modus operandi. Worse, many of the efforts we read about in class were probably futile from the outset. I often say as much. But can my students afford to agree?

Not surprisingly, students can come up with all sorts of insightful and eerie parallels between what the Vietnam War literature conveys (just to pick one body of literature) and what they have spent the last number of years experiencing themselves. But even when our readings make it more than evident that waging war alongside a government that lacks legitimacy and is corrupt has rarely paid off, it is still hard for them to want to connect *all* the dots between Afghanistan (or Iraq) and similar wicked problems from the past.

Not only do the officers I teach have a personal stake in today's fights (they've all lost close friends), but many clearly feel they have a generational stake in 9/11. At the same time, they are virtually all career officers in the combat arms. That means most are fully vested in the conviction that things *can* be improved. Otherwise, not even the most cynical among them would be sticking it out when, in today's all-volunteer force, none has to.[8] In fact, if students in our program weren't so "onward and upward"–oriented, few of them would be sitting in our classrooms in Monterey.

At the same time, neither Iraq nor Afghanistan has officially been considered lost. Iraq is actually considered a victory in some quarters. Thus, the arc of conflict has not yet begun to look as though it is heading toward defeat, as Vietnam did in the late 1960s. And certainly there has been no antimilitary sentiment in the United States. Thus, though some of our students are quite open about having no desire to go back to Kandahar to "eat more moon dust," most still have a can-do attitude about the *operational* challenges that lie ahead. Though they might have little faith in Washington, morale remains high; they have faith in themselves.

So, again, is it really my job to prod them to ask truly discomfiting questions? Where, after all, would such questions really get them, let alone the rest of us? The short answer is nowhere. At least not immediately.

Yet, this is the pool from which tomorrow's senior leaders will come. Or, to put this in slightly different terms, the senior leadership of the future can only come from those in uniform today. If cadets and junior and midgrade officers aren't encouraged to think sufficiently critically now, when will that habit be cultivated?

Granted, some among my colleagues might contend that this is exactly what we are already doing: helping to cultivate critical thinking. But are we? Or, by unduly privileging the unconventional, are we only planting the seeds for new iterations of groupthink?

Subverting "The" Unconventional

Here is another catch: our students, who are self-selected in more ways than most, are incomparably sophisticated when it comes to assessing one another's capabilities. They can thin-slice and skewer one another in nanoseconds. But 18 months is hardly sufficient time for them to learn how to adequately separate the wheat from the chaff when it comes to Ph.D.s and subject matter experts, particularly on subjects about which they are not as knowledgeable.

Compounding this is that our students also come to graduate school somewhat uncertain about academicians (as they call us), but primed to want to listen to individuals who *can* speak authoritatively and who must know more than they do, thanks to those three letters, P-h-D. Most, too, are anxious for anything we can offer that will help them cut through the Gordian knot of twenty-first century warfare in places like Afghanistan. All of this renders them almost automatically deferential, which is good—it makes for polite students—but also bad, since it leads them to accept large chunks of what they hear, read, or are told at face value without subjecting it to their normal withering scrutiny. This, I suspect, has something to do with the nature of officerdom, hierarchy, and military conditioning. But also, we do not teach hard sciences and we proclaim, right up front, that there are no right answers, just better and worse arguments.

Without question, our students immediately reject anything that flies in the face of their personal experiences. But, on the whole, we faculty don't talk tactics or operations (at least not in the military sense of the word "operations"). Instead, when we're critical we're critical of policy. Some of us even know policy makers. Thus, faculty members' "presentation of self" can be quite impressive, so much so it can make smart officers even more susceptible, especially when they are generationally predisposed to think in terms of sound bites: pithy formulations that *sound* convincing, especially when said with authority, can be utterly seductive.

This is why I sometimes fear we teach ideal indoctrinees, though I most definitely do not mean that in the way most civilians might imagine. Rather, my concern is that the more we tout the unconventional, the more routine whatever we present as unconventional becomes.

The conventionalization of the unconventional has been under way for quite some time: at least since I first did fieldwork with U.S. Army Special Forces in the early 1990s. Since 9/11, the institutionalization of "the" unconventional has only intensified. Proof positive comes in the 2007 publication of the University of Chicago Press–issued counterinsurgency field manual. At the same time, SOF numbers have grown substantially and the business of doing SOF-like things is booming throughout the military. But, whereas all things SOF may have gained renewed prominence, it is not clear that SOF has any better an idea today about what to do with, or how to nurture or protect, truly unconventional thinkers.

Also, although SOFs are said to excel at "dealing in the gray," there is a critical distinction to be made between the gray of no clear national policy and granting SOF officers the latitude they need to conduct operations. Give SOF units a coherent strategy, provide them with clear intent, and they will come up with 16 different ways to skin the cat or, depending on the situation, the only two that make sense. But, offer them nothing more than strategic ambiguity and they'll do no better at escaping Groundhog Day than anyone else.

Strategy requires clearly defined goals, along with clearly aligned ends, ways, and means. To be effective, strategy also needs to be easy for everyone up and down the chain of command to understand so that they can repeat it back to one another and know exactly what the other means. Anything else becomes too complex and/or confusing to execute. Thus, it shouldn't be surprising that when our national security strategy is ambiguous, the default is to gravitate back toward what the doctrine says to do. Although doctrine is only meant to serve as a set of guidelines, not a template, as far as those who promulgate it are concerned, when there is no clear guidance about what the U.S. military is supposed to achieve, at least doctrine offers clarity; without being given a compelling "why" to work toward, officers can punt pretty far (though never far enough) by concentrating instead on "how."

Meanwhile, once the unconventional is boiled down to a well-defined doctrine, SOF loses its flair. Others have written recently about the American military's preoccupation with the operational art (e.g., Strachan

2010). They see this as both cause and effect of our chronic strategic incoherence. At my level, what I see is worse: a waste. We are grinding up lives and alienating talent.

Here is why: at least some of the officers sitting in my classes *will* be among those responsible for helping to devise strategy and advise policy makers one day. Surely, it is not too soon to ask them how they might do this, while the best way I have found to try to de-conventionalize the unconventional is to be subversive about who or what really *is* unconventional: a most delicate task with men who have been conditioned to regard themselves as plenty unconventional already.

Editorial Commentary

Anna Simons offers a perspective on education and training at the NPS, in this case teaching SOF operatives, based on long experience. Like Fujimura, Simons' tenure at an elite institution in the Professional Military Education system antedates the events of 9/11 or the military's increased interest in anthropology since the mid-2000s. As such, she is able to reflect on what it means to teach "critical thinking" to operators in the military, while in a way taking account of how the multiple tours of many of these personnel in Iraq and Afghanistan have influenced their openness to new thinking in ways that complicate her responsibilities as an instructor, a mentor, and a translator of cultural anthropology into the domain of military engagement.

Her account can also be read alongside, and productively compared with, other narratives in this volume provided by anthropologists working in military education and training institutions, including those of Clementine Fujimura, Paula Holmes-Eber, and Jessica Turnley. Each of these accounts, however, is notably different, in part since the institutional contexts for each are not identical. Unlike her counterparts, Simons does not offer us an entrance narrative: instead, she dives right into the challenging problems she faces in the present tense. However, like Fujimura and Holmes-Eber, she also interacts with her work space in ethnographic terms, which doubles as a scene of research and reflection: as noted in her biography here, Simons has published extensively on the U.S. Army's Special Forces.

At the same time, these are her students. It is notable that, as an anthropologist teaching in an interdisciplinary department, what the discussion she offers of "critical thinking" is in her account is not in any obvious way related to anthropology's particular critical discourse. In fact, although Simons is a subtle commentator on pedagogy in this context, it is not so evident what her anthropological training has to do with it. This makes us curious about whether, and how, her status as the lone anthropologist in her department might have mattered in any way.

With Fujimura, Simons also notes tensions between teaching and indoctrination. Simons quips that it might be better to think of her students as "indoctrinees." For Simons, this quip leads to interesting pedagogical reflection on what it means to teach in the shadow of military doctrine, how to reference doctrine, and the risks in doing so. As a particular form of Department of Defense knowledge production, doctrine is at once a distillation of military policy into practice, framework for how the military thinks about the world, and a guideline for how to get things done. Simons notes that "doctrine offers clarity," particularly when there is no strategic clarity for operators to fall back on in circumstances of ambiguity. In a teaching context, the problem with doctrine, however, is that it "essentializes"—to use her term—when uncritically consumed by users.

Her attention here to the pitfalls of essentialization, even "strategic essentialisms" (to borrow this term from discussions of nationhood), does seem to mobilize a disciplinary sensibility. In Simons' narrative, learning counterinsurgency lingo—as summarized in the new U.S. Army *Counterinsurgency Manual*, for example—can be in tension with critical thinking. Here, then, in a way Simons is reflecting awareness of the different expectations for kinds of knowledge production of the military and academia, differences that have come up in other places (if not in the same ways), as more intractable contradictions between military and academic practice. For example, the exchanges among Roberto González, Montgomery McFate, David Price, and David Kilcullen in 2007 in *Anthropology Today* about whether the *Counterinsurgency Manual* is properly categorized as doctrine, scholarship, or plagiarism, illustrates this tension. Simons, in contrast, seeks the best balance.

She is particularly concerned with the "specter of the cult of the unconventional," as this is historically cultivated by the SOF and as more recently represented by the supposedly "out of the box" thinking summarized in the *Counterinsurgency Manual*. She is concerned with what happens when the "unconventional" becomes the new "groupthink," a trend she calls the "conventionalization of the conventional." In conjunction with this, she also identifies another trend that has cropped up in successive accounts offered by our authors; namely, a direct association among her students between knowledge acquisition and problem-solving utility. She tellingly notes, "Without question, our students immediately reject anything that flies in the face of their personal experiences." This comment is interesting in a number of ways. First, it rings a change on one classical anthropological narrative of professionalization, that of "being there," where the field and fieldwork separate the students from the professionals. In Simons's case, her students have been there, often multiple times—a theme echoed in Turnley's essay as well. This experience, and role reversal, appears to have particular authority for how she is able to teach them.

Another way it is interesting is that students' experience on their tours takes the form of "what works" and what doesn't. And they are concerned with what has worked. Simons tellingly notes that whereas as faculty she pitches her teaching at the policy level (analogous, in its way, to a theoretical approach), her students are typically more interested in the tactical and operational levels (e.g., the utility of knowledge as informed by their experience of successive tours). This poses a challenge for Simons: how does one appropriately teach "outside-the-box" critical thinking to SOF-type operators who need such skills more than most, without either providing too much criticality in ways that undermine their morale or aiding and abetting a groupthink-type, tactical-level problem-solving, and utilitarian relationship to knowledge that—doctrine-like—all too easily can become a dangerously uncritical status quo? This seems to be a significantly different challenge than those faced by teachers in nonmilitary academic institutions.

How a military education "is" and "is not" the same as that in a "normal" university setting is a theme addressed by multiple authors in this volume. This theme, however, deserves some more attention. After reading Simons, we came away wanting to know more about what value an M.S. in Defense Analysis, or any degree for that matter, holds for the officer-student. Specifically, we wondered who qualifies for these programs and what they expect from the program in terms of career advancement. The extent to which "schoolroom" knowledge measures up to "real-life" frontline experience is also interesting; for example, when officers study scenarios from Vietnam, what are they expected to learn about differences between past and present military campaigns? We ask this because Simons notes the difficulty her students face in connecting "all the dots between Afghanistan [or Iraq] and similar wicked problems from the past."

If Simons is concerned with the cult of the unconventional, we also wonder about another cult, that of "leadership." A common theme emerging from several cases is how a military education is about—among other things—cultivating "leaders" (think of Holmes-Eber and Fujimura's accounts). At first glance, this makes sense, as their students are officers and de facto or intended leaders (in the case of the U.S. Naval Academy). But more is at stake than having a well-run military. Several authors, for instance, remark upon the fact that from the pool of military officers will come many of the future's top decision makers; as such, they all recognize the gravity of their teaching obligations. In fact, the opportunity to shape the outlook and thinking of the nation's senior leaders (military and otherwise) seems a large part of the appeal and/or moral obligation of teaching in a military educational setting. Does Simons agree?

Simons Response

I write this response on the eve of a trip to Baghdad to visit one of the commanders of U.S. SOF forces in Iraq. He has done as well as it is possible to do thus far in SOF.

Whenever I get to travel to visit our graduates I invariably say that seeing how well they are doing in the field is the best part of my job. But that's actually not quite true. Building the relationships that lead to these visits is no less rewarding, as is the impetus behind the invitations to travel "downrange": graduates in command positions *want* us to see what their units are doing. They want us to return to the classroom as well informed as possible so that what we teach and the questions we raise remain relevant for the next generation of commanders. No one is more interested in making the armed forces more effective than are some of those who are charged with running it—except maybe those in the running to run it.

I like to think that, by this point in time, I can distinguish between pure careerists and officers who strive to make a difference, both to others and for the country. It is hard to be around the latter and not work as hard as they do. It is also hard not to want to offer them every possible form of assistance, to include exposure to as many useful anthropological approaches as quarter-long courses permit.

Among the core courses I teach are Anthropology of Conflict and Military Advisor. In the former I focus on what motivates groups to fight. We pay particular attention to identity. I introduce students to concepts like "emic" and "etic," and we read accounts that range from Lincoln Keiser's ethnography of the Kohistani (a book that my pre-9/11 students turned out to especially appreciate after 9/11) to Ed Husain's personal journey through Islamism. In the Military Advisor class our focus is, as the title might suggest, on working *with* others. We delve into a series of cross-cultural advisory encounters. Among other things, we analyze the significance of cross-cultural affinity, linguistic ability, empathy, what "going native" might mean, and all manner of other topics that would be familiar to anthropologists.

I teach other courses with a heavy anthropological bias. Students love this. Indeed, this year for the first time a young colleague whom I first taught as an undergraduate at UCLA is teaching Anthropology of Conflict with me. He tells me almost every week how enthused his students are about the subject matter, how they wish they could take more anthropology courses, and how refreshingly different—but relevant—they find the material.

This, I'd say, reveals something very healthy about our military, or at least the slice of the military we teach. It is one of the distinct benefits of affording midcareer officers (as well as select warrant officers and, soon, noncommissioned officers) 18 months in which to step back from day-to-day operational pressures to reflect, synthesize, question, debate, and be able to put their experiences into a broader context and examine them from different frames. Without question, this particular generation of officers deserves time to reacquaint themselves with their families. I am just finishing a project undertaken with 13 of them. We counted up their total number of deployments since 9/11: 82. SOF has never had so many experienced individuals. At the same time, it is difficult for anyone to make sense of these experiences without being granted the time and tools to think about them critically—which is what graduate programs enable. If even we faculty, who think about these issues full-time, have difficulty working our way through the thicket of the past decade, imagine those who have been in the thick of it.

Of course, I also know that I'm about to be flummoxed once again in Iraq. There are so many moving pieces and parts, so many players, and so many operations that have to be juggled, managed, and monitored that it is never clear to me there is anyone who *can* see the forest *and* the trees. This, too, is an issue I keep raising with students and graduates, knowing that already, some of them are filling positions where this is what they have to try to do. How, then, can one not want to try to help them? Especially when one considers anthropology's strong suits: thinking holistically and from multiple angles.

Notes

1. Lieutenant commander in the Navy.
2. This includes numerous of our international officers, who likewise tend to be SOF-oriented.
3. Or, if they don't, they should.
4. Worth noting is that U.S. Army Special Forces (commonly referred to as Green Berets) are just one among a number of SOF forces. Their traditional specialization has been working with, training, and advising foreign forces, whether insurgents or counterinsurgents, guerrillas, or government troops.
5. World War II is actually replete with examples: both of synergies, and division of labor nightmares.
6. On Luzon there were a whole series of bands, some of which amalgamated over time, and some of which did not.
7. Battles yes, campaigns maybe, but not a war.
8. I need to be careful about not overstating this. The personnel system, for all its faults, is still shrewd, and keeps officers hooked with half-pay at retirement after 20 years, along with other benefits. Among these are generous health benefits, which prove especially important to families with children with special needs.

References

González, Roberto
2007 Toward a Mercenary Anthropology? *Anthropology Today* 23(3):14–19.
Hart, Basil Liddell
1954 Strategy. New York: Praeger.
Kilcullen, David
2007 Ethics, Politics and Non-State Warfare: A Response to González in This Issue. *Anthropology Today* 23(3):20.
McFate, Montgomery
2007 Building Bridges or Burning Heretics? A Response to González in This Issue. *Anthropology Today* 23(3):21.
Price, David
2007 Anthropology as Lamppost? *Anthropology Today* 23(6):20–1.
Simons, Anna
1995 Networks of Dissolution: Somalia Undone. Boulder, CO: Westview Press.
1997 The Company They Keep: Life Inside the U.S. Army Special Forces. New York: Free Press.
Strachan, Hew
2010 Strategy or Alibi? Obama, McChrystal and the Operational Level of War. *Survival* 52(5):157–82.

Conclusion

"Be All That You Can Be...": The Anthropological Vocation in the Securityscape

George E. Marcus

Our casebook arises from and within a period of controversy—the totalizing atmosphere of fear since 9/11, after the four years of work by the American Anthropological Association (AAA) Commission on the Engagement of Anthropology with the U.S. Security and Intelligence Communities (CEAUSSIC), the appeal of anthropology to the military's counterinsurgency doctrine, the Human Terrain System's use of anthropologists in military operations—but it would otherwise be very worth doing even in calmer times because it contributes to making visible the blurring boundaries and common concerns of an anthropological profession that increasingly operates as much outside academia as within it. And indeed, the terrains of research interest of both academic and nonacademic anthropologists overlap as well. The securityscape, as we term it, is a distinctive sphere in which anthropological work occurs, but is by no means an exotic one. In fact, I will want to argue that careers in this arena satisfy some of the keenest desires for involvement in the public anthropology that is much called for, and referred to, today at the core of the discipline.

The practice of a public anthropology is not only limited to speaking out in the media of the classically conceived public sphere, or to working for activist causes and social movements. It depends at base on the practice of an anthropological vocation wherever and however it is situated. The debates and controversy over the roles of anthropologists in the military and other defense and security institutions have focused on the concept and standards of ethics (at base, "do no harm," and its problems and complications in application). Questions of ethics are undeniably important, and quite intricate in their situational complexity (see Faubion 2011). They particularly focus the issues about which anthropology, as an organization with professional standards of conduct, should be concerned. But the concept of vocation is broader and more personal at the same time; it merges personal motivation, outlook, and commitments with one's professional pursuits. It goes more to the emotional core of the professional ethos of anthropology and of what might be controversial about anthropological careers in the securityscape. And certainly, it is what is either most strongly expressed, or muted, in the cases that are presented and discussed in this volume.

So, in this reflection on our casebook project, I want to encourage discussion about the practice of a distinctive anthropological vocation rather than a more narrowly focused ethical standard of conduct. The classic reference to the vocational is Max Weber's 1918 essay, "Science as a Vocation" (he wrote in the same year "Politics as a Vocation" partly to mark the difference), and it has often been used as a source and inspiration for rethinking the forms of the pursuit of knowledge as disinterested inquiry (though not implying that it is value-free) in changing or challenging circumstances. In his recent book, *The Scientific Life,* the historian of science, Steven Shapin, inspired by Weber's essay, observes the substantial movement of scientific inquiry generally from the university to the product- and profit-minded corporation, much to the regret and suspicion of the social theorist (Shapin 2008). While acknowledging that the degree of toleration for uncertainty and patience as to "actionable" results are much greater in the academy than in industry, Shapin argues provocatively against the tendency for social theorists to judge this trend negatively in a reactive way. The realization that a substantial amount of anthropology is practiced in defense, intelligence, military, and security organizations, under several rubrics, including policy analysis and humanitarian assistance, has seemed to arouse a similar level of concern and suspicion in the academy. In the same way as Shapin, we are committed to an open assessment of the pursuit of an anthropological vocation in the securityscape.

For Weber, such a vocation would consist of practices of open-ended scholarly or scientific inquiry and the teaching of the products, methods, and value of such inquiry. According to Barbara Herrnstein-Smith in her review of Shapin's book (2009), "For that vocation to be honored in Weber's sense, the scientific life would have to be, as it was for him, the life of the dedicated pedagogic researcher…wherever it was pursued…." The same could be said for the practice of the anthropological vocation in the securityscape. Our cases in dialogic form probe when, how, and in what circumstances the pursuit of such a vocation is possible, or not.

In selecting and developing cases for inclusion in our volume, we intentionally avoided those that reflected the "hot button" of recent controversy, such as anthropologists' participation in Human Terrain Teams (which represents, in any case, a very small minority of such participation in the securityscape and which has received considerable, detailed attention elsewhere) in favor of a diversity and range of career situations (only Dawson and Goolsby, I believe, had any association with the Human Terrain program). We selected cases to show different functions that anthropologists perform prominently as well as routinely (teaching, training, analysis, research, program administration) and also to define a number of angles of participation within the scape, but not necessarily within the security apparatus (for example, Omidian as a nongovernment organization [NGO] worker in Afghanistan, Albro as a university researcher and coordinator of programs) to demonstrate the variety—indeed, tangle—of ways in which anthropologists might be caught up in security policies and programs.

My own position is as a curious outsider without a function or sustained research project that would give me a role in the securityscape. It was service on CEAUSSIC from membership on the AAA Executive Board that led me to join Laura McNamara, Rob Albro, and Monica Schoch-Spana in this post-CEAUSSIC project. As a "type," I perhaps represent a senior-generation academic exploring anthropology for its own sake, with its own conceits, ways of thinking, and habits of scholarship, but who is keenly aware that this exploration is more worldly, so to speak, than it ever has been before, and merges at many points with the thinking and work of those anthropologists who have developed careers outside academia. I have come to appreciate deeply that we share a vocation, perhaps with different practical stakes, purposes, and challenges.

My greatest pleasure and sense of intellectual stimulation in working on this project occurred during our several conference calls, especially in the first few minutes of "catching up" before we got down to business, and when filling in the background of this or that case, once we did. For example: Monica mentioned a seminar on nuclear detonation that she had attended that morning; Laura spoke of the government's interest in behavioral studies of the conditions under which people might respond to emergencies by self-organization, as in United Flight 93 on 9/11, and told us of her most recent study on satellite imagery analysts at White Sands, one of many that she does on the informal problem-solving cultures of experts and scientists at work; and Rob gave valuable insights into how military thinking was shaped by the genre of "doctrine," and mentioned his recent participation with "defense intellectuals" at National Research Council (NRC) meetings, etc. All seem to be peripatetic, going from one conference or research setting to another, thinking reflectively about those routine events with ethnographic subtlety and scope, defining a vast but recursive network of government and other security institutions by their participations. Toward the end of the process, we devoted one long call to developing background information on each of our case subjects, an extended exercise in overview, mapmaking, and contextualizing. Mainly, I just listened. This was working, everyday knowledge of a world, the dimensions and details of which were constantly being referenced in our conversations, some of which has found expression in the dialogic form through which we developed cases, but mainly is evanescent in the solidarity building and the enjoyment of shared company and commentary on which our work has been based.

Rob, Laura, and Monica composed case narratives of their own, developed in dialogic form as with the others. I myself have no case narrative to offer—only this collection of second-order reflections from having observed more informed participant observers observing in working along with a most remarkable performance of the anthropological vocation as a collaborative effort.

The Trope of the Securityscape as a Parallel World

As anthropologists compiling this casebook, we needed a working concept of the terrain, a rough map, in which to position our subjects. This is a habit of the professional craft of the ethnographer, who knows all along how provisional this scaffolding conception of a bounded space, a culture, or a community is. It is always a problem of engaged ethnographic research of imagining the "forest" while concentrating on seeing the "trees." Ultimately, we let the narratives of the case subjects and our dialogues with them reshape and test initial characterizations of a bounded space, a culture, or a system that we presume to be investigating. Now, claiming that our cases are charting, or reflecting, the dimensions and expansion of a "national security state" would have been one obvious mode of conceiving the system in which we are developing this volume. It would certainly conform to a very popular critical reference as to what structurally is occurring in the United States after 9/11, and much of what we present may inform this argument, for and against. But instead, we preferred a working conception for ourselves of the distinctive space that our subjects inhabit, which was both more naive perhaps than "national security state" and more sensitive to the range of conceptions that our case subjects themselves have of the world, culture, or system in which they were working. Whereas it might be a covert category for them, none, to my knowledge, had as broadly an inclusive working concept as the one we chose.

So, borrowing from Arjun Appadurai's improvised concept—the scape—when he was producing early views of globalization suitable for the messy and micro ways that anthropologists are comfortable understanding systems and processes, we early on adopted the term "securityscape." It gave us a good enough concept of a bounded space that, taken together, our cases have collectively but not comprehensively filled in. Otherwise, according to their own purposes and perceptions, we invite readers of these cases on their own to "connect the dots," so to speak.

I found it useful in my own thinking to posit the securityscape as a parallel world—seemingly alike, but of course very different from that of the many anthropologists who base themselves in universities, academic departments, and whose careers are defined by the requirements of teaching and scholarship and that depend on achieving individual cultivation of distinction in these tasks. We think of the anthropological vocation as being typically associated with the particular, largely academic institutional forms of publishing and recognition. Being myself thoroughly raised and having grown up in the academic context, I was immediately impressed with the parallelisms in some of the key institutions of the securityscape in which a number of anthropologists are situated—military and defense universities, graduate schools, research institutes, conferences, seminars, publishing expectations and venues—and whose paths rarely cross those of academic anthropologists, or for that matter other practicing anthropologists in corporations and consulting firms, except perhaps at large professional gatherings such as the AAA annual meeting. And although there are clumps and networks of association and acquaintanceship among anthropologists within the securityscape, I observed how relatively little of this there seemed to be. Several of our case subjects had to be found, or were only known by the surveys produced for the CEAUSSIC reports. Although there are many anthropologists who work throughout the institutions of the securityscape, disciplinary identity does not seem to be a consistently strong source of mutual association and recognition within it. Indeed, it seems to have been the controversies of "anthropology in the military" of recent years that have markedly raised this level of acquaintanceship and mutual awareness.

Although it was attractive to me to posit the securityscape as a parallel world of anthropological practice of which the academic anthropologist has been generally unaware—a recognition to be made; a horizon to be developed—still it would be distorting to push this idea of parallel or mirroring—as separate and similar—too far. As our cases show, the securityscape is hardly separate. Academia in a variety of ways is very linked to the securityscape, even structurally and financially so. At least four of our subjects move fluidly in their work across lines that would seem to divide the securityscape from other institutions. The securityscape still has its obvious centers and clusters of organizations, but it is by no means an apparatus apart. Its boundaries are permeable with many cross-cutting relations.

Moreover, the situation of anthropologists in apparent academic positions of research and teaching is not all that similar either to that of counterparts outside the securityscape. There are unique features of surveillance and personnel classification, especially in the civilian domains of the securityscape, that make apparently similar academic environments distinctively "other" rather than parallel to the environments of work in which academic anthropologists operate. For one thing, work in the securityscape is distinguished and enabled by the almost universal assignment of security clearances to individuals—the personal refusal of which (as in one of our cases) would seem to be substantial career impairment. Such a system of graded, formal trust partly redefines the actors and their ethical constructions in routine as well as exceptional meetings and interactions. Though understandable and necessary, there is nothing like this in the civilian university. For another, the writing for a public or readership other than designated must be vetted—as were a number of the pieces in this volume, and the volume itself, for at least one of the coeditors. And finally, for a third, in one case, the ability to revise and produce a second edition of a very successful manual-like volume was hampered by concerns that it would change "doctrine"—a key genre or form for the production and dissemination of thought in the military which Rob Albro has studied. So there are indeed constraints on basic norms of academic freedom and the flow of information that in itself would challenge the attractiveness of the securityscape containing within it a parallel world of anthropological activity that could be mutually recognized. The basis for this recognition is still worth discussing as encouraging of discussion across "scapes," but the realities of difference must be acknowledged as well.

What the Cases Show, and Don't Show

Originally, our cases were to have been about ethical issues in the actual practices and jobs that anthropologists do as they are situated in the securityscape. Only a couple of the cases actually expose this in detail—Flagg Miller's, the first developed, about dilemmas of disclosure in the course of his research comes especially to mind. Though there is a sketching in the other cases of what one's work entails, they are mainly reflections about position, identity, and self-fashioning in pursuing careers of varying kinds in the securityscape. And there is a considerable and interesting range of intensity and commitment with which the case subjects claim an identity as an anthropologist. That is why the volume has turned out to be a highly detailed and nuanced source for understanding the range of expressions of an anthropological vocation in the securityscape, rather than a casebook of dilemmas of ethical decision in specific situations. In my view, the vocational ethos precedes and encompasses the question of ethical practice, and is far more revealing of the sort of thinking, effects, and critique that the work of anthropologists, variously situated, can produce in the securityscape.

We did not plan for the cases to be more about the function of anthropologists in a range of contexts, and somewhat less about what they do. Our subjects themselves seemed generally more inclined to discuss their situations and commitments than to describe the details of their work. But this fortuitous shift in the direction of cases seems even more valuable for current discussions about the role of anthropologists in the securityscape. These cases do not so much probe the micro-ethics of their work, but rather how they are positioned—what they do as anthropologists, sometimes job-classified as such, but more often not, working in and on agendas not, or very only partially, of their own making.

Given the recent public controversy about the work of anthropologists—especially in military counterinsurgency doctrine and operations—an atmosphere of defensiveness, sensitivity, and self-justification in choosing a practicing securityscape career colors our collection and development of cases, yet not as much as I would have expected. Sensitivity to self-justification ranges widely from the highly explicit ("why I chose this career" after 9/11), to the subtle, to the barely detectable, and even to the indifferent.

There is also a considerable range of variation expressed in the cases about the valuation of and caring for an explicit identity as an anthropologist in the securityscape. Work associates or supervisors may appreciate (or not) that their colleague's disciplinary training is as an anthropologist, but the jobs themselves have other classifications. So one may be more or less appreciated as an anthropologist in different situations—and again to our subjects, this may be a matter of great sensitivity, of subtle concern, or of none at all. Situationally, it can be quite disturbing to some not to be credited as an anthropologist. Yet for others, what is troublesome is the lack of consistency and predictability in how one is accorded standing: sometimes one is seen as speaking as an anthropologist, and sometimes not, and there are no rules or consistency about this. What is clear is that for the purposes of our casebook conversations, the subjects are with varying intensity and enthusiasm reflexively attending to their anthropological vocations. Identifications with anthropology have a distinctly sectarian feel to me—with a range of passionate, moderate, and lapsed expressions of affiliation.

In the cases of a passionate identification with an anthropological vocation, there is a distinct doubling of identity, the practice of "a said and an unsaid" in one's work, and the effort to "translate" anthropological sensibilities, and especially its critical inflections of recent years, into bureaucratic rationality and modes of thinking. It is not that these latter modes are not fairly valued, but that they are hegemonic (see the next section). But here it is interesting to note at what point, say, anthropology *in* the securityscape might become anthropology *of* the securityscape (that is, being an anthropologist of one's own work conditions), or to what degree this possibility is an ultimate compensation for those who are constantly trying to make a home for anthropological sensibilities in a securityscape tending toward a discourse of the hyperrational and the programmed. Indeed, in some of the cases, this move has already been made (one has published on the ethnography of the military; others plan to make the securityscape eventually a subject of such independent research, written in the genre of memoir or ethnography). And this casebook itself is an enactment of such a move from the "in" to the "of." It is infused with the impulse toward autoethnography in its cases and its rationale. The personal narratives presented here, and the way that we have dialogically engaged them, can be read as such.

Credit for one's contribution as an anthropologist in securityscape careers is certainly quite different than in academia. In the academic training of social/cultural anthropologists (including most of those who have written case narratives), the ideal, real, and required form of self-expression is ethnography, as dissertation, article, or eventually a book. Whereas the character of the ethnography has changed in recent years, going from apprentice to professional means successfully cultivating a highly individualistic project, and claiming or "owning" it as ethnography with critique as its purpose and contribution—creating new knowledge by revising conventions and settled ways of thinking. If this is the contemporary anthropological vocation, then we can see it is practiced with commitment and ingenuity in the securityscape, but not in the forms of its academic expression or reception. One's credit or reputation in securityscape careers seems to depend most on skills for working effectively (including communication skills, more like business than academia) in collaborations and collective projects. There is a considerable amount of writing to be done, but little of it redounds to the credit of authorship ("doctrine" trumps authorial "signature"). One might have the satisfaction of seeing one's ideas having effect, but this rarely redounds to enduring personal reputation, which is perhaps not as welcome as it is in academia, in any case. Individual regard, reputation, and recognition of insight seem to be blended into projects, participations, collaborations where the play of ideas—especially in abstract forms or based on fieldwork insights that are not subject to modeling and quantification—has little value. The across-the-board modesty as anthropologists expressed in our casebook narratives is impressive (though it seems to be compensated for in two or three cases by the accumulation of institutional, administrative power—not that different in the academic setting, in the rare cases when the ethnography-minded anthropologist becomes a dean!).

What is Asked of Anthropology; What is Offered

What securityscape agencies want from anthropology is usually in the framework of missions, projects, assignments, programs of various scope, and in the military, activities governed by doctrine. Most explicitly when anthropology is identified as such, what seems to be asked for is expertise in training and education as it relates to specific and general aspects of cultural sensitivity and knowledge. Among our cases, the most common and easily identified function is in this capacity, across a range of military educational institutions. Anthropologists have specific culture-area expertise, or they are experts in the study of cultures. This might also be the arena in which what anthropologists do and what agencies expect of them is most in tension, especially if the latter expect cultural skills and knowledge to be literal, scientific, and precise, and cultures to be definable in this way. Obviously, working with students in the military—soldiers who have been or will be deployed—is where anthropologists can be, and have a long record of being, the most effective. This is the fulfillment of the pedagogical aspect of the anthropological vocation at its most explicit.

There also seems to be some understanding in securityscape agencies that anthropologists can provide subtle knowledge of informal cultures of expertise, contextual problem-solving, and decision-making; that they can investigate organizational cultures in the same way for which they are known in the study of the cultural systems of peoples and places. Still, time frames of investigation are relatively short and more certain or actionable results are expected than anthropologists are inclined to otherwise give. Further, if anthropologists are recognized as such, securityscape agencies may look to them as "walking archives" of generalized behavioral traits of humans, so that there may be the expectation that anthropologists can provide reliable generalizations, or even educated guesses, about how people (in general!) will behave in certain situations of interest. Although there is ample evidence in the cases in this volume that the actual expectations of anthropologists, recognized as such, in their everyday work in the securityscape is much more nuanced, calibrated, and mutually negotiated in line with the actual capabilities of anthropological expertise, still the stereotyping of the anthropologist lingers.

The situation is quite different when the identity of the anthropologist is secondary to, or submerged in, a primary identity that is defined by internal securityscape job categories and expectations. The anthropologist is valuable for language skills, knowledge of particular regions, or research abilities, without any expectation related to the ethos or ideology of anthropology as a profession. Such situations stimulate in anthropologists, especially where their disciplinary identity is particularly salient to them, a kind of doubling, where they give an official account of what they do in their work cultures, and another, different sort of account to those who think of and understand them as anthropologists. This doubling is visible and enacted in many of the narratives and our engagements with them in this volume. And it is interesting to note the range in expressions of feeling and justification about the nature of the gaps between the requirements and achievements of the job as defined in the securityscape and the ethos of a variously submerged anthropological vocation.

In our cases, what anthropologists seem to have distinctively to offer in their jobs, however they are defined, is variously characterized in our narratives as holistic thinking; pragmatism tied to a sensitivity to subjects' perceived motivations and assumptions in everyday life activities; "out of the box," lateral, unconventional thinking; and a sensitivity to and concern for the effects of policies, programs, and missions on the lives of people affected by them. This work seems to be most interesting when it is relevant to the great number of projects in the securityscape that are about preparedness, engage in scenario-thinking, and are anticipatory of near and conceivable futures. This orienting temporality of much securityscape research in fact relates to the same temporality as well in which many of the most innovative research agendas in contemporary academic anthropology (Rabinow et al. 2009) want to cast themselves (often spoken as emergent practices, norms, and systems). The orientation toward the scenario is thus another terrain on which the conversation between academic and securityscape anthropologists might develop. For example, Monica Schoch-Spana's effort, among others, to build understandings of how people are as likely to self-organize as to panic in the face of catastrophes, as a contribution to planning and policy-making that might otherwise tend to assume that populations will need tight controls, if not martial law, in disasters, is as much a practice of constructive critique within the securityscape as a contribution to the sorts of questions that academic research in anthropology is pursuing.

So, it is often the case that the securityscape in its research pursuits and curiosities asks remarkably good questions. But, perhaps from the anthropological perspective, it is inclined to provide "thin," inadequate answers. This has to do with the knowledge culture, so to speak, of the securityscape and its preferred and prestige modes of operating (quantitative modeling enhanced by advances in computing, etc.). Thus, what anthropologists have to offer from their own research traditions (which is more than what they are usually asked for), is surplus knowledge of a particular kind (expressed by them, as noted, as holistic thinking, unconventional pragmatism, etc.). Actually, this distinctiveness of anthropology has been interestingly characterized by Marilyn Strathern as she herself became engaged as ethnographer within the complexity of a major technoscience project at her home university (Strathern 2004:5): "What research strategy could possibly collect information on unpredictable outcomes? Social anthropology has one trick up its sleeve: the deliberate attempt to generate more data than the investigator is aware of at the time of collection. Anthropologists deploy open-ended, non-linear methods of data collection which they call ethnography…."

Surplus, then—"the trick up its sleeve"—is what anthropologists potentially have to contribute in their participations in the securityscape, as well; they generate more data (and insights) than their employers are prepared to acknowledge or use. There are indications that this "added value"—what anthropologists have to offer, more than they are asked for—is sometimes appreciated and absorbed. But, given the control of agenda, constraints on the flow of information, and demand for certain results in this arena, there is a lot of the surplus on offer that remains as such—in reserve, unexpressed, even repressed. How, then, are anthropologists to think about this surplus, beyond what they can skillfully introduce in their genres, requirements, and constraints of work in the securityscape? Critique is one channel for this surplus, which sometimes gets a hearing, and even successfully gets integrated in or at least has an effect on the flow of projects in the securityscape (again I think here of Monica Schoch-Spana's work, and also of Laura McNamara's in participating in a substantial debate about the use of computer-generated modeling and social analysis in various agencies of the securityscape). But critique is often frustrated as well and remains a silent or repressed dimension of thinking. Another option is to begin thinking about such surplus on offer by anthropologists as a resource that might gain expression in a domain of public anthropology, to which the anthropological profession currently would like to give thematic definition and substance.

In What Senses Is or Could Anthropology in the Securityscape be a Form of Public Anthropology?

Public anthropology, at least in kernel, is scaled to the level at which anthropological research operates—observed social action, dialogue, sustained relationships with subjects—according to the virtues of the ethnographic method. Inside research, or the spaces in which anthropology is practiced, the public emerges in a pattern of conversations, transactions, and exchanges that might be understood as engaged receptions and responses to the articulation of anthropological ideas and insights. Whether or not this context of reception and exchange goes further—whether it enters the conventional public sphere by the anthropologist playing the role of a public intellectual or advocate in some context—the idea and reality of public anthropology begins granularly in conversations and exchanges in the very same situations or scenes wherever anthropology is practiced.

Traditionally, public anthropology arises from the long-standing work of anthropologists mediating between peoples they have studied, and with whom they have lived, and major agents of external change (now a sphere occupied by thousands of NGOs). More recently, the terrains of research and how they are structured for anthropologists make it difficult to find such a distinctive mediating role. Trajectories of critique guide affiliations and interventions in different spaces where anthropologists are situated. And the securityscape, even with its special defining and restrictive characteristics, should be seen as one of several possible venues in which a public form of anthropology can granularly gain traction. What are the affordances as well as obstacles in such an arena for the emergence in context and situation of a public anthropology scaled to the conditions for the expression of the anthropological vocation? The same question could be asked about any framework in which anthropological work occurs today. The securityscape is not exceptional in this regard. If I were reconceiving today the idea of circumstantial activism that I proffered in evoking the emergence of a multisited anthropology in the mid-1990s (Marcus 1995), it would now be in terms of how the embedding of anthropological research generates at its core a public of unknown dimensions. The public begins in the movements and dialogues of such practice.

How then can a public anthropology be expressed, what forms can it take, and what is its potential to morph and grow in scale, and in terms of what issues and debates? Indeed, we have seen anthropology of the securityscape grow into a kind of public anthropology brought into being by controversy. By what sort of self-generated ways from within the variety of engagements of anthropologists in the securityscape, as chronicled in this volume, can such issues of an expanded public sphere arise?

In the dialogic spirit of this project, I have pulled a quote from Rob Albro's narrative and copied below our brief exchange about it which seems to go to the heart of how the special contribution that anthropology, as it is practiced as a vocation in the securityscape, can exceed a desire for critique within—which has limited outlets of full expression—toward a related practice of much desired, yet vaguely defined public anthropology. Rob's comments reflect on his attendance at an NRC conference, where he was definitely working within the securityscape, but as a guest, a visitor. Though he reflects on the kind of situational doubling of identity already mentioned (conflicted about how the culture concept is being deployed among defense intellectuals), he imagines a different outcome based on the potentials of dialogue in which he is invested:

ROB: To call these engagements public because they address looming extradisciplinary social issues is insufficient. Nor, as has been argued, is it enough to suggest that a more effective public anthropology needs to tell better or more accurate stories than, say, the punditocracy. The error this makes is that it still assumes a unilateral projection of a recognizable disciplinary "voice" and makes no accommodation for the plural voices of consociates in a conversation. In disciplinary ethical terms, it is notable that there is little legible room for public engagements except in this way.... If the AAA's CoE [Code of Ethics] notes the importance of doing "dialogue and negotiation" with research subjects and on the matter of informed consent, with publics it restricts comment to an unproblematic concept of dissemination. As important are the terms of reference of our interlocutors, their discursive habits and language ideologies. Stripping away all of the meta-talk, this amounts to an injunction to meet people where they are rather than just on our own terms.

GEORGE: A very good portrait indeed of anthropologists being among "defense intellectuals," and also the inevitable discomfort of us so being. You offer a very effective notion of the dialogic, a critique of the presumption of being public that anthropology, or official anthropology (AAA), so much likes to thematize now. As you say, "The error this makes is that it still assumes a unilateral projection of a recognizable disciplinary 'voice' and makes no accommodation for the plural voices of consociates in conversations." But what is the alternative? Quite a predicament: we (you) sit through these meetings that you find difficult—and could easily lead to an unvoiced sense of contempt for hyperrational discourses...or something more constructive? As you say, the possibility of pushing back against impoverished understandings of culture seems to be the calling of the anthropologist wherever situated."

ROB: Thanks for this.... I think you've captured the sentiments nicely. My sense is that at present anthropology, as a discipline, has paid relatively scant attention to these spaces, forums, conversations, entanglements, somewhere in between "academic critique of" and "directly working for" (and where you aren't being paid). In fact they appear vaguely under suspicion. But I suspect these scenarios were not uncommon in earlier generations. So, our conversations are significantly narrower than previously in some ways....

The securityscape, even given its many restrictions and constraints, affords also, as our cases attest, many opportunities for productively occupying the kinds of forums that through bridge-building and nourishing can enter from the ground up, so to speak, a sphere that could be called and easily recognized as public. As such, our volume is foremost a contribution, not to the defense or explanation of anthropology in the securityscape, but to anthropology in the public sphere, which is built up from situated accounts of practice and arguments that through granular, dialogic engagement, gradually attracts a public of open-ended dimension and possibility.

References

Faubion, James D.
2011 An Anthropology of Ethics. Cambridge: Cambridge University Press.

Herrnstein-Smith, Barbara
2009 It's like Getting Married: Review of *The Scientific Life* by Steven Shapin. *The London Review of Books*, February 12, pp. 10–12.

Marcus, George E.
1995 The Emergence of Multisited Ethnography: Anthropology in/of the World System. *Annual Review of Anthropology* No. 11. Stanford: Annual Review Press.

Rabinow, Paul, George E. Marcus, James Faubion, and Tobias Rees
2009 Designs for an Anthropology of the Contemporary. Durham, NC: Duke University Press.

Shapin, Steven
2008 The Scientific Life: a Moral History of a Late Modern Vocation. Chicago: University of Chicago Press.

Strathern, Marilyn
2004 Commons and Borderlands: Working Papers on Interdisciplinarity, Accountability and the Flow of Knowledge. Oxford, UK: Sean Kingston Publishing.

Index

N

O

S

T

U

ABOUT THE EDITORS

Robert Albro received his Ph.D. in sociocultural anthropology from the University of Chicago in 1999. Since 1991, Dr. Albro has maintained long-term ethnographic research and published widely on popular and indigenous politics in Bolivia, with a particular focus on the changing terms of citizenship, democratic participation, and indigenous movements in this country. His current research is concerned with global cultural policy-making as it meaningfully shapes the ongoing terms of globalization, including the relevance of culture in contexts of security. Dr. Albro's research and writing have been supported over the years by the National Science Foundation, the Mellon Foundation, the Rockefeller Foundation, and the American Council for Learned Societies, among others. Dr. Albro has also been a Fulbright scholar, and has held fellowships at the Carnegie Council for Ethics in International Affairs, the Kluge Center of the Library of Congress, and the Smithsonian Institution. Dr. Albro has held several leadership positions in the American Anthropological Association (AAA), including Chair of the Committee for Human Rights and Chair of the Ad Hoc Commission on the Engagement of Anthropology with the U.S. Security and Intelligence Communities. He was given the AAA's President's Award in 2009 for outstanding contributions to the Association. Most recently, he has taught at Wheaton College (MA) and at George Washington University. He currently teaches in the School of International Service at American University.

George E. Marcus is Chancellor's Professor of Anthropology at the University of California at Irvine (UCI). He has conducted ethnographic studies of elites and elite cultures in a variety of settings: kings and nobles in modern Tonga of the South Pacific; contemporary political and business dynasties in the United States, Europe, and Latin America; art collectors; Portuguese aristocrats; and, most recently, the workings of the World Trade Organization. Since the mid-1990s, he has been working with the idea of "multisited ethnography," which involves direct and long-term contact and inquiry amid both cultures of experts and elites and those of ordinary people in everyday life. Through his founding of a Center for

Ethnography at UCI, he has conducted experiments with the classic form of anthropology's distinctive method of inquiry and its teaching to meet the challenge of new topics and contexts of research. Marcus's projects continue to be explicitly collaborative, and he is interested generally in the nature of collaborations at the core of the contemporary practice of diverse ethnographic research. In recent collaborations, he pursued this interest in inquiries involving Portuguese nobles, European politicians, Latin American artists, U.S. bankers, and Brazilian intellectuals.

Laura A. McNamara is a Principal Member of Technical Staff in the Exploratory Simulation Technologies Organization at Sandia National Laboratories. Trained in cultural anthropology, McNamara conducts field studies in national security environments to assess barriers and opportunities for new technology development and adoption. She has worked with nuclear weapon experts, intelligence analysts, and cybersecurity experts, focusing on issues of expert knowledge elicitation and representation, verification and validation in computational social science, uncertainty quantification, user-centered design strategies, innovation adoption, and software evaluation. Dr. McNamara received her Ph.D. in cultural anthropology from the University of New Mexico in 2001, with a dissertation on the problem of knowledge loss in the post–Cold War nuclear weapons programs at Los Alamos National Laboratory (LANL). Dr. McNamara is a Fellow of the Society for Applied Anthropology and spent two years on the AAA's Commission on the Engagement of Anthropology with the U.S. Security and Intelligence Communities (CEAUSSIC). McNamara was recently appointed to the National Research Council's Committee on Improving the Decision Making Abilities of Small Unit Leaders (2010–2011). In addition, she serves on Sandia's Human Studies Board. She is coeditor (with Robert Rubinstein) of the forthcoming book *Dangerous Liaisons: Anthropologists and the National Security State*, to be published by SAR Press in 2011.

Monica Schoch-Spana, a medical anthropologist, is a Senior Associate with the Center for Biosecurity of the University of Pittsburgh Medical Center (UPMC) and an Assistant Professor in the School of Medicine Division of Infectious Diseases. For more than 10 years, Schoch-Spana has briefed numerous federal, state, and local officials as well as medical, public health, and public safety professionals on critical issues in biosecurity. National advisory roles include serving on the Steering Committee of the Disaster Roundtable of the National Research Council (NRC), the Institute of Medicine Standing Committee on Medical Readiness, and the NRC Committee on Increasing National Resilience to Hazards and Disasters. She serves on the faculty and steering committee for the National

Consortium for the Study of Terrorism and Responses to Terrorism (START), a university-based center of excellence supported by the U.S. Department of Homeland Security. Archival and ethnographic case studies inform Dr. Schoch-Spana's perspective on community reactions to public health and terrorist crises, including Anthrax Attacks 2001, World Trade Center Attack 2001, and Pandemic Influenza 1918. Select publications include "Community Engagement: Leadership Tool for Catastrophic Health Events" (*Biosecurity and Bioterrorism,* 2007), "Leading during Bioattacks and Epidemics with the Public's Trust and Help" (*Biosecurity and Bioterrorism,* 2004), "Educating, Informing and Mobilizing the Public" (in *Terrorism and Public Health*, B. Levy and V. Sidel, eds., Oxford University Press, 2003), and "Bioterrorism and the Public: How to Vaccinate a City against Panic?" (*Clinical Infectious Diseases,* 2002). In 2003, Dr. Schoch-Spana helped establish the Biosecurity Center of UPMC; prior to that, she worked at the Johns Hopkins University Center for Civilian Biodefense Strategies starting in 1998. She received her Ph.D. in cultural anthropology from Johns Hopkins University (1998) and B.A. from Bryn Mawr College (1986).

Left Coast Press, Inc. is committed to preserving ancient forests and natural resources. We elected to print this title on 30% post consumer recycled paper, processed chlorine free. As a result, for this printing, we have saved:

2 Trees (40' tall and 6-8" diameter)
1 Million BTUs of Total Energy
248 Pounds of Greenhouse Gases
1,120 Gallons of Wastewater
71 Pounds of Solid Waste

Left Coast Press, Inc. made this paper choice because our printer, Thomson-Shore, Inc., is a member of Green Press Initiative, a nonprofit program dedicated to supporting authors, publishers, and suppliers in their efforts to reduce their use of fiber obtained from endangered forests.

For more information, visit www.greenpressinitiative.org

Environmental impact estimates were made using the Environmental Defense Paper Calculator. For more information visit: www.papercalculator.org.